# REVISION WORKBOOK

# Criminal Law

**Third Edition**

**OLD BAILEY PRESS**

OLD BAILEY PRESS
at Holborn College, Woolwich Road,
Charlton, London, SE7 8LN

First published 1997
Third edition 2002

ISBN 1 85836 461 2

**British Library Cataloguing-in-Publication.**

A CIP Catalogue record for this book is available from the British Library.

Printed and bound in Great Britain.

# Contents

Acknowledgement     v

Introduction     vii

Studying Criminal Law     ix

Revision and Examination Technique     xi

Table of Cases     xvii

Table of Statutes and Other Materials     xxv

1   Actus Reus, Omissions and Automatism     1

2   Mens Rea     17

3   Homicide     38

4   Non-fatal Offences against the Person     58

5   Sexual Offences and Consent     78

6   Theft     97

7   Deception and Related Offences     114

8   Robbery, Burglary, Blackmail and Related Offences     133

9   Criminal Damage     153

10   Inchoate Offences and Accessorial Liability     169

11   General Defences – Insanity and Intoxication     188

12   General Defences – Compulsion     202

# Contents

Acknowledgement

Introduction

Surviving Criminal Law

Revision and Examination Techniques

1 Liability Basics

Failure Situations and Other Matters

6 Actus Reus, Omissions and Automatism

2 Mens Rea

3 Homicide

4 Non-fatal Offences against the Person

5 Sexual Offences and ... assault

6 Theft

7 Deception and Related Offences

8 Robbery, Burglary, Blackmail and Related Offences

9 Criminal Damage

10 Inchoate Offences and ... Secondary Liability

11 General Defences - General Introduction

12 General Defences - Compulsion

# Acknowledgement

Some questions used are taken or adapted from past University of London LLB (External) Degree examination papers and our thanks are extended to the University of London for their kind permission to use and publish the questions.

## Caveat

The answers given are not approved or sanctioned by the University of London and are entirely our responsibility.

They are not intended as 'Model Answers', but rather as Suggested Solutions.

The answers have two fundamental purposes, namely:

a) to provide a detailed example of a suggested solution to an examination question; and

b) to assist students with their research into the subject and to further their understanding and appreciation of the subject.

# Introduction

This Revision WorkBook has been designed specifically for those studying criminal law to undergraduate level. Its coverage is not confined to any one syllabus, but embraces all the major criminal law topics to be found in university examinations.

Each chapter contains a brief introduction explaining the scope and overall content of the topic covered in that chapter. There follows, in each case, a list of key points which will assist the student in studying and memorising essential material with which the student should be familiar in order to fully understand the topic.

Additionally in each chapter there is a key cases and statutes section which lists the most relevant cases and statutory provisions applicable to the topic in question. These are intended as an aid to revision, providing the student with a concise list of materials from which to begin revision.

Each chapter usually ends with several typical examination questions, together with general comments, skeleton solutions and suggested solutions. Wherever possible, the questions are drawn from the University of London external criminal law papers, with recent questions being included where possible. However, it is inevitable that, in compiling a list of questions by topic order rather than chronologically, not only do the same questions crop up over and over again in different guises, but there are gaps where questions have never been set at all.

Undoubtedly, the main feature of this Revision WorkBook is the inclusion of as many past examination questions as possible. While the use of past questions as a revision aid is certainly not new, it is hoped that the combination of actual past questions from the University of London LLB external course and specially written questions, where there are gaps in examination coverage, will be of assistance to students in achieving a thorough and systematic revision of the subject.

Careful use of the Revision WorkBook should enhance the student's understanding of criminal law and, hopefully, enable you to deal with as wide a range of subject matter as anyone might find in a criminal law examination, while at the same time allowing you to practise examination techniques while working through the book.

# Studying Criminal Law

Unlike many other 'compulsory' areas of law, criminal law is generally remembered by students as being one of the most interesting and therefore studying it becomes so much easier than some other disciplines. That is not to say, though, that it is an 'easy' subject, and there are certain crucial aspects of it which require a great deal of attention in order to understand them fully.

A considerable amount of criminal law appears in statutes and it is vital to be familiar with these enactments and their more important sections. Students must have a good working knowledge of which statutes create certain offences and which sections lay down criteria for determining questions arising from alleged offences (eg ss1–7 Theft Act 1968). You must know the ingredients of all the main offences covered by their respective syllabuses together with any defences.

Care should be taken not to confuse elements from one offence with those of another, such as 'reasonable excuse', 'lawful authority' and 'dishonesty'. One of the most difficult areas of Criminal law is that of mens rea. Which type of mens rea is applicable in a given case? The different types of mens rea must be clearly understood together with the various objective and subjective tests which have been developed by the courts.

Problems in this area are nowhere more apparent than in the area of murder – still governed by the common law – and the epithet 'malice aforethought' which most laymen associate with 'pre-meditation' has had a turbulent and confusing passage through the courts over recent years.

When considering an accused's liability, one must not be blinkered; the facts will often reveal several (sometimes overlapping) offences. Some instances of criminal damage may also amount to theft. Separate offences of burglary and robbery may be disclosed on the same facts. Consider, too, how an offence has been committed; were any instruments, disguises, or 'props' used? If so, then other offences may have been made out. How many people were involved? Were they all acting voluntarily? Are they equally culpable? Were they acting in concert?

If you were able to defend the accused what possible defences, however remote, may be available? How restrictive are they and how have the courts interpreted them? Is there an essential element missing from the facts as presented thereby obviating the need for a defence?

In asking these questions one must establish the elements required in order to attract liability, and then consider each individual part in the light of statutory guidance and case law.

So, in an alleged burglary one should proceed logically through the facts to discover whether there has been an 'entry'; whether it was into a 'building'; whether it was made as a 'trespasser'; whether the accused had the requisite 'intent' and so on. One must then look at the attendant (possibly mitigating) circumstances, eg the accused had got drunk, he had been drugged, he was mistaken, he was acting under duress, he did it for a joke, etc. In other words, once the basic principles have been grasped from a thorough reading of the textbooks and cases, one should approach specific instances of alleged criminal conduct from the point of view of both prosecutor and defence counsel, finally weighing up the respective merits of each argument and coming to a conclusion.

As with any other legal topic, students should have a sufficient number of authorities in their 'armoury' to support the arguments they propose and by repeatedly practising the application of what they have learned to hypothetical cases, students can become competent and confident in answering problem questions favoured by examiners, and also in discussing broader concepts of criminal law such as impossibility and strict liability.

Finally it is suggested that students read the *Criminal Law Review* which, apart from containing the most recent cases on the subject, also has regular articles of interest to academics and practitioners alike.

# Revision and Examination Technique

## Revision Technique

### Planning a revision timetable

In planning your revision timetable make sure you do not finish the syllabus too early. You should avoid leaving revision so late that you have to 'cram' – but constant revision of the same topic leads to stagnation.

Plan ahead, however, and try to make your plans increasingly detailed as you approach the examination date.

Allocate enough time for each topic to be studied. But note that it is better to devise a realistic timetable, to which you have a reasonable chance of keeping, rather than a wildly optimistic schedule which you will probably abandon at the first opportunity!

### The syllabus and its topics

One of your first tasks when you began your course was to ensure that you thoroughly understood your syllabus. Check now to see if you can write down the topics it comprises from memory. You will see that the chapters of this WorkBook are each devoted to a syllabus topic. This will help you decide which are the key chapters relative to your revision programme, though you should allow some time for glancing through the other chapters.

### The topic and its key points

Again working from memory, analyse what you consider to be the key points of any topic that you have selected for particular revision. Seeing what you can recall, unaided, will help you to understand and firmly memorise the concepts involved.

### Using the WorkBook

Relevant questions are provided for each topic in this book. Naturally, as typical examples of examination questions, they do not normally relate to one topic only. But the questions in each chapter will relate to the subject matter of the chapter to a degree. You can choose your method of consulting the questions and solutions, but here are some suggestions (strategies 1–3). Each of them pre-supposes that you have read through the author's notes on key points and key cases and statutes, and any other preliminary matter, at the beginning of the chapter. Once again, you now need to practise working from memory, for that is the challenge you are preparing yourself for. As a rule of procedure constantly test yourself once revision starts, both orally and in writing.

### Strategy 1

Strategy 1 is planned for the purpose of quick revision. First read your chosen question carefully and then jot down in abbreviated notes what you consider to be the main points at issue. Similarly, note the cases and statutes that occur to you as being relevant for citation purposes. Allow yourself sufficient time to cover what you feel to be relevant. Then study the author's skeleton solution and skim-read the suggested solution to see how they compare with your notes. When comparing consider carefully what the author has included (and concluded) and see whether that agrees with what you have written. Consider the points of variation also. Have you recognised the key issues? How relevant have you been? It is possible, of course, that you have referred to a recent case that is relevant, but which had not been reported when the WorkBook was prepared.

### Strategy 2

Strategy 2 requires a nucleus of three hours in which to practise writing a set of examination answers in a limited time-span.

Select a number of questions (as many as are normally set in your subject in the examination you are studying for), each from a different chapter in the WorkBook, without consulting the solutions. Find a place to write where you will not be disturbed and try to arrange not to be interrupted for three hours. Write your solutions in the time allowed, noting any time needed to make up if you are interrupted.

After a rest, compare your answers with the suggested solutions in the WorkBook. There will be considerable variation in style, of course, but the bare facts should not be too dissimilar. Evaluate your answer critically. Be 'searching', but develop a positive approach to deciding how you would tackle each question on another occasion.

### Strategy 3

You are unlikely to be able to do more than one three hour examination, but occasionally set yourself a single question. Vary the 'time allowed' by imagining it to be one of the questions that you must answer in three hours and allow yourself a limited preparation and writing time. Try one question that you feel to be difficult and an easier question on another occasion, for example.

#### Misuse of suggested solutions

Don't try to learn by rote. In particular, don't try to reproduce the suggested solutions by heart. Learn to express the basic concepts in your own words.

#### Keeping up-to-date

Keep up-to-date. While examiners do not require familiarity with changes in the law during the three months prior to the examination, it obviously creates a good impression if you can show you are acquainted with any recent changes. Make a habit of looking through one of the leading journals – *Modern Law Review*, *Law Quarterly Review* or the *New Law Journal*, for example – and cumulative indices to law reports, such as the *All England Law Reports* or *Weekly Law Reports*, or indeed the daily law reports in *The Times*. The *Law Society's Gazette* and the *Legal Executive Journal* are helpful sources, plus any specialist journal(s) for the subject you are studying.

## Examination Skills

### Examiners are human too!

The process of answering an examination question involves a communication between you and the person who set it. If you were speaking face to face with the person, you would choose your verbal points and arguments carefully in your reply. When writing, it is all too easy to forget the human being who is awaiting the reply and simply write out what one knows in the area of the subject! Bear in mind it is a person whose question you are responding to, throughout your essay. This will help you to avoid being irrelevant or long-winded.

### The essay question

Candidates are sometimes tempted to choose to answer essay questions because they 'seem' easier. But the examiner is looking for thoughtful work and will not give good marks for superficial answers.

The essay-type of question may be either purely factual, in asking you to explain the meaning of a certain doctrine or principle, or it may ask you to discuss a certain proposition, usually derived from a quotation. In either case, the approach to the answer is the same. A clear programme must be devised to give the examiner the meaning or significance of the doctrine, principle or proposition and its origin in common law, equity or statute, and cases which illustrate its application to the branch of law concerned. Essay questions offer a good way to obtain marks if you have thought carefully about a topic, since it is up to you to impose the structure (unlike the problem questions where the problem imposes its own structure). You are then free to speculate and show imagination.

### The problem question

The problem-type question requires a different approach. You may well be asked to advise a client or merely discuss the problems raised in the question. In either case, the most important factor is to take great care in reading the question. By its nature, the question will be longer than the essay-type question and you will have a number of facts to digest. Time spent in analysing the question may well save time later, when you are endeavouring to impress on the examiner the considerable extent of your basic legal knowledge. The quantity of knowledge is itself a trap and you must always keep within the boundaries of the question in hand. It is very tempting to show the examiner the extent of your knowledge of your subject, but if this is outside the question, it is time lost and no marks earned. It is inevitable that some areas which you have studied and revised will not be the subject of questions, but under no circumstances attempt to adapt a question to a stronger area of knowledge at the expense of relevance.

When you are satisfied that you have grasped the full significance of the problem-type question, set out the fundamental principles involved.

You will then go on to identify the fundamental problem (or problems) posed by the question. This should be followed by a consideration of the law which is relevant to the problem. The source of the law, together with the cases which will be of assistance in solving the problem, must then be considered in detail.

Very good problem questions are quite likely to have alternative answers, and in advising a party you should be aware that alternative arguments may be available. Each stage of your answer, in this case, will be based on the argument or arguments considered in the previous stage, forming a conditional sequence.

If, however, you only identify one fundamental problem, do not waste time worrying that you cannot think of an alternative – there may very well be only that one answer.

The examiner will then wish to see how you use your legal knowledge to formulate a case and how you apply that formula to the problem which is the subject of the question. It is this positive approach which can make answering a problem question a high mark earner for the student who has fully understood the question and clearly argued their case on the established law.

### Examination checklist

a) Read the instructions at the head of the examination carefully. While last-minute changes are unlikely – such as the introduction of a compulsory question or an increase in the number of questions asked – it has been known to happen.

b) Read the questions carefully. Analyse problem questions – work out what the examiner wants.

c) Plan your answer before you start to write.

d) Check that you understand the rubric before you start to write. Do not 'discuss', for example, if you are specifically asked to 'compare and contrast'.

e) Answer the correct number of questions. If you fail to answer one out of four questions set you lose 25 per cent of your marks!

### Style and structure

Try to be clear and concise. Fundamentally this amounts to using paragraphs to denote the sections of your essay, and writing simple, straightforward sentences as much as possible. The sentence you have just read has 22 words – when a sentence reaches 50 words it becomes difficult for a reader to follow.

Do not be inhibited by the word 'structure' (traditionally defined as giving an essay a beginning, a middle and an end). A good structure will be the natural consequence of setting out your arguments and the supporting evidence in a logical order. Set the scene briefly in your opening paragraph. Provide a clear conclusion in your final paragraph.

# Table of Cases

A (Children) (Conjoined Twins: Surgical
  Separation), Re [2000] 4 All ER 961    *51,
  202, 205, 211, 216, 217*
Abbott v R [1977] AC 755    *204*
Albert v Lavin [1981] 1 All ER 628    *35*
Alphacell Ltd v Woodward [1972] AC 824
  *19, 28, 29, 30*
Anderton v Ryan [1985] AC 567; [1985] 2
  WLR 968    *183*
Atkinson v Sir Alfred McAlpine & Son Ltd
  [1974] Crim LR 668    *28, 30*
Attorney-General for Northern Ireland v
  Gallagher [1963] AC 349    *188*
Attorney-General's Reference (No 1 of 1974)
  [1974] 1 QB 744; [1974] 2 WLR 891    *136*
Attorney-General's Reference (No 1 of 1975)
  [1975] 3 WLR 11; (1975) 61 Cr App R 118
  *70, 84, 171, 174*
Attorney-General's References (Nos 1 and 2
  of 1979) [1979] 2 WLR 577    *124, 145, 147*
Attorney-General's Reference (No 6 of 1980)
  [1981] QB 715    *62, 80, 81, 95*
Attorney-General's Reference (No 1 of 1983)
  [1985] QB 182; [1984] 3 All ER 369    *98,
  110, 148*
Attorney-General's Reference (No 2 of 1992)
  [1993] 3 WLR 982    *1, 3, 10, 83, 190, 209*
Attorney-General's Reference (No 3 of 1994)
  [1997] 3 All ER 936    *20, 21, 208*
Attorney-General's Reference for Northern
  Ireland (No 1 of 1975) [1977] AC 105    *49*

B v DPP [2000] 1 All ER 833    *19, 20, 21, 23,
  35, 79*
Balogh v St Albans Crown Court [1975] QB 73
  *118*
Beckford v R [1988] AC 130; [1987] 3 WLR
  611; [1987] 3 All ER 425    *35, 37, 54, 204,
  206*
Blakeley and Others v DPP [1991] Crim LR
  763    *70*
Bratty v Attorney-General for Northern
  Ireland [1963] AC 386; [1961] 3 WLR 965;
  [1961] 3 All ER 523    *3, 10, 13, 83, 189, 190,
  191, 192, 198, 209*

Buckoke v Greater London Council [1971] 1
  Ch 655    *202, 214*

Chandler v DPP [1964] AC 763    *17*
Chief Constable of Avon and Somerset v
  Shimmen (1987) 84 Cr App R 7    *19, 20,
  163, 164*
Cole v Turner (1705) 6 Mod Rep 149    *67, 69*
Collins v Wilcock [1984] 1 WLR 1172; [1984] 3
  All ER 374    *50, 72, 95*
Commissioner of Police of the Metropolis v
  Caldwell [1982] AC 341; [1981] 2 WLR 509;
  [1981] 1 All ER 961    *9, 11, 18, 19, 21, 22,
  23, 32, 45, 74, 122, 154, 158, 162, 163, 164,
  165, 166, 168*
Corcoran v Anderton [1980] Crim LR 385
  *133*
Coward v Baddeley (1859) 28 LJ Ex 260    *69*

Davies v DPP [1954] AC 378    *174, 187*
Davies v Flackett (1972) 116 SJ 526    *102, 116*
Dip Kaur v Chief Constable for Hampshire
  [1981] 1 WLR 578    *101, 102*
DPP v Beard [1920] AC 479    *190*
DPP v Camplin [1978] AC 705; [1978] 2 All ER
  168    *159*
DPP v Doot [1977] 1 WLR 1406    *193*
DPP v Huskinson [1988] Crim LR 620
  *97*
DPP v Lavender [1994] Crim LR 297    *98,
  107*
DPP v Majewski [1977] AC 443; [1976] 2 All
  ER 142    *10, 22, 23, 83, 84, 189, 190, 194,
  195, 200*
DPP v Morgan [1976] AC 182; [1975] 2 All ER
  347    *21, 22, 23, 34, 36, 70, 81, 85, 96, 194*
DPP v Newbury and Jones [1977] AC 500
  *15, 20, 41, 43, 57, 74*
DPP v Nock [1978] AC 979    *170, 173*
DPP v Pittaway [1994] Crim LR 600    *203*
DPP v Ray [1974] AC 370    *114, 116, 118, 149*
DPP v Smith [1961] AC 290; [1960] 3 All ER
  161    *7, 22, 26, 48, 50, 59, 73, 75, 93, 121,
  164, 179, 184*

DPP *v* Stonehouse [1978] AC 55    *127*
DPP for Northern Ireland *v* Lynch [1975] AC
    653; [1975] 1 All ER 913    *204*
DPP for Northern Ireland *v* Maxwell; [1978] 3
    All ER 1140; (1978) 68 Cr App R 128    *174*

Edwards *v* Ddin [1976] 1 WLR 942    *98, 122,
130*
Elliot *v* C [1983] 1 WLR 939; 2 All ER 1005
    *18, 21, 33, 45, 163*

Fagan *v* Metropolitan Police Commissioner
    [1969] 1 QB 439; [1968] 3 All ER 442    *12,
25, 48, 49, 53, 58, 75, 92, 118, 120, 179*
Farrell *v* Secretary of State for Defence [1980]
    1 All ER 166    *37*
Faulkner *v* Talbot [1981] 3 All ER 468    *78*

Gammon (Hong Kong) Ltd *v* Attorney-
    General for Hong Kong [1985] AC 1; (1984)
    80 Cr App R 194    *19, 21*

Hardman *v* Chief Constable of Avon and
    Somerset Constabulary [1986] Crim LR 330
    *154, 166, 167*
Harding *v* Price [1948] 1 KB 695    *28*
Haughton *v* Smith [1975] AC 476    *136, 182,
183*

Invicta Plastics Ltd *v* Clare [1976] RTR 251
    *169, 173, 177, 186*

JJC (A Minor) *v* Eisenhower [1984] QB 331;
    [1983] 3 WLR 537    *7, 59, 60, 63, 66, 93, 184*
Jaggard *v* Dickinson [1981] QB 527; [1981] 2
    WLR 118; [1980] Crim LR 717    *142, 153,
154, 189*
James & Son Ltd *v* Smee [1955] 1 QB 78    *77*
Johnson *v* DPP [1994] Crim LR 673    *154*
Johnson *v* Youden [1950] 1 KB 544    *7, 171,
174*

Lawrence *v* Metropolitan Police
    Commissioner [1972] AC 626; [1972] 2 All
    ER 1253    *97, 98, 104, 112*
Lloyd *v* DPP [1991] Crim LR 904    *154*
Logdon *v* DPP [1976] Crim LR 121    *58, 165*
Low *v* Blease (1975) 119 SJ 695    *98*

McNaghten's Case (1843) 10 Cl & F 200    *13,
62, 189, 190, 191, 197, 198*
Metropolitan Police Commissioner *v* Charles
    [1977] AC 177; [1976] 1 All ER 659; [1977]
    Crim LR 615    *114, 116, 123, 130*
Moloney *v* Mercer [1971] 2 NSWLR 207    *93*
Morphitis *v* Salmon [1990] Crim LR 48    *122,
153, 154, 213*
Moynes *v* Cooper [1956] 1 QB 439    *110, 148*

Neal *v* Gribble [1978] RTR 409; (1977) 64 Cr
    App R 54    *134*
Norfolk Constabulary *v* Seekings and Gould
    [1986] Crim LR 167    *137*

Oxford *v* Moss [1979] Crim LR 119; (1978) 68
    Cr App R 183    *97, 98*

Palmer *v* R [1971] AC 814    *121, 204, 206*
Pharmaceutical Society of Great Britain *v*
    Logan [1982] Crim LR 443    *19*

R *v* Abdul-Hussain and Others [1999] Crim
    LR 570    *203, 204*
R *v* Adomako [1994] 3 WLR 288    *6, 14, 19,
24, 41, 43, 51, 68, 74, 77, 161, 163, 164*
R *v* Ahluwalia [1992] 4 All ER 889; [1993]
    Crim LR 63    *40*
R *v* Aitken and Others [1992] 1 WLR 1066
    *63, 80, 81*
R *v* Ali [1995] Crim LR 303    *204*
R *v* Allen [1985] AC 1029; [1985] 3 WLR 107;
    [1985] 2 All ER 641    *98, 123, 129*
R *v* Allen [1988] Crim LR 698    *203*
R *v* Anderson [1986] AC 27; [1985] 2 All ER
    961    *141, 170, 173, 178, 180, 182*
R *v* Anderson and Morris [1966] 2 QB 110
    *174*
R *v* Andrews and Hedges [1981] Crim LR 106
    *115*
R *v* Armstrong [1989] Crim LR 149    *39*
R *v* Arobieke [1988] Crim LR 314    *5*
R *v* Ashford and Smith [1988] Crim LR 682
    *154*
R *v* Atakpu; R *v* Abrahams [1993] 3 WLR 812
    *105*
R *v* Atwal [1989] Crim LR 293    *115, 116*
R *v* Bailey (1800) Russ & Ry 1, CCR    *34*

R *v* Bailey (1977) 66 Cr App R 31    *40*

R *v* Bailey [1983] 2 All ER 503; (1983) 77 Cr
App R 76    *2, 3, 10, 12, 15, 188, 201*

R *v* Bainbridge [1960] 1 QB 129; [1959] 3 WLR
356; (1960) 43 Cr App R 194    *120, 156,
160, 171, 176, 183, 184*

R *v* Baker and Wilkins [1997] Crim LR 497
*118, 211*

R *v* Baldessare (1930) 22 Cr App R 70    *171*

R *v* Ball [1989] Crim LR 730    *181*

R *v* Bamborough [1996] Crim LR 744    *174*

R *v* Barnard (1837) 7 C & P 784    *116*

R *v* Bashir (1982) 77 Cr App R 59    *25*

R *v* Becerra and Cooper (1975) 62 Cr App R
212    *173, 174, 176*

R *v* Bernard [1938] 2 KB 264    *110*

R *v* Betts and Ridley (1930) 22 Cr App R 148
*171, 174*

R *v* Billinghurst [1978] Crim LR 553    *80, 82,
95*

R *v* Blaue [1975] 1 WLR 1411; [1975] 3 All ER
446; (1975) 61 Cr App R 271    *3, 14, 39, 42,
45, 47, 55, 64, 66, 84, 157*

R *v* Bloxham [1983] 1 AC 109; [1982] 1 All ER
582    *136, 137*

R *v* Bogacki [1973] QB 832    *134, 137, 150,
214*

R *v* Bow [1977] Crim LR 176; (1976) 64 Cr
App R 54    *134, 137, 150, 214*

R *v* Bowden [1993] Crim LR 380    *195*

R *v* Bowen [1996] 2 Cr App R 157    *204*

R *v* Boyea [1992] Crim LR 574    *63*

R *v* Bradish (1990) 90 Cr App R 271    *19, 22,
29*

R *v* Brooks and Brooks [1983] Crim LR 188
*98, 129*

R *v* Brown (1776) Leach 148    *142, 144*

R *v* Brown [1970] 1 QB 105; [1969] 3 WLR 370
*135*

R *v* Brown [1985] Crim LR 212    *134*

R *v* Brown [1993] 2 WLR 556; [1993] 2 All ER
75; [1993] Crim LR 961    *63, 80, 82, 88, 89,
90, 95*

R *v* Brown and Stratton [1998] Crim LR 485
*195*

R *v* Bulduc and Bird [1967] 3 ccc 294    *94*

R *v* Bundy [1977] 1 WLR 914; [1977] 2 All ER
382    *135*

R *v* Bunyan and Morgan (1844) 1 Cox CC 74
*93*

R *v* Burgess [1991] 2 WLR 1206; [1991] 2 All
ER 769; (1991) 93 Cr App R 41    *190, 198*

R *v* Burstow *see* R *v* Ireland; R *v* Burstow

R *v* Byrne [1960] 2 QB 396; [1960] 3 All ER 1
*40, 43, 209*

R *v* Callender [1992] 3 All ER 51    *116*

R *v* Cato [1976] 1 WLR 110; [1976] 1 All ER
260; (1976) 62 Cr App R 41    *43, 60, 69,
94*

R *v* Cavendish [1961] 1 WLR 1083    *135*

R *v* Chan Fook [1994] 1 WLR 689; [1994] Crim
LR 432; (1994) 99 Cr App R 147    *12, 26,
48, 50, 55, 59, 73, 75, 93, 118, 120, 164, 179,
184*

R *v* Charlson [1955] 1 All ER 859    *198*

R *v* Cheshire [1991] 1 WLR 844; [1991] 3 All
ER 670; (1991) 93 Cr App R 251    *3, 39, 50,
181*

R *v* Church [1966] 1 QB 59; [1965] 2 All ER 72
*6, 15, 20, 24, 27, 41, 45, 48, 51, 54, 74, 157,
181, 208*

R *v* Clarence (1888) 22 QBD 23    *33, 71 ,72,
73, 75, 94*

R *v* Clarke [1972] 1 All ER 219    *189*

R *v* Clarkson [1971] 1 WLR 1402    *7, 171,
174, 217*

R *v* Clear [1968] 1 QB 670    *108, 136, 140,
151, 157, 212*

R *v* Clegg [1995] 2 WLR 80    *204, 206*

R *v* Clucas [1949] 2 KB 226    *123*

R *v* Coady [1996] Crim LR 518    *130*

R *v* Cogan and Leak (1975) 61 Cr App R 217
*71*

R *v* Cole [1994] Crim LR 582    *51, 203, 205,
210*

R *v* Collins [1973] QB 100; [1972] 2 All ER
1105    *67, 134, 137, 142, 143, 144*

R *v* Collis-Smith [1971] Crim LR 716    *114,
126*

R *v* Collister and Warhust (1955) 39 Cr App R
100    *136*

R *v* Coney (1882) 8 QBD 534    *7, 95, 171, 217*

R *v* Conway [1989] QB 290; [1988] 3 All ER
1025    *51, 203, 205, 210, 214*

R *v* Court [1989] AC 28; [1987] 1 All ER 20
*78, 81, 83, 142, 143*

R *v* Culyer (1992) The Times 12 April    *142, 143*

R *v* Cunningham [1957] 2 QB 396; (1957) 41 Cr App R 155    *9, 18, 19, 21, 22, 23, 24, 50, 55, 69, 76, 84, 164, 165*

R *v* Curr [1968] 2 QB 944; [1967] 1 All ER 478    *169, 173, 177, 180, 186*

R *v* D [1984] AC 778    *184*

R *v* Dalby [1982] 1 WLR 425; [1982] 1 All ER 916    *8, 39, 48*

R *v* Davies (Leslie) [1983] Crim LR 741    *200, 201*

R *v* Dawson [1976] Crim LR 692; (1976) 64 Cr App R 170    *133, 136*

R *v* Dawson (1985) 81 Cr App R 150    *15, 41, 43, 45, 64, 157, 208*

R *v* Dear [1996] Crim LR 595    *39, 42, 64*

R *v* Denton [1982] 1 All ER 65; (1982) 74 Cr App R 81    *153, 154*

R *v* Donovan [1934] 2 KB 498    *62, 80, 82, 87, 91*

R *v* Doughty [1986] Crim LR 625    *57*

R *v* Doukas [1978] 1 WLR 372; [1978] 1 All ER 1061    *116, 118, 121*

R *v* Dudley [1989] Crim LR 57    *154*

R *v* Dudley and Stephens (1884) 14 QBD 273    *51, 202, 205, 207, 208, 210, 216*

R *v* Duffy [1949] 1 All ER 932    *39, 47, 56, 159, 180*

R *v* Dunnington [1984] QB 472    *176*

R *v* Dytham [1979] QB 722; [1979] 3 All ER 641    *2, 3, 8*

R *v* Easom [1971] 2 QB 315    *127*

R *v* Elbekkay [1995] Crim LR 163    *79*

R *v* Emmett (1999) The Times 15 October    *82*

R *v* Feely [1973] 1 QB 530    *113, 125, 126, 127, 129, 131*

R *v* Fenton (1830) 1 Lew CC 179    *5*

R *v* Fitzmaurice [1983] 2 WLR 227; [1983] 1 All ER 189    *169, 173, 178, 182*

R *v* Fitzpatrick [1977] NI 20    *205*

R *v* Fletcher (1859) 8 Cox CC 131    *25*

R *v* Franklin (1883) 15 Cox CC 163    *5*

R *v* Gamble [1989] NI 268    *172*

R *v* Garwood [1987] 1 WLR 319; [1987] 1 All ER 1032; [1987] Crim CR 476    *134, 136, 140*

R *v* Geddes [1996] Crim LR 894; (1996) The Times 16 July    *176*

R *v* George [1956] Crim LR 52    *78, 81*

R *v* Ghosh [1982] QB 1053; [1982] Crim LR 608; (1982) 75 Cr App R 154    *8, 98, 99, 101, 102, 105, 108, 110, 111, 112, 113, 115, 116, 118, 120, 123, 125, 127, 129, 131, 139, 145, 147, 149, 151, 152, 207, 213*

R *v* Gibbens and Proctor (1918) 13 Cr App R 134; (1918) 82 JP 287    *2, 3*

R *v* Gilks [1972] 3 All ER 280    *113, 131*

R *v* Gillard (1988) 87 Cr App R 189    *60, 69*

R *v* Gilmour (2000) The Times 21 June    *174*

R *v* Gittens [1984] QB 698    *40*

R *v* Gomez [1993] AC 442; [1992] 3 WLR 1067; [1993] 1 All ER 1    *87, 89, 97, 99, 100, 104, 110, 112, 114, 130, 139, 148, 152, 157, 207*

R *v* Goodfellow (1986) 83 Cr App R 23    *41, 43, 48*

R *v* Gotts [1992] 2 AC 412; [1992] 1 All ER 832 (HL); [1991] 2 WLR 878 (CA)    *204, 205*

R *v* Graham [1982] 1 All ER 801; (1982) 74 Cr App R 235    *108, 176, 203, 205, 212*

R *v* Groak [1999] Crim LR 669    *195*

R *v* Gullefer [1987] Crim LR 195    *109, 129*

R *v* Gullefer [1990] 3 All ER 882; (1990) 91 Cr App R 356    *53, 147, 170, 174, 176, 183*

R *v* Hale (1978) 68 Cr App R 415    *8, 133, 136, 140, 146*

R *v* Hall [1973] QB 126; [1972] 3 WLR 381    *97, 125*

R *v* Hall (1985) 81 Cr App R 260    *135, 138*

R *v* Hammond [1982] Crim LR 611    *98*

R *v* Hancock and Shankland [1986] AC 455; [1986] 2 WLR 257; [1986] 1 All ER 641    *17, 53, 73*

R *v* Hardie [1985] 1 WLR 64; [1984] 3 All ER 848    *10, 15, 188, 189, 191*

R *v* Harris (1987) 84 Cr App R 75    *135*

R *v* Harry [1974] Crim LR 32    *134, 151*

R *v* Harvey (1980) 72 Cr App R 139    *134, 136*

R *v* Hayward (1833) 6 C & P 157    *40*

R *v* Hayward (1908) 21 Cox CC 692    *47*

R *v* Hegarty [1994] Crim LR 353    *205*

R *v* Hennessy [1989] 1 WLR 287; (1989) 89 Cr App R 10    *12, 190, 192, 199*

R *v* Hensler (1870) 22 LT 691    *3, 114*

R *v* Hill [1986] Crim LR 815; (1986) 83 Cr App R 386   *69*

R *v* Hinks [2000] 4 All ER 833 (HL); [1998] Crim LR 904 (CA)   *97, 99, 104, 148, 149*

R *v* Holden [1991] Crim LR 478   *127, 131*

R *v* Holland (1841) 2 Mood & R 351   *39, 42*

R *v* Holt and Lee [1981] 2 All ER 854   *116*

R *v* Hopley (1860) 2 F & F 202   *95*

R *v* Horseferry Road Magistrates' Court, ex parte K [1997] Crim LR 129   *193*

R *v* Howe [1987] AC 417; [1987] 2 WLR 568; [1987] 1 All ER 771   *204, 205*

R *v* Hudson and Taylor [1971] 2 QB 202 *177, 203, 205, 212*

R *v* Humphreys [1995] 4 All ER 1008   *42*

R *v* Hunt [1977] Crim LR 740; (1977) 66 Cr App R 105   *154*

R *v* Hurley and Murray [1967] VR 526   *203*

R *v* Hussey (1924) 18 Cr App R 160   *54, 206, 207*

R *v* Ibrams and Gregory [1982] Crim LR 229; (1981) 74 Cr App R 154   *43, 57*

R *v* Instan [1893] 1 QB 450   *2, 5, 8*

R *v* Ireland; R *v* Burstow [1998] AC 147; [1997] 3 WLR 534; [1997] 4 All ER 225   *33, 55, 58, 59, 60, 66, 71, 73, 84, 161, 166*

R *v* Jackson [1983] Crim LR 617   *115, 116*

R *v* Johnson [1968] SASR 132   *142, 143*

R *v* Jones and Smith [1976] 3 All ER 54   *67, 101, 110, 128, 134, 137, 140, 145, 147, 156, 158*

R *v* Jordan (1956) 40 Cr App R 152   *39, 42*

R *v* Julien [1969] 1 WLR 839   *62, 206*

R *v* K [2001] 3 All ER 897   *81*

R *v* Kaitamaki [1985] AC 147   *81*

R *v* Kanwar [1982] 1 WLR 845; [1982] Crim LR 532   *135, 138*

R *v* Kelly [1993] Crim LR 763; (1993) 97 Cr App R 245   *134*

R *v* Kelly [1998] 3 All ER 741   *99*

R *v* Kemp [1957] 1 QB 399; [1956] 3 All ER 249 *189, 190, 192, 198*

R *v* Khan [1990] Crim LR 519; (1990) 91 Cr App R 29   *170, 174*

R *v* Kimber [1983] 1 WLR 1118   *35, 80*

R *v* King [1979] Crim LR 122   *119*

R *v* King and Stockwell [1987] Crim LR 398 *126*

R *v* Kingston [1994] 3 WLR 519; [1994] 3 All ER 353; [1994] Crim LR 846   *93, 189, 191, 194, 195, 200, 201*

R *v* Kitson (1955) 39 Cr App R 66   *210*

R *v* Kovacs [1974] 1 WLR 370; [1974] 1 All ER 1236   *126*

R *v* Lamb [1967] 2 QB 981; [1967] 2 All ER 1282   *41, 58*

R *v* Lambie [1981] 1 All ER 332; [1981] Crim LR 712   *114, 124*

R *v* Langford (1842) Car & M 642   *42*

R *v* Larsonneur (1933) 24 Cr App R 74; (1933) 97 JP 206   *19*

R *v* Latimer (1886) 17 QBD 359   *20, 21, 33, 47, 184*

R *v* Lawrence [1982] AC 510; [1981] 2 WLR 524   *41*

R *v* LeBrun [1991] 3 WLR 653; [1991] 4 All ER 673   *20*

R *v* Linekar [1995] 3 All ER 69   *94*

R *v* Lipman [1970] 1 QB 152   *191*

R *v* Lloyd and Ali [1985] QB 829; [1985] 3 WLR 30   *98, 99, 107, 108*

R *v* McDavitt [1981] Crim LR 843   *98, 99, 129, 141*

R *v* McDonough (1962) 47 Cr App R 37   *173*

R *v* McInnes [1971] 1 WLR 1600; [1971] 3 All ER 295   *206*

R *v* McNamara (1988) 87 Cr App R 246   *29*

R *v* Majoram [2000] Crim LR 372   *42*

R *v* Malcherek and Steel [1981] 2 All ER 422; (1981) 73 Cr App R 173   *3, 39, 42*

R *v* Marchant (1985) 80 Cr App R 361   *134, 137*

R *v* Marcus [1981] 1 WLR 774; [1981] 2 All ER 833   *60, 69, 84, 94*

R *v* Marriott (1838) 8 C & P 425   *8*

R *v* Marshall; R *v* Coombes; R *v* Eren [1998] 2 Cr App R 282   *99*

R *v* Martin (1881) 8 QBD 54   *55, 66*

R *v* Martin [1989] 1 All ER 652; (1988) 88 Cr App R 343   *203, 205, 208, 210, 214, 217*

R *v* Martin [2000] Crim LR 615   *203, 205, 212*

R *v* Martindale [1986] 1 WLR 1042   *29*

R *v* Michael (1840) 9 C & P 356   *85*

R *v* Miller [1954] 2 QB 282   *7, 60, 63, 166*

R *v* Miller [1983] 2 AC 161; [1983] 2 WLR 539; [1983] 1 All ER 978   *2, 4, 5, 10, 67*

R *v* Minor (1987) 52 JP 30   *135*

R *v* Mitchell [1983] 2 WLR 938   *41*

R *v* Mohan [1976] QB 1   *160*

R *v* Moloney [1985] AC 905; [1985] 1 All ER 1025   *53*

R *v* Morgan [1975] 2 All ER 347   *79*

R *v* Morris [1984] AC 320; [1983] 3 WLR 697; [1983] 3 All ER 288   *12, 97, 99, 100, 101, 107, 111, 112, 130, 139, 145, 147, 207*

R *v* Most (1881) 7 QBD 244   *173*

R *v* Mowatt [1968] 1 QB 421; [1967] 3 All ER 47; (1967) 51 Cr App R 402   *33, 45, 46, 55, 60, 62, 66, 71, 73, 84, 158*

R *v* Nedrick [1986] 1 WLR 1025; [1986] 3 All ER 1; [1986] Crim LR 742; (1986) 83 Cr App R 267   *18, 53, 73*

R *v* Nicholls (1874) 13 Cox CC 75   *8*

R *v* Oatridge [1992] Crim LR 205; (1991) 94 Cr App R 397   *26, 54, 204*

R *v* O'Connor [1991] Crim LR 135   *188, 195*

R *v* O'Grady [1987] 3 WLR 321; (1987) Cr App R 315   *36, 189*

R *v* O'Leary (1986) 82 Cr App R 341   *134*

R *v* Olugboja (1981) 73 Cr App R 344   *79, 81*

R *v* Owino [1996] 2 Cr App R 128   *49, 121*

R *v* Pagett (1983) 76 Cr App R 279   *39, 42*

R *v* Palmer [1971] AC 814   *57*

R *v* Parmenter (1991) 92 Cr App R 68 (*see also* R *v* Savage; R *v* Parmenter)   *165*

R *v* Peart [1970] 2 QB 672   *134, 137*

R *v* Pembliton (1874) LR 2 CCR 119   *20, 21, 34*

R *v* Phipps and McGill [1970] RTR 209   *134, 137*

R *v* Pitchley [1972] Crim LR 705; (1973) 57 Cr App R 30   *135, 138*

R *v* Pittwood (1902) 19 TLR 37   *2, 4, 5*

R *v* Pommell [1995] 2 Cr App R 607   *118, 203, 205, 211, 217*

R *v* Powell and Daniels; R *v* English [1997] 3 WLR 959; [1997] 4 All ER 545   *172, 175, 185, 187*

R *v* Price [1990] Crim LR 200; (1990) 90 Cr App R 409   *125*

R *v* Quick & Paddison [1973] QB 910; [1973] 3 All ER 347   *3, 190, 198, 199*

R *v* Rabey (1977) 37 CC (2d) 461 (Ont)   *190, 199*

R *v* Rahman (1985) 81 Cr App R 349   *184, 212*

R *v* Rai [2000] 1 Cr App R 242   *116*

R *v* Ransford (1874) 13 Cox CC 9   *186*

R *v* Rashid [1977] 1 WLR 298; [1977] 2 All ER 237   *114, 118, 121, 135, 137*

R *v* Reed [1982] Crim LR 819   *173*

R *v* Reid [1992] 1 WLR 793; [1992] 3 All ER 673; [1992] Crim LR 814   *21, 23, 158, 164*

R *v* Richardson [1999] Crim LR 62; [1998] 2 Cr App R 200   *80, 82*

R *v* Richardson and Irwin [1999] Crim LR 494; [1999] 1 Cr App R 392   *82*

R *v* Roberts [1972] Crim LR 27; (1971) 56 Cr App R 95   *26, 39, 42, 48*

R *v* Robinson [1977] Crim LR 173   *133*

R *v* Rook [1993] 1 WLR 1005; [1993] 2 All ER 955   *173, 175*

R *v* Rose (1884) 15 Cox CC 540   *34, 206*

R *v* Sangha [1988] 1 WLR 519; [1989] 2 All ER 385   *21, 33*

R *v* Sargeant [1997] Crim LR 50   *78, 81*

R *v* Satnam; R *v* Kewal (1983) 78 Cr App R 149   *70, 81, 94*

R *v* Saunders [1985] Crim LR 230   *60, 65, 70, 71, 158*

R *v* Saunders and Archer (1573) 2 Plowd 473   *172, 175*

R *v* Savage; R *v* Parmenter [1992] 1 AC 699; [1991] 3 WLR 914; [1991] 4 All ER 698   *7, 24, 26, 33, 48, 50, 55, 59, 60, 66, 73, 75, 92, 121, 161, 179, 185*

R *v* Scott [1975] AC 819   *170*

R *v* Shannon (1980) 71 Cr App R 192   *57*

R *v* Shendley [1970] Crim LR 49   *8*

R *v* Shepard [1987] Crim LR 686; (1987) 86 Cr App R 47   *177, 205*

R *v* Shivpuri [1987] AC 1; [1986] 2 WLR 988; [1986] 2 All ER 334   *109, 147, 170, 174, 176, 183, 212*

R *v* Shortland [1995] Crim LR 893   *115*

R *v* Sibartie [1983] Crim LR 470   *115, 116*

R *v* Silverman [1987] Crim LR 574   *116, 120*

R *v* Singh (Gurpal) [1999] Crim LR 582   *67*

R *v* Siracusa (1990) 90 Cr App R 340   *141, 170, 173, 177, 178, 180, 182*

R *v* Slingsby [1995] Crim LR 570   *95*

R *v* Smith (1850) 1 Den 510   *135*

R v Smith [1959] 2 QB 35    *3, 39, 42, 50, 181*

R v Smith [1974] QB 354    *142, 154*

R v Smith [1982] Crim LR 531    *198*

R v Smith (Morgan) [2000] 4 All ER 289    *14, 39, 43, 47, 54, 56, 180*

R v Smith (Sandie) [1982] Crim LR 531    *1, 3*

R v Speck (1977) 65 Cr App R 161    *79*

R v Spratt [1991] 2 All ER 210; (1990) 91 Cr App R 362    *165*

R v Steer [1988] AC 111; [1987] 3 WLR 205; [1987] 2 All ER 833    *45, 154, 155, 158, 166*

R v Stephenson [1979] QB 695    *32*

R v Stewart (1982) The Times 14 December    *98*

R v Stewart and Scholfield [1995] 1 Cr App R 441    *172*

R v Stokes [1982] Crim LR 695    *150*

R v Stone and Dobinson [1977] QB 354    *2, 4, 5, 8*

R v Sullivan [1984] AC 156; [1983] 1 All ER 577    *190, 192, 193*

R v T [1990] Crim LR 256    *3, 190, 199*

R v Tabassum [2000] Crim LR 686    *80, 81*

R v Tandy [1989] 1 WLR 350; [1989] 1 All ER 267; (1988) 87 Cr App R 45    *40, 43*

R v Thornton [1992] 1 All ER 306    *40*

R v Tolson (1889) 23 QBD 168    *36*

R v Turner (No 2) [1971] 1 WLR 901; [1971] 2 All ER 441    *99*

R v Valderrama-Vega [1985] Crim LR 220    *108, 203*

R v Velumyl [1989] Crim LR 299    *98, 213*

R v Venna [1976] QB 421; [1975] 3 All ER 788; (1975) 61 Cr App R 310    *25, 50, 58, 145, 165, 212*

R v Vickers [1957] 2 QB 664    *47*

R v Vinagre (1979) 69 Cr App R 104    *40*

R v Vincent [2001] Crim LR 488    *99*

R v Waites [1982] Crim LR 369    *115*

R v Walker [1996] 1 Cr App R 111    *93*

R v Walker and Hayles (1990) 90 Cr App R 226    *160, 170, 174, 185*

R v Walkington [1979] 2 All ER 716; (1979) 68 Cr App R 427    *134, 147*

R v Wall (1802) 28 State Tr 51    *39*

R v Waterfield [1964] 1 QB 164    *37*

R v Warner (1970) 55 Cr App R 93    *107, 108*

R v Wellard (1884) 14 QBD 63    *93*

R v White [1910] 2 KB 124    *3, 5, 38, 42, 47, 64, 66, 157*

R v Whitefield (1983) 79 Cr App R 36    *173*

R v Whiteley (1991) 93 Cr App R 25    *213*

R v Whybrow (1951) 35 Cr App R 141    *179, 185*

R v Whyte [1987] 3 All ER 416    *37, 57*

R v Willer (1986) 83 Cr App R 225    *51, 203, 205, 210, 214*

R v Williams [1923] 1 KB 340; (1923) 17 Cr App R 56    *79*

R v Williams [1968] Crim LR 678    *48, 49*

R v Williams [1983] 3 All ER 316; (1983) 78 Cr App R 276    *22, 23, 26*

R v Williams [1987] 3 All ER 411    *13, 209*

R v Williams [1992] 1 WLR 380; [1992] 2 All ER 183    *42*

R v Williams (Gladstone) [1987] 3 All ER 411; [1984] Crim LR 163; (1984) 78 Cr App R 276    *35, 37, 204, 206*

R v Wilson [1955] 1 All ER 744    *58*

R v Wilson; R v Jenkins [1984] AC 242; [1983] 3 WLR 686 (HL); [1983] 1 All WE 993 (CA)    *50, 67, 75, 187*

R v Wilson [1996] 3 WLR 125    *63, 64, 80, 82, 95*

R v Windle [1952] 2 QB 826    *62, 190, 193*

R v Woodman [1974] 2 All ER 955    *97*

R v Woods (1981) 74 Cr App R 312; [1982] Crim LR 42    *24, 25*

R v Woollin [1998] 4 All ER 103    *5, 14, 18, 21, 23, 24, 39, 42, 51, 53, 56, 62, 64, 66, 71, 73, 157, 158, 159, 163, 180, 185, 216*

R v Woolven [1983] Crim LR 632    *127*

R v Wootten and Peake [1990] Crim LR 201    *127, 132*

Race Relations Board v Applin [1973] QB 815    *108, 169, 173, 177, 180, 182, 186*

Rance v Mid Downs Health Authority [1991] 1 All ER 801    *60*

Riley v DPP (1989) The Times 13 December    *37*

Scott v Shepherd (1773) Wm Bl 892    *58*

Scudder v Barrett [1979] 3 WLR 591    *147*

Simpson v Peat [1952] 2 QB 24    *9, 214*

Smedleys Ltd v Breed [1974] AC 839    *19, 22*

Smith *v* Hughes (1871) LR 6 QB 597    *110, 120*

Smith *v* Superintendent of Woking Police Station (1983) 76 Cr App R 234    *60*

Southwark London Borough Council *v* Williams [1971] 2 All ER 175    *202, 210*

Stevens *v* Gourley (1859) 7 CBNS 99    *52*

Sweet *v* Parsley [1970] AC 132; [1969] 1 All ER 347    *29, 30*

Thorne *v* Motor Trade Association [1937] AC 797    *108*

Thornton *v* Mitchell [1940] 1 All ER 339    *175*

Treacy *v* DPP [1971] AC 537    *134, 151*

Troughton *v* Metropolitan Police Commissioner [1987] Crim LR 138    *98*

Tuberville *v* Savage (1669) 1 Mod Rep 3    *58*

Wai Yu-Tsang *v* R [1991] 3 WLR 1006    *170*

Westminster City Council *v* Croyalgrange [1986] 2 All ER 353    *36*

Whittaker *v* Campbell [1984] QB 318; [1983] 3 WLR 676    *134, 137*

Williams *v* Phillips (1957) 41 Cr App R 5    *97, 99*

Wrothwell (FJH) *v* Yorkshire Water Authority [1984] Crim LR 43    *19*

Yeandel *v* Fisher [1966] 1 QB 440    *28, 29*

Yip Chiu-Cheung *v* R [1994] 3 WLR 514; [1994] 2 All ER 924; [1994] Crim LR 824    *170, 180, 181, 182*

# Table of Statutes and Other Materials

Abortion Act 1967    60
Accessories and Abettors Act 1861
    s8    7, 93, 108, 120, 160, 171, 175, 183,
      184, 212
Asbestos Regulations 1969    28

Children and Young Persons Act 1933    4,
  5
Crime and Disorder Act 1998
    s29    60
    s34    20, 21, 33, 44, 108, 150, 161
Criminal Attempts Act 1981    170, 176, 177,
  177–178
    s1    7, 53, 109, 129, 160, 168, 176, 179,
      182, 185, 212
    s1(1)    102, 145, 174, 207
    s1(2)    102, 109, 170, 174, 176, 183, 212
    s1(3)    102, 126, 170, 174
    s1(4)    67
    s4(3)    53, 183
Criminal Damage Act 1971    45, 153, 162,
  168
    s1    9, 11, 74, 122, 124, 162, 183, 213
    s1(1)    10, 31, 32, 44, 83, 87, 89, 142, 155,
      158, 166, 167
    s1(1)(b)    32
    s1(2)    10, 11, 31, 32, 154, 155, 158, 163,
      166, 167, 194
    s1(3)    10, 154, 162
    s3    9, 154, 167, 168
    s5    96, 167, 210
    s5(2)    202
    s5(2)(a)    153
    s5(2)(b)    153
    s5(3)    153
    s10    74
    s10(1)    153, 167, 213
    s10(1)(a)    74
    s10(2)    153
    s27    154
Criminal Justice Act 1967
    s8    14, 17, 21, 23
    s91    142
Criminal Justice Act 1988
    s39    69

Criminal Justice and Public Order Act 1994
  25
    s142    69, 79, 85
Criminal Law Act 1967
    s3    36, 37, 54, 55, 57, 59, 121, 204
    s3(1)    206, 208
Criminal Law Act 1977    150, 171, 177, 187
    s1    52, 150, 170, 180, 182, 184
    s1(1)    174, 177, 186
    s1(1)(b)    170
    s5    186
Criminal Procedure (Insanity) Act 1964    197
    s1    190, 193
Criminal Procedure (Insanity and Unfitness
  to Plead) Act 1991    13, 197

Education Act 1986
    s47    95

Family Allowance Act 1945
    s9(b)    186
Firearms Act 1968    19
    s5(1)(b)    29

Homicide Act 1957
    s1    42
    s2    40, 57
    s2(1)    43, 64, 193, 209
    s3    39, 43, 54, 56, 159, 180

Indecency with Children Act 1960
    s1(1)    79
Infant Life (Preservation) Act 1929    60

Law Reform Act (Year and a Day Rule) Act
  1996    38, 155, 158

Misuse of Drugs Act 1971    29, 30

Offences Against the Person Act 1861    24,
  26, 55, 58, 59, 95, 145
    s4    50
    s18    7, 8, 24, 26, 31, 33, 45, 46, 48, 50,
      59, 61, 62, 63, 66, 67, 71, 73, 75, 83, 84,
      85, 93, 121, 158, 164, 179, 184, 187

Offences Against the Person Act 1861 (*contd.*)
s20    *7, 8, 9, 10, 15, 24, 26, 31, 33, 45, 46,*
*48, 50, 55, 56, 59, 61, 62, 63, 66, 67, 71,*
*73, 74, 75, 76, 83, 84, 85, 93, 121, 158,*
*161, 164, 166, 179, 184, 187*
s23    *60, 61, 68, 69, 71, 73, 76, 83, 84, 85,*
*164*
s24    *60, 61, 68, 69, 71, 73, 83, 84, 85, 94*
s47    *7, 8, 9, 10, 12, 24, 26, 37, 45, 46, 48,*
*50, 55, 56, 59, 61, 63, 66, 71, 72, 73, 75,*
*92, 118, 120, 161, 164, 165, 166, 179, 184*
s58    *60*

Police Act 1964
s51    *36, 118*
Police Act 1996
s89    *36*
s89(1)    *36, 37, 59*
s89(2)    *37*
Protection from Harassment Act 1997    *61*
Public Order Act 1986    *142*
s4    *118*

Road Traffic Act 1972
s1    *41*
Road Traffic Act 1988    *14*
s1    *41*
s2    *9, 214*
s3    *9, 214*
s170    *2*
Road Traffic Act 1991    *9, 14, 214*

Sexual Offences Act 1956    *78, 80, 81*
s1    *79*
s1(1)    *69, 85, 86, 80*
s1(2)    *25*
s1(3)    *79*
s2(1)    *80*
s3(1)    *80*
s4(1)    *80*
s5    *79, 81*
s6    *79, 81*
s14    *78, 81, 143*
s14(1)    *83*
s15    *78, 81, 94*
s15(1)    *83*
Sexual Offences Act 1985    *343*

Sexual Offences (Amendment) Act 1976    *69,*
*81*
s1(2)    *70, 79*
Sexual Offences (Amendment) Act 2000    *80,*
*81*

Theft Act 1968    *97, 104, 125, 126, 130, 132,*
*133, 153, 155*
ss1–7    *125, 128*
s1    *7, 11, 107, 110, 111, 112, 114, 122,*
*124, 125, 126, 127, 130, 131, 133, 145,*
*213*
s1(1)    *44, 89, 100, 103, 104, 139, 207*
s2    *99, 113, 125, 126, 127, 128, 131, 132,*
*147*
s2(1)    *101, 102, 105, 123, 139, 207*
s2(1)(a)    *98, 101, 102, 110, 111, 139, 148,*
*149, 213*
s2(1)(b)    *96, 98, 139*
s2(1)(c)    *98*
s2(2)    *105*
s3    *8, 44, 99, 107, 111, 112, 139, 145,*
*207, 213*
s3(1)    *12, 100, 103, 130, 147, 156*
s4    *99, 107, 139, 207*
s4(1)    *97, 147, 156*
s4(4)    *113*
s5    *99, 139, 207*
s5(1)    *97, 100, 111, 112, 113, 147, 149,*
*156*
s5(3)    *97, 125*
s5(4)    *97, 110, 111, 112, 113, 131, 146,*
*148*
s6    *99, 132*
s6(1)    *98, 107, 126*
s8    *7, 8, 133, 145, 150, 152*
s8(1)    *136, 140*
s9    *101, 125, 127, 140, 142*
s9(1)    *137, 155*
s9(1)(a)    *44, 54, 67, 70, 87, 89, 101, 109,*
*120, 134, 140, 144, 145, 147, 148, 158,*
*176, 182, 186, 187, 212*
s9(1)(b)    *65, 67, 70, 101, 134, 140, 143,*
*144, 145, 146, 147, 148, 156, 186, 187,*
*213*
s10    *134*
s11    *134, 144*

Theft Act 1968 (*contd.*)
    s12    *134, 137, 150, 160, 214*
    s12(6)    *150, 14*
    s12A    *160*
    s13    *99*
    s15    *102, 104, 114, 116, 118, 119, 121,*
    *123, 124, 125, 126, 128, 130, 149, 150, 151*
    s15(1)    *104*
    s15(2)    *114*
    s15(4)    *111, 113, 114, 117, 118, 126, 130,*
    *151*
    s16    *114, 115, 126*
    s16(1)    *111, 113, 116, 126*
    s16(2)    *111, 113*
    s16(2)(b)    *126*
    s21    *108, 134, 137, 150, 152, 212*
    s21(1)    *137, 140, 156*
    s22    *44, 123, 138*
    s24(2)    *136*
    s25    *135, 137*

Theft Act 1968 (*contd.*)
    s30(1)    *126*
    s30(2)    *126*
    s30(4)    *126*
    s34(2)    *137*
Theft Act 1978    *97, 125, 126, 130, 133,*
  *153*
    s1    *115, 117, 125, 126*
    s1(1)    *115, 116, 127*
    s1(2)    *117, 127*
    s2    *114, 128, 131*
    s2(1)    *115, 116*
    s2(1)(a)    *115*
    s2(1)(b)    *115, 130*
    s2(1)(c)    *115, 116*
    s2(3)    *115*
    s3    *98, 99, 102, 123, 128, 129, 130, 140*
Traffic Signs Regulations and General
  Directions 1975
    reg 34    *210*

# Chapter 1

# Actus Reus, Omissions and Automatism

1.1    Introduction

1.2    Key points

1.3    Key cases and statute

1.4    Questions and suggested solutions

## 1.1  Introduction

Criminal liability normally requires proof of two elements, the actions of the defendant (actus reus) and a guilty state of mind (mens rea). Some offences can be committed without mens rea – these are normally referred to as strict liability offences (see Chapter 2). It remains a basic principle, however, that criminal liability will always require proof of an actus reus. As outlined below, actus reus can take a number of forms. It should be remembered that it does not always require proof of a positive act by the accused – liability can be imposed for failing to act. It is also a basic principle that actus reus must be freely willed, hence the 'defence' of automatism is considered in this chapter. Strictly speaking the issue of causation is also an aspect of actus reus, but most students find it easier to deal with in the context of result crimes, like homicide, rather than in the abstract – hence causation is covered more fully in Chapter 3.

## 1.2  Key points

### Acts must be freely willed

A defendant may escape liability if there is evidence to show that his actions were not freely willed – ie he was in a state of automatism. In *Attorney-General's Reference (No 2 of 1992)* [1993] 3 WLR 982 the court held that the defence of automatism requires that there must have been a total destruction of voluntary control on the defendant's part. Impaired, reduced or partial control is not enough.

a)  The defendant bears an evidential burden in establishing the defence, which means that he must provide sufficient evidence of automatism for a jury to act upon – this means providing expert medical evidence.

b)  The categories of automatism are not closed but the courts will be cautious in allowing the defence as it results in a complete acquittal where successfully pleaded: see *R* v *Sandie Smith* [1982] Crim LR 531.

c) A defendant may be prevented from raising the defence of automatism where there is evidence to show that he was in some way at fault in bringing about the state of automatism: see *R* v *Bailey* (1983) 77 Cr App R 76.

## Types of actus reus

Offences can be classified on the basis of the type of actus reus involved.

### Conduct

Some offences do not require proof of any result or consequence. The action of the defendant is all that has to be proved. A typical example is the offence of 'dangerous driving'.

### Circumstances

The actus reus of an offence can consist of elements which are almost entirely external to the physical actions of the defendant, eg: whether or not another person is consenting to sexual intercourse; the age of the person the defendant had sexual intercourse with; and whether property belongs to another.

### Result crimes

These are offences where the prosecution has to prove that the accused caused the prohibited result. Examples include homicide, assault and criminal damage. It is not sufficient that the defendant's act can be shown to have been a factual cause of the prohibited act. It must be shown that the act is also a cause in law of the result.

### Omissions

Although generally a failure by the accused to act will not be sufficient to establish the actus reus for an offence, there are occasions where an omission will suffice:

a) where the accused's relationship with another imposes a legal duty to act, eg parent-child (*R* v *Gibbens and Proctor* (1918) 13 Cr App R 134) or where an accused has taken it upon himself to look after another: *R* v *Stone and Dobinson* [1977] QB 354;

b) where the accused has a legal duty by virtue of his office to act (eg police officer): *R* v *Dytham* [1979] QB 722;

c) where a statute imposes such a duty, eg the duty to stop after a road traffic accident (RTA 1988, s170) or where the accused is under a contractual duty (eg by virtue of his terms of employment: *R* v *Pittwood* (1902) 19 TLR 37) or other agreement: *R* v *Instan* [1893] 1 QB 450;

d) where an accused is under a common law duty to act after accidentally causing harm eg where he accidentally sets fire to a room and, on realising what he had done goes to sleep elsewhere and omits to put the fire out: *R* v *Miller* [1983] 2 AC 161.

Remember that where a 'result' crime is charged the prosecution will have to prove that the omission caused the harm.

## Causation

The accused must voluntarily act or pursue a course of conduct that brings about the proscribed consequences/circumstances. If what he does fails to bring those consequences/circumstances about, there is no actus reus (although there may be a charge of attempt): *R* v *Hensler* (1870) 22 LT 691; *R* v *White* [1910] 2 KB 124.

If the accused's conduct initiates a sequence of events which are overtaken by a subsequent supervening event, then he has not caused the circumstances/consequences that follow that event and they cannot form part of the actus reus: *R* v *Smith* [1959] 2 QB 35; *R* v *Blaue* [1975] 3 All ER 446; *R* v *Malcherek and Steel* [1981] 2 All ER 422. The accused's acts need not be the sole cause of the proscribed result (for example, death or serious injury), it being sufficient if the accused's acts contribute significantly to that result: *R* v *Cheshire* [1991] 3 All ER 670.

## 1.3 Key cases and statute

*Automatism*

- *Attorney-General's Reference (No 2 of 1992)* [1993] 3 WLR 982
  What is automatism?

- *Bratty* v *Attorney-General for Northern Ireland* [1963] AC 386
  What is automatism?

- *R* v *Bailey* [1983] 2 All ER 503
  Self-induced automatism

- *R* v *Quick* [1973] QB 910
  Diabetes and automatism

- *R* v *Sandie Smith* [1982] Crim LR 531
  Pre-menstrual tension and automatism

- *R* v *T* [1990] Crim LR 256
  Post-traumatic stress disorder as automatism

*Omissions*

- *R* v *Dytham* [1979] 3 All ER 641
  Liability for omissions based on holding an office

- *R* v *Gibbens and Proctor* (1918) 13 Cr App R 134
  Liability for omissions based on relationship/reliance

- *R* v *Miller* [1983] 1 All ER 978
  Liability for omissions based on causing harm

- *R* v *Pittwood* (1902) 19 TLR 34
  Liability for omissions based on contract

- *R* v *Stone and Dobinson* [1977] QB 354
  Liability for omissions based on relationship/reliance

- Children and Young Persons Act 1933 – parental statutory duty to care for children

## 1.4 Questions and suggested solutions

QUESTION ONE

J's young son had been attacked by K, an older boy who, at the time, had been recovering from an epileptic fit. J was very anxious because the school would not expel K or arrange for proper supervision. J was driving down a lonely country lane when he saw K on the side of the road having a fit. K was near a puddle of water. J stopped and watched K writhing on the ground until K's face went under the water of the puddle. J watched as K drowned.

Advise J of his criminal liability, if any. What difference, if any, would it make to your advice if J had driven to a point from which an ambulance was coming and by driving slowly had delayed its arrival to the scene of the accident?

University of London LLB Examination
(for External Students) Criminal Law June 1998 Q3

### General Comment

This is a very difficult, not to say odd, question. Much of the consideration is based around liability for failing to act and killing by gross negligence. Issues of causation also arise. The question asks to advise on J's liability so do not be tempted to discuss K. In any event K dies, making his liability purely academic. Although rather fanciful given the facts, the external examiner's report indicates that self-defence ought to be considered.

### Skeleton Solution

Liability for omission – failure to act – any duty arising? – alternatively base liability on a positive act – consider chain of causation in fact and in law – go through various types of homicide with a particular reference to killing by gross negligence – does J have any defences – anxiety not enough – consider self-defence as in defence of others.

### Suggested Solution

Does J incur any liability for homicide as a result of his failure to prevent the death of K? The law will only impose liability based upon a defendant's failure to act where there is a positive legal duty resting upon the defendant to take steps to prevent the harm. Such a duty can arise under statute, eg Children and Young Persons Act 1933, or under a contract: see *R* v *Pittwood* (1902) 19 TLR 34. Neither could form the basis for any legal duty resting on J given the facts. At common law a duty to act can arise if the defendant is a blood relative of the victim: see *R* v *Instan* [1893] 1 QB 450, or if there is a special relationship between the parties: see *R* v *Stone and Dobinson* [1977] QB 354. For such a relationship to arise it would have to be shown that J had undertaken the duty of caring for K, that he was aware of his condition, and that K had become reliant on J. Again the facts do not suggest this. The only other basis at common law for imposing a liability based on failure to act is as set out by the House of Lords in *R* v *Miller* [1983] 1 All ER 978. This decision states that liability can arise where J accidentally commits an act that causes harm, becomes aware of what he has done, and it lies within his power to take steps, either himself or by calling for assistance to prevent or minimise the harm. If J does nothing in such a situation liability can arise. On the facts this could not be invoked against J as there is no evidence that he causes the harm to K in the first place. In short there would appear to be no basis on which liability for failing to act could be imposed on J, hence no liability for the consequences of his failure to act can arise.

The prosecution would have a much stronger case if it could be shown that J had committed some positive act. J's deliberately slowing down the ambulance might provide a basis for this but there are many problems for the prosecution. Does J's action in fact cause K's death? Consider *R* v *White* [1910] 2 KB 124 – that is, but for J's actions would K have died? If it can be shown that K was already dead before the ambulance was delayed by J there will be no causation in fact. Assuming there is causation in fact the prosecution will have to establish causation in law. On the facts this should not be problematic – applying a basic test of reasonable foreseeability. There is no evidence of any novus actus interveniens. Assuming causation is made out, what type of homicide could J be charged with?

The most serious charge would be murder. This would require evidence that J intended to kill or cause grievous bodily harm to K by delaying the ambulance. The meaning of intent for these purposes has been clarified by the House of Lords in *R* v *Woollin* [1998] 4 All ER 103. A jury would be entitled to infer intention if there was evidence that J foresaw death or grievous bodily harm as a virtually certain consequence of his actions in delaying the ambulance. Such foresight is not mens rea as such but is evidence from which the mens rea can be inferred. On the facts this may be the case, but in reality the prosecution will find it very difficult to prove in the absence of a confession by J.

If the mens rea for murder cannot be established the prosecution would have to consider unlawful act manslaughter. The difficulty here is, as the name suggests, that the prosecution have to base liability on an unlawful act. Unlawful for these purposes means criminal – a mere tort would not be enough: see *R* v *Fenton* (1830) 1 Lew CC 179 and *R* v *Franklin* (1883) 15 Cox CC 163. A specific criminal act would have to be identified: see *R* v *Arobieke* [1988] Crim LR 314. On the facts it is hard to see what the criminal act could be. There is a vague possibility of obstruction of the highway, but using the road to drive a vehicle, albeit slowly, is not going to give rise to an obstruction charge. In any event, even if obstruction was used as the unlawful act, it would be difficult to show that it was 'dangerous' as defined in *R v Church* [1965] 2 All ER 72 – such as all sober and reasonable people would inevitably recognise must subject the other person to, at least, the risk of some harm resulting therefrom, albeit not serious harm.

A better basis for liability would be a charge of killing by gross negligence. The prosecution would have to show that J owed K a duty of care. This could be difficult, but the assertion would be that he owes every other road user a duty of care, including those lying injured on the highway. What is gross negligence? This is defined in *R v Adomako* [1994] 3 WLR 288. The prosecution must prove that J's conduct departed from the proper standard of care incumbent upon him, involving a risk of death to K such that it should be judged criminal. It is submitted that this could be established on the facts.

What of defences available to J? There is no defence of revenge, neither is there any defence of anxiety as such. On the facts there is no obviously available defence. J might argue that his worry about the safety of his son amounted to some sort of neurosis that resulted in a defence of diminished responsibility in respect of any murder charge but this seems far fetched.

Alternatively, he might contend that in causing K's death he was in fact protecting other pupils at the school. At common law J would be allowed to use reasonable force to protect his family, but the defence would only apply where there was a real threat and J's actions would have to be proportionate. It is very unlikely that any such defence could be made out here.

## QUESTION TWO

K was attacked in a street by a group of youths. L, who was the leader, caused K to be thrown to the ground where several of the gang kicked him until he became unconscious. They then left the scene. Whilst K was on the ground M passed by and removed K's wallet to see if there was anything worth stealing. M took five pounds from the wallet and kicked K twice before leaving causing severe bruising. N who was next to pass the scene saw that K was seriously ill but did nothing, deciding that he did not want to become involved. O, a doctor, also passed by without rendering assistance. P finally came over to K's aid but because of his inexperience in such matters, he moved K which in turn caused K's internal injuries to become severe.

Advise the parties of their criminal liability.

University of London LLB Examination
(for External Students) Criminal Law June 1987 Q4

## General Comment

Although primarily concerned with the offences of assault and theft, this question is a good illustration of some of the different types of mens rea in criminal law.

It is a complicated question involving a number of parties and students should take care not to get bogged down in generalities.

## Skeleton Solution

L: meaning of cause; assault; incitement; accomplice – youths: ss47, 20, 18 OAPA 1861; causation – M: ss1 and 8 Theft Act 1968; ss47, 20 and 18 Offences Against the Person Act 1861 – N: causation; assault; omission.

## Suggested Solution

K was attacked and left unconscious. The question does not provide details of the exact harm done – grievous bodily harm under s18 of the Offences Against the Person Act 1861 will require proof of 'serious bodily harm': see *DPP* v *Smith* [1961] AC 290 There is nothing to indicate that K suffered a wound, which requires a break in the external skin: *JJC (A Minor)* v *Eisenhower* [1984] QB 331. The most likely charge here would be one of causing actual bodily harm contrary to s47 of the 1861 Act. Actual bodily harm requires proof of a hurt or injury that interferes with the health and comfort of the victim: see *R* v *Miller* [1954] 2 QB 282. The mens rea required would be that for assault – L and the other gang members would have to foresee at least a risk of K being battered or apprehending immediate physical violence: *R* v *Savage*; *R* v *Parmenter* [1991] 3 WLR 914. There would seem to be little difficulty with this on the facts.

L could be charged with aiding and abetting the attack. An aider or abettor is a person present assisting or encouraging at the scene of the offence: *R* v *Coney* (1882) 8 QBD 534; *R* v *Clarkson* [1971] 1 WLR 1402. He must have full knowledge of the circumstances of the offence: *Johnson* v *Youden* [1950] 1 KB 544. Section 8 of the Accessories and Abettors Act 1861 provides that for the purposes of trial and punishment accomplices are to be treated as principal offenders.

When M removes K's wallet to see if there is anything worth stealing he may commit an attempted theft. Section 1 Theft Act (TA) 1968 provides that theft is committed where an accused dishonestly appropriates property belonging to another with intention to permanently deprive the other of it. In order to establish attempted theft the prosecution must show that M has done an act more than merely preparatory (s1 Criminal Attempts Act 1981) with full mens rea. M takes the wallet to see if there is anything worth stealing. This is an example of 'conditional' intention. Provided the indictment is drafted broadly without reference to particular items, eg M attempted to steal from the contents of the wallet, the mens rea for attempted theft will be satisfied. In practice, as M proceeds to the full offence it is unlikely the prosecution would pursue an attempted charge.

The full offence will be complete when M removes £5 from the wallet – at that time there is an assumption of the rights of an owner (s3 TA 1968) and this would amount to an appropriation. There seems no doubt that the mens rea is satisfied. He has an intention to permanently deprive and he is clearly dishonest. Were there to be any difficulties in relation to dishonesty the jury should be directed in line with: *R v Ghosh* [1982] 1 QB 1053.

After he commits theft M kicks K twice causing severe bruising. At that point M commits an assault either under s47, s20 or possibly s18. If the bruising amounts to grievous bodily harm a charge under s20 or s18 could be sustained. The difficulty would be establishing mens rea for s18 which requires an intent to do grievous bodily harm. More likely is a charge under s20 where the prosecution must prove that M was malicious – meaning that he must have foreseen at least the risk of some physical harm occurring to K. This seems to be beyond doubt. It should be noted that M is not liable for robbery. Section 8 TA 1968 provides that a person commits robbery 'if he steals, and immediately before or at the time of doing so and in order to do so, he uses force on any person or puts or seeks to put any person in fear of being then and there subjected to force.' M undoubtedly uses force. However, this occurs after the theft is complete. Even allowing for the prosecution to argue that there is a continuing actus reus (*R v Hale* (1978) 68 Cr App R 415) it could still not amount to robbery as the force used is gratuitous force and not force in order to steal: *R v Shendley* [1970] Crim LR 49.

N would appear to have no liability in this matter. Undoubtedly certain crimes may be committed by omission. But there can be no liability by this means unless there is a duty to act in law. In these circumstances N has no duty to act in law and therefore would have no liability. N was under no legal liability to help K. Where English criminal law does impose a duty to act, there must be a close relationship ie family, a business or similar: *R v Marriott* (1838) 8 C & P 425; *R v Nicholls* (1874) 13 Cox CC 75; *R v Instan* [1893] 1 QB 450; *R v Stone and Dobinson* [1977] 1 QB 354; *R v Dalby* [1982] 1 WLR 425.

Similarly, O would not be liable unless he stood in such a special relationship to K (ie his family doctor). He has a moral duty to act but, in these circumstances, that is not automatically translated into a duty under criminal law. One could argue, on the lines of *R v Dytham* [1979] QB 722 where a police officer was determined to be liable, virtue officii, to intervene and stop an assault, that O has a similar duty to act by virtue of his 'office', in which case his omission would be sufficient to attract liability.

When P moves K causing his internal injuries to become severe, he would not become liable in criminal law. There are two main reasons for taking this view. First, as a matter of law he would not be regarded as the legal cause of the injuries. The chain of causation will not be broken in these circumstances – P would be regarded as an innocent or non-responsible intervener. Where such a person intervenes by an act instinctively done to assist someone he would not break the chain of causation and the harm resulting would not be in law attributable to him but rather to those who started the chain of causation. Furthermore, the offences contained in ss47, 20 and 18 are crimes of maliciousness, and from the facts patently P is not acting in a malicious manner. It would not be sufficient mens rea to allege that P is reckless. Although recklessness may be sufficient mens rea for s47, it is *Cunningham* recklessness (*R* v *Cunningham* [1957] 2 QB 396) and not *Caldwell* recklessness (*Commissioner of Police of the Metropolis* v *Caldwell* [1982] AC 341) that must be established. On the facts this is not shown.

## QUESTION THREE

Dan was driving one afternoon and felt increasingly drowsy. He fell asleep and his car mounted the pavement, crashed into a wall and trapped a young boy against the wall, seriously injuring him. The crash woke Dan who, seeing the trapped boy, decided not to move his car. After some time he did decide to move, reversed and drove away. Jack, a passing pedestrian, witnessed the event and was very upset by the occurrence. In his efforts to erase the memory of the injured boy, Jack drank a large quantity of brandy and became extremely drunk. He stumbled into a hotel and did not realise that he had dropped his cigarette on the hall carpet. The hotel caught fire and two of the occupants died in the blaze. Jack escaped.

Discuss their criminal liability.

University of London LLB Examination
(for External Students) Criminal Law June 1981 Q3

### General Comment

The question centres mainly on the respective mens rea of both Dan and Jack, particularly with regard to automatism, intoxication and recklessness. The issue of liability for failing to act also arises.

### Skeleton Solution

Dan: ss2 and 3 Road Traffic Act 1988; automatism; ss47 and 20 Offences Against the Person Act 1861; failure to act – Jack: s1 Criminal Damage Act 1971; recklessness.

### Suggested Solution

Dan may commit a number of road traffic offences when his car mounts the pavement and injures a boy. Under s3 of the Road Traffic Act 1988 (as amended by the Road Traffic Act 1991), if a person drives a motor vehicle (or mechanically propelled vehicle) on a road without due care and attention or without reasonable consideration for other persons using the road, he shall commit an offence. A person could be driving 'without due care and attention' if he fails to exercise the degree of care and attention that a reasonable and prudent driver would exercise in the circumstances: *Simpson* v *Peat* [1952] 2 QB 24. This is an objective standard and it is an example of one of the few crimes of negligence in English criminal law. Section 2 of the Road Traffic Act 1988 provides that a person who drives a motor vehicle on a road dangerously shall be guilty of an offence. Again liability is based on an objective assessment of whether or not Dan drove in a manner that the reasonable motorist would regard as dangerous. At the point of collision with the boy Dan may have caused grievous bodily harm, wounding or actual bodily harm. The problem for the prosecution is that Dan was asleep at the time and therefore lacked mens rea. Dan will presumably assert the defence of automatism, defined in *Bratty* v *Attorney General for Northern Ireland* [1963] AC 386 as a state where something was done by the defendant's muscles without the control of his mind, including spasms, reflex actions, sleepwalking, nightmares, fits and so on. Dan will have to produce evidence that he was not capable of responding to gross stimuli at the time of the crash: see *Attorney General's Reference (No 2 of 1992)* [1993] 3 WLR 982 where the Court of Appeal rejected the appellant's contention that he had been in a state of automatism, referred to as 'driving without awareness', induced by 'repetitive visual stimulus experienced on long journeys on straight flat roads'. Where a defendant becomes increasingly drowsy whilst driving his car, and instead of pulling over to the side of the road continues to drive, eventually falling asleep at the wheel, and causes an accident, the prosecution will argue that it was his fault because he could have avoided the problem by ceasing to drive when he first became drowsy. Dan should be advised that, on the basis of *R* v *Bailey* [1983] 2 All ER 503 the defence of automatism will not be available in relation to basic intent crimes, such as wounding or inflicting grievous bodily harm contrary to s20 of the Offences Against the Person Act 1861, or actual bodily harm contrary to s47, if it can be shown that he was reckless in failing to stop when he became drowsy, in the sense that he was aware of the risk of what might happen if he continued. On this basis it is submitted that Dan will be convicted of offences under either s20 or s47, depending on the extent of the injuries.

By not reversing away from the boy immediately Dan may have caused him further injuries, although the facts provided do not indicate that this is the case. If further harm is caused after he leaves the scene the prosecution may choose to base his liability on his failure to act when he became aware of the harm he had caused: see *R* v *Miller* [1983] 2 AC 161, where it was stated that D is under a duty to limit the harmful effect of his accidental acts, once he becomes aware that they are causing harm.

Jack may commit an act of criminal damage contrary to s1(1) of the Criminal Damage Act 1971, where intentionally or recklessly he destroys or damages property belonging to another with intent or being reckless as to whether such property is destroyed. Prima facie, there is the more serious offence within s1(2) of the Criminal Damage Act, in that he destroys or damages property intentionally or recklessly with intention to endanger life or being reckless as to whether life is endangered. Because the offence is performed by fire, then it will come within s1(3) – arson. There may be difficulties in showing that Jack had the necessary mens rea in his drunken state. However, he will not be able to plead this as a defence unless it can be shown that the offences with which he could be charged are crimes of specific intent. In these circumstances, drunkenness may be a defence if it can be shown that the drunkenness totally negatives the mens rea required: *DPP* v *Majewski* [1977] AC 443. If it is a crime of basic intent, then drunkenness will normally be no defence (see *R* v *Hardie* [1985] 1 WLR 64) even though the accused is incapable of forming mens rea. The House of Lords considered the defence of drunkenness in relation to the Criminal Damage Act in *Commissioner of Police of the Metropolis* v *Caldwell* [1982] AC 341, holding that the term 'reckless' within s1 of the Act held a meaning which it bore in ordinary speech. That meaning included not only deciding to ignore the risk of harmful consequences resulting from one's acts that one recognises as existing but also failing to give any thought to whether or not there was such risk in circumstances where, if any thought were given to the matter, it would be obvious that there was. Therefore, the fact that Jack was unaware of the risk of endangering lives owing to his voluntary intoxication would be no defence if the risk would have been obvious to him had he been sober. The result is that if Jack was charged under s1(2) of the Criminal Damage Act, with criminal damage being reckless as to whether life was endangered, he would not be able to claim drunkenness as a defence. However, if he were charged under s1(2) of the Criminal Damage Act, intending to endanger life, evidence of self-induced intoxication could be relevant as a defence, as this is a specific intent crime.

## QUESTION FOUR

D was in a self-service shop when she began to feel very unwell. She was a diabetic who had taken her insulin as prescribed but had afterwards eaten a lighter breakfast than usual. She put a tin of cat food in her handbag and not into the shop basket which she was carrying. She saw E, her neighbour, with whom she was on bad terms, coming towards her. D mistakenly thought that E was going to attack her. She hit E over the head with her umbrella and E sustained a grazed face.

Advise D of her criminal liability. What difference, if any, would it make to your advice if, instead, D had failed to take her insulin as usual at breakfast time?

*University of London LLB (Examination)*
*(for External Students) Criminal Law June 1995 Q7*

### General Comment

A more traditional question concentrating on the distinction between automatism and insanity in the complicated context of diabetes.

### Skeleton Solution

Theft – actual bodily harm – insanity – automatism.

### Suggested Solution

By putting the can of cat food in her handbag, D may have committed theft contrary to s1 of the Theft Act 1968, which is made out where D dishonestly appropriates property belonging to another with the intention of permanently depriving the other of it. It should be noted that D may have committed theft merely by putting the can in her bag – it is unnecessary to show that she left the shop with the can. This is because *R* v *Morris* [1984] AC 320, interpreting s3(1) of the 1968 Act, held that an appropriation took place when the accused usurped any of the owner's rights, which D has clearly done by placing the can in her handbag.

When D hit E over the head with an umbrella she may have committed an assault, which was defined in *Fagan* v *Metropolitan Police Commissioner* [1969] 1 QB 439 as where the accused causes the victim to apprehend immediate personal violence. It is also possible that she may be guilty of an assault occasioning actual bodily harm contrary to s47 of the Offences Against the Person Act 1861. The problem here would be to establish that a grazed face amounts to 'actual bodily harm' which was defined in *R* v *Chan Fook* [1994] Crim LR 432 as any injury which is more than trivial.

In relation to both the theft and assault charges D may raise issues related to the absence of mens rea. If D's mental state was such that she did not know what she was doing then it is possible that her condition could amount to automatism – essentially a condition where she is not controlling or aware of her actions. A person who successfully raises the defence of automatism is acquitted of the charge and the courts have no powers to make any orders in relation to that person – hence the courts are careful to distinguish between those defendants who have conditions which might endanger others, and those who pose no such threat.

In *R* v *Bailey* [1983] 2 All ER 503 the court indicated that a defect of reason due to an internal cause, such as illness, should be classified as a disease of the mind and therefore was likely to be classified as insanity, but an external cause such a blow to the head or drugs should be classified as automatism. It was also held in Bailey that if a diabetic failed to consume food after taking insulin the subsequent hypoglycaemic state was due to the insulin, not the diabetes, and was therefore an external cause, giving rise to the defence of automatism rather than insanity. Consequently, it would appear that D is entitled to the defence of automatism. However, it was also held in Bailey that self-induced automatism would not necessarily be a defence to a charge of basic intent – the question is whether the accused was reckless in allowing him or herself to enter the state of automatism. Therefore, it would be important to discover whether D was aware of a tendency to be affected as she was by her failure to eat a proper breakfast. If she was so aware, then it may be said that she was reckless in not ensuring that she ate properly and, consequently, she may be convicted of the offence under s47 of the 1861 Act (which is an offence of basic intent). Theft is an offence of specific intent since it requires an intention to permanently deprive. Self-induced automatism (whether reckless or not) will be a defence to such a charge where it deprives the accused of the mens rea for that offence.

If D had failed to take insulin after breakfast then she would have to rely on the defence of insanity rather than automatism. This is because it was held in *R* v *Hennessy* (1989) 89 Cr App R 10 that a mental aberration caused by the failure to take insulin was due to the diabetes, which was an internal cause and therefore a disease of the mind.

The court may, in any event, be tempted to look carefully at D's plea of automatism in respect of the assault charge and consider whether or not a finding of insanity would be more appropriate. Insanity was defined in *McNaghten's Case* (1843) 10 Cl & F 200 as arising where the accused was labouring under such a defect of reason from disease of the mind as not to know the nature and quality of the act he was doing; or if he did know it, he did not know that it was wrong. Under the Criminal Procedure (Insanity and Unfitness to Plead) Act 1991, although a verdict of insanity is technically an acquittal, the courts do have powers to make various orders with respect to the accused, and may, for example, order detention at a mental institution, or a supervision or treatment order. The distinction between insanity and automatism involving diabetes is a complex one. In *Bratty* v *Attorney-General for Northern Ireland* [1961] 3 WLR 965 Lord Denning said that any condition which was likely to recur, and thus pose a threat to the public, should be classified as insanity. If diabetes was to be regarded as a disease of the body that affected the mind and manifested itself in violence the way would be open for the courts to refuse to allow D to put forward the defence of automatism in respect of the assault charge, and indicate that the only defence it would allow to go before the jury was one of insanity.

D may attempt to argue that she is entitled to the defence of self-defence because she believed that she was acting to repel an attack by E. Under *R* v *Williams* [1987] 3 All ER 411 a person who mistakenly believes that they are under attack should have their liability judged as if they were under such an attack. The danger for D is that if she puts her state of mind in issue (by pleading mistake) the prosecution can lead evidence of insanity (ie that she made the mistake because of her mental abnormality).

## QUESTION FIVE

J had visited K, his hypnotherapist for treatment of relief of pain. After treatment J was still under the influence of hypnosis though he gave no signs of this. Whilst driving home J ran down and killed L, a child aged six years who had run out in front of J's car. Unaware of the accident, J walked away to his home nearby. J then went for a walk and met M who called him a 'thick idiot'. J lost his temper and hit M over the head with his walking stick. M had a thin skull and died from the blow.

Advise J and K as to their criminal liability.

*Adapted from University of London LLB Examination*
*(for External Students) Criminal Law June 1985 Q4*

### General Comment

A difficult question. The range of the question is wide, covering a number of fairly difficult aspects of the syllabus including recklessness. Furthermore, the difficulties are aggravated because of the need to consider the defence of automatism.

A student should take great care to ensure that his answer is clear and well planned. Although there is no one correct approach a student would probably find that the best approach would be to explain all the possible offences committed by J first and only then go on to consider and apply the defence of automatism.

*Skeleton Solution*

Causing death by dangerous driving – Road Traffic Act 1991 – overlap with involuntary manslaughter – murder and the defence of provocation – alternative charge of constructive manslaughter – the defence of non-insane automatism – limits on such a defence – *R* v *Bailey* whether K could be the legal cause of the deaths – liability of K for manslaughter by gross negligence – doctrine of innocent agency.

*Suggested Solution*

J may be guilty of causing death by dangerous driving contrary to s1 of the Road Traffic Act 1991 which abolished and replaced the offence of causing death by reckless driving contrary to the Road Traffic Act 1988. J may be guilty of this offence if the way he drove fell far below what would be expected of a competent and careful driver. Although J ran down L and killed him there is no information as to the manner in which he was driving and therefore whether the 'accident' was due to J's poor driving or L's own carelessness in running across the road. If J's driving did fall below this standard it must also be proven that it would have been obvious to a competent and careful driver that driving in that way would be dangerous.

J could also be charged with manslaughter by gross negligence as defined in *R* v *Adomako* [1994] 3 WLR 288. As a driver he clearly owes other road users (including pedestrians) a duty of care; this duty is likely to have been broken by driving in a hypnotic state. It will be for a jury to decide whether this conduct is so negligent that it amounts to a criminal act.

J may be liable for either murder or manslaughter when he strikes and kills M. He will not be able to claim that he did not cause the death because an accused must take his victim as he finds him and a characteristic like a thin skull will not break the chain of causation: *R* v *Blaue* [1975] 1 WLR 1411.

J will be liable for murder if he kills while intending to kill or intending to do grievous bodily harm. If he did the act foreseeing that it was virtually certain that he would kill or do grievous bodily harm that will be evidence from which the jury can infer that he had the necessary mens rea: see *R* v *Woollin* [1998] 4 All ER 103 and s8 Criminal Justice Act 1967.

If J had the necessary mens rea for murder, but was provoked by M, he may be able to claim the defence of provocation, which would reduce murder to voluntary manslaughter. Provocation may be established if an accused can show that he lost his self control as a result of actions or words of the victim or a third party. Furthermore, it must be shown that in reacting to the provocation he displayed the self-control that it was reasonable to expect from him, bearing in mind the relevant factors having a bearing on his ability to exercise self-control: *R* v *Smith (Morgan)* [2000] 4 All ER 289.

Although there is no evidence of any particular characteristic of J that would be especially relevant to the provocation, his low intelligence could be taken into account as a factor having a bearing on his emotional stability.

An alternative charge to murder is that of constructive manslaughter. The prosecution must establish that J committed a dangerous criminal act that caused death. The term dangerous in this context means that it must be an act that such as all sober and reasonable people would inevitably recognise must subject the other person to, at least, the risk of some harm resulting therefrom, albeit not serious harm: *R v Church* [1966] 1 QB 59. In *R v Dawson* (1985) 81 Cr App R 150 this was further clarified to indicated that what the jury must be directed to consider is the possibility of physical harm to the victim as opposed to merely 'emotional disturbance'. The test is applied on the basis of the knowledge gained by a sober and reasonable man as though he were present at the scene of the crime and watched the unlawful act being performed, ie he has the same knowledge as the man attempting to rob and no more: see further *R v Watson* [1989] 1 WLR 684. On the facts it is likely that the jury would conclude that the attack by J satisfied the test for dangerousness, but some thought must be given to the 'thin skull' point. If the blow from J was fairly trivial, such that a reasonable person (who we must assume would not have known that the victim had a thin skull unless this was visible to J) would not have foreseen physical harm, then the test for dangerousness would not be satisfied. Assuming it is satisfied, the mens rea for unlawful act manslaughter would be the mens rea for the unlawful act. There is no need to prove that J foresaw any risk of death: see *DPP v Newbury and Jones* [1977] AC 500. In short, subjective recklessness as regards assault, or foresight of the possibility of some physical harm, albeit slight (for s20), would suffice. On the facts the prosecution should not have any difficulty establishing either on the part of J.

It is now necessary to consider whether J can claim a defence resulting from his hypnotised state. Whatever offence under criminal law is being alleged it must be shown that an accused acted 'voluntarily', ie that his mind was in control of his body. If this is not the case he will be acting as an automaton. On the facts in question the automatism does not arise from a disease of the mind (insane automatism) and therefore non-insane automatism may be pleaded as a defence. It should, however, be noted that where the automaton state arose as a result of the accused's own recklessness he will be unable to claim it as a defence to a crime where recklessness is sufficient mens rea: *R v Bailey* [1983] 2 All ER 503; *R v Hardie* [1985] 1 WLR 64. The defence of automatism would therefore only be available to J if he can show that he has not acted 'voluntarily' through no fault of his own. While this might possibly be the case where L is killed, it is not as easy to apply the principles where M's death is considered. Intoxication and automatism are acting in conjunction with each other. The need to protect the public would probably result in the principles relating to voluntary intoxication being applied.

For K to incur any liability it will have to be shown that there is some causal link between his actions and the deaths of L and M. Whilst cause in fact can be seen in both cases, cause in law may be more problematic. As regards the death of L it could be argued that, because J was under hypnosis, he was acting as K's innocent agent. There is no evidence, however that K had any mens rea. In respect of M's death, K will argue that the killing resulted from J losing his temper, not from the hypnosis. Again there would be considerable evidential difficulties in showing that K had any relevant mens rea at the time of the hypnosis.

# Chapter 2

# Mens Rea

2.1   **Introduction**

2.2   **Key points**

2.3   **Key cases and statutes**

2.4   **Questions and suggested solutions**

## 2.1 Introduction

It is often stated as a fundamental rule of criminal law that a man cannot be guilty on the basis of his actions alone – he must also have a guilty mind. This is summed up in the Latin phrase 'actus non facit reum nisi mens sit rea'. In reality there are, of course, important exceptions to this rule. Strict liability offences may require no mens rea at all, or at least only a limited form of mens rea. Crimes based on concepts such as negligence and 'dangerousness' will involve reference to what the hypothetical reasonable person would have thought, rather than what the accused actually thought.

Where mens rea is required the problem arises of defining the various expressions used to denote various states of mind. In doing so it should be remembered that mens rea can exist quite independently of any ill will or malice on the part of the accused. Normally motive will be irrelevant in establishing mens rea.

## 2.2 Key points

### Intention

a) Intention can be based on proof of purpose, ie what end the defendant wanted to achieve – but this is difficult for the prosecution to establish: see *Chandler* v *DPP* [1964] AC 763.

b) More usually, where a crime requires proof of intention it will be established by evidence of what the defendant foresaw. Section 8 of the Criminal Justice Act 1967 provides that a court or jury in determining whether a person has committed an offence shall decide whether he intended or foresaw a prohibited result. In other words, the test for foresight is subjective – what did the defendant foresee – rather than objective – what would the reasonable person have foreseen.

c) Key decisions on intention based on foresight are: *R* v *Hancock and Shankland* [1986]

2 WLR 257; *R v Nedrick* (1986) 83 Cr App R 267; and *R v Woollin* [1998] 4 All ER 103. In *Woollin* the House of Lords confirmed that the jury should not infer that a defendant intended a consequence unless there was evidence that he foresaw its occurrence as a virtually certain consequence of his actions.

d) Specific and basic intent

Basic intent is the mens rea that relates to the actus reus committed by the defendant. An offence of specific intent is one where the mens rea goes beyond the actus reus in the sense that the defendant has some ulterior purpose in mind. An example is provided by the offence of 'aggravated' criminal damage. This offence is committed where a defendant causes damage or destruction to property with the intention of thereby endangering life. The actus reus it will be noted is almost identical to that of the simple offence, the differentiating factor is the further or specific intent that the defendant must possess, to endanger life.

### Recklessness

Recklessness, in general terms, involves a defendant who acts not caring about the consequences of his actions. The key distinctions is between advertent (subjective) recklessness, where the defendant is aware of the risk he is taking, and inadvertent (objective) recklessness where the defendant has not thought of the risk.

a) Subjective recklessness

*R v Cunningham* [1957] 2 QB 396: recklessness involved the defendant in being aware of the risk that his actions might cause the prohibited consequence.

b) Objective recklessness

*Commissioner of Police of the Metropolis* v *Caldwell* [1982] AC 341: a majority of Law Lords endorsed a new form of recklessness – based not simply on the defendant's foresight of a risk, but one that encompassed also his failure to consider a risk that would have been obvious to the reasonable man. The House of Lords held, inter alia (Lords Wilberforce and Edmund-Davies dissenting), that a defendant was to be regarded as reckless where he created an obvious risk of a particular type of harm occurring, and either went on to take that risk, or failed to give any thought to its existence. The decision has had harsh consequences – see *Elliott v C* [1983] 1 WLR 939 – where an educationally subnormal 14-year-old schoolgirl was convicted of reckless criminal damage even though there was evidence to suggest that she could not have appreciated the risk of harm even if she had stopped to think about it.

c) The lacuna argument

It has been contended that a defendant might escape liability where he is not *Cunningham* reckless (because he does not think that he is taking a risk), yet neither is he *Caldwell* reckless because, far from having given no thought to the risk, he has given considerable thought to it, albeit coming to the wrong conclusion as to its significance: see *Chief Constable of Avon and Somerset v Shimmen* (1987) 84 Cr App R 7. In *R v Reid* [1992] 3 All ER 673 the House of Lords accepted (obiter) that a defendant could escape liability if, for example, he was the driver of a left-hand drive car overtaking on the brow of a hill and was misinformed as to the safety of doing so by his passenger, resulting in damage to a car travelling in the opposite direction. In the circumstances his actions would not be reckless.

d) *Cunningham* or *Caldwell* recklessness?

*Caldwell* now only applies to criminal damage – but note that it might yet have a role to play in manslaughter where the unlawful act causing death is criminal damage.

## Negligence

Very few significant crimes utilise negligence as the fault element – this is not surprising given that it is the basis of civil liability not criminal. The key exception is killing by gross negligence. The House of Lords in *R v Adomako* [1994] 3 WLR 288 confirmed that liability for this form of manslaughter could arise where the negligence causing death fell so far below the standard of care to be expected of the reasonable person that it deserved to be labelled 'criminal': see further Chapter 3.

### Strict liability

Absolute liability arises where an offence requires no proof of mens rea whatsoever: eg *R v Larsonneur* (1933) 24 Cr App R 74. Strict liability offences may require some mens rea, but not full mens rea in respect of each element of the offence (eg the defendant must know that he is having sexual intercourse with a girl, but need not know that she is under the age of 13). The courts will presume that an offence requires proof of mens rea even where the statute is silent on this point: see *B v DPP* [2000] 1 All ER 833. This presumption is, however, rebuttable either on the basis of the clear wording of the statute in question, or by necessary implication. If the prosecution can show that it really was the intention of Parliament that mens rea should be excluded in respect of one or more elements of an offence the courts will dispense with it as appropriate. Relevant factors will include the following:

a) Danger to society – see *R v Bradish* [1990] Crim LR 271 – possession of a prohibited weapon contrary to the Firearms Act 1968.

b) Offence not truly 'criminal' – see *Smedleys Ltd v Breed* [1974] AC 839; *Pharmaceutical Society of Great Britain v Logan* [1982] Crim LR 443.

c) The offence is designed to prevent a public nuisance such as pollution – see *Alphacell Ltd v Woodward* [1972] AC 824 and *FJHWrothwell v Yorkshire Water Authority* [1984] Crim LR 43 – and also enforcement of building regulations enacted for public safety: see *Gammon (Hong Kong) Ltd v Attorney-General for Hong Kong* [1985] AC 1.

## Mistake

Although it is common to talk of the 'defence of mistake' this is something of a misnomer – it is in fact a denial of mens rea. If the defendant is charged with an offence of absolute liability, a mistake of fact is unlikely to avail him as the offence will need proof only of his actus reus. Where mens rea has to be established the defendant is entitled to be judged on the facts a she/he honestly believed them to be: see *B* v *DPP* (above) and *DPP* v *Morgan* [1976] AC 182.

## Infancy

A child under the age of ten cannot incur criminal liability. Further to the enactment of s34 of the Crime and Disorder Act 1998 the rebuttable presumption of criminal law that a child aged between ten and 14 was incapable of committing an offence has been abolished. The change came into effect in September 1998.

## Transferred malice

Under the doctrine of transferred malice, where a defendant fires a gun intending to kill X, but misses and instead kills Y, he will not be able to escape liability for the murder of Y simply because it was his intention was to kill X. The defendant has still committed the actus reus that he intended, namely to cause the death of a human being. In this sense it might be said that the 'malice' against X can be transferred to Y: see *R* v *Latimer* (1886) 17 QBD 359 and *Attorney-General's Reference (No 3 of 1994)* [1997] 3 All ER 936. The limitation placed on the doctrine of transferred malice is that the mens rea can only be 'transferred' from one victim to another, or one item of property to another, within the same offence: see *R* v *Pembliton* (1874) LR 2 CCR 119.

## Coincidence of actus reus and mens rea

As a general rule the accused must commit the act or omission at the same time as he has the requisite mens rea. Thus, an accused who knocks a victim unconscious and then, wrongly believing her to be dead, throws her in the river where she drowns would apparently not be guilty of murder because at the time of doing the act which actually caused death the accused no longer intended to kill since he believed his victim to be already dead. The obvious injustice of this rule has been avoided by use of the 'continuing act' doctrine where all of the accused's acts are seen as part of a series of acts, it being sufficient if he had the requisite mens rea at any stage in that series: see *R* v *Church* [1966] 1 QB 59 and *R* v *LeBrun* [1991] 4 All ER 673.

## 2.3 Key cases and statutes

*Mens rea terms*

- *Chief Constable of Avon and Somerset* v *Shimmen* (1987) 84 Cr App R 7
  The lacuna in recklessness

- *Commissioner of Police of the Metropolis* v *Caldwell* [1982] AC 341
  Objective recklessness

- *Elliot* v *C* [1983] 2 All ER 1005
  Objective recklessness

- *R* v *Cunningham* [1957] 2 QB 396
  Subjective recklessness

- *R* v *Reid* [1992] 3 All ER 673
  The lacuna in recklessness

- *R* v *Sangha* [1988] 1 WLR 519
  Objective recklessness

- *R* v *Woollin* [1998] 4 All ER 103
  Direction on intent

- Criminal Justice Act 1967, s8 – nature of foresight

### The 'defence' of mistake

- *B* v *DPP* [2000] 1 All ER 833
  Mistake viewed subjectively

- *DPP* v *Morgan* [1976] AC 182
  Mistake viewed subjectively

### Infancy

- Crime and Disorder Act 1998, s34 – age of criminal responsibility

### Transferred malice

- *Attorney-General's Reference (No 3 of 1994)* [1997] 3 All ER 936
  What can be transferred

- *R* v *Latimer* (1886) 17 QBD 359
  Same result different victim

- *R* v *Pembliton* (1874) LR 2 CCR 119
  Different result/different object

### Strict liability

- *B* v *DPP* [2000] 1 All ER 833
  Presumption in favour of mens rea

- *Gammon (Hong Kong) Ltd* v *Attorney-General for Hong Kong* [1985] AC 1
  Factors determining strict liability imposition

- *R* v *Bradish* [1990] Crim LR 271
  Danger of offence

- *Smedleys Ltd* v *Breed* [1974] AC 839
  Regulatory offence

## 2.4 Questions and suggested solutions

QUESTION ONE

a) 'Mistake in the sense of a failure to foresee a consequence and mistake in the sense of a lack of knowledge of a surrounding circumstance are treated differently in law.'

   Discuss.

b) U was an excellent shot. He was demonstrating his skills at a shooting match when a bullet ricocheted off a target hitting V who was in the crowd watching the match. An expert described the event 'as one in a million'. U had considered the possibility of such an eventuality but had concluded, wrongly, that such an outcome was impossible, given his levels of skill, the distance of the crowd from the targets and the safe placing of the targets themselves.

   Advise U.

University of London LLB Examination
(for External Students) Criminal Law June 1996 Q8

*General Comment*

A question that should not be attempted without having first considered the wider aspects of mistake and mens rea. The distinctions drawn in part (a) of the question are fine and may not be immediately apparent.

*Skeleton Solution*

a) Failure to foresee a consequence; subjective tests for intention – *Caldwell and Cunningham* recklessness – *DPP* v *Majewski*; mistake as to circumstances – *R* v *Williams*; *DPP* v *Morgan* – drunken mistake.

b) Liability for murder – manslaughter – non-fatal offences against the person.

*Suggested Solution*

a) Prior to 1967 it had been held in *DPP* v *Smith* [1961] AC 290 that there was an irrebutable presumption that a person intended or foresaw the natural consequences of his acts. Consequently, an accused who did not intend or foresee a prohibited consequence would still be convicted of an offence requiring intention if the jury was of the opinion that such a consequence was the natural result of the accused's act. In other words, an accused's mistake as to the consequences of his act would not afford him a defence. This position was essentially reversed by s8 Criminal Justice Act 1967 which effectively provides that the test for intention or foresight is subjective. Consequently, a person who does not intend or foresee the obvious consequences of his act because he has made a mistake (for example, mistakenly believing a gun to be unloaded) will no longer be convicted of an offence requiring that intention or foresight simply because the prosecution will have failed to establish the mens rea necessary for the offence: see further *R v Woollin* [1998] 4 All ER 103.

A similar result would be arrived at where an accused mistakenly does not foresee the prohibited consequences of his act and is charged with an offence of *Cunningham* recklessness (*R v Cunningham* [1957] 2 QB 396) since this is framed to require subjective foresight of the risk.

The position is somewhat less clear with respect to *Caldwell* recklessness (*Commissioner of Police of the Metropolis v Caldwell* [1982] AC 341) where Lord Diplock did not deal with the possibility of the accused considering whether there was a risk and then mistakenly concluding that there was none. However, there is authority to suggest that someone who makes such a positive mistake should be acquitted: see *R v Reid* [1992] 1 WLR 793.

An accused charged with an offence requiring specific intent must be acquitted if, through a mistaken belief, he does not have the required intent, even if the mistake was due to voluntary intoxication: *DPP v Majewski* [1977] AC 443.

An accused may also make a mistake as to the circumstances surrounding the alleged offence. This mistake may afford a 'defence' either by amounting to a denial of part of the mens rea of the offence (other than a denial of intention or foresight discussed above) or because the facts as the accused believed them to be may give rise to a defence. An example of the former would be on a charge of rape, where the accused believes the victim has consented to the sexual intercourse and therefore does not know and is not reckless as to her consent. *DPP v Morgan* [1976] AC 182 puts the law on such a mistake, which prevents an essential element in the mens rea from arising, on a par with mistake or intention or foresight. It was held in Morgan that the accused's mens rea must be judged subjectively and consequently; if the accused mistakenly (even if unreasonably) believed the victim to be consenting he is entitled to an acquittal: see further *B v DPP* [2000] 1 All ER 833. A similar position has now been reached in the latter scenario by *R v Williams* (1983) 78 Cr App R 276 where it was held that an accused who uses reasonable force to protect someone whom he wrongly believes to be under attack would be entitled to the defence of self defence.

It can be seen, therefore, that case law has developed such that a mistake of circumstances will be treated in a similar fashion as a mistake of consequences. However, an important difference does exist in that it is established that although voluntary intoxication is highly relevant to mistake negating intention, it is a factor which must be ignored when considering mistake as to surrounding circumstances: *R v Woods* (1981) 74 Cr App R 312.

b) It is unclear whether the victim died from the gunshot wound. If the victim died it is unlikely that U would be convicted of murder since it is clear that he had no intention to kill or cause grievous bodily harm: *R v Woollin* 1998] 4 All ER 103. A charge of unlawful act manslaughter is also unlikely since there appears to be no unlawful criminal act: *R v Church* [1966] 1 QB 59. A charge of manslaughter by gross negligence as defined in *R v Adomako* [1994] 3 WLR 288 is also unlikely to succeed, since although the offence is essentially one of strict liability we are told that the incident was a 'one in a million' event and therefore unlikely to be considered as grossly negligent.

If the victim survived the incident U may face charges under the Offences Against the Person Act 1861 such as assault occasioning actual bodily harm contrary to s47, maliciously inflicting grievous bodily harm under s20 or intentionally causing grievous bodily harm contrary to s18.

A charge under s47 is unlikely to succeed since there is no evidence of an assault, which is an essential ingredient of this offence. A charge under s18 would also be unsuccessful because U clearly did not intend to cause grievous bodily harm. Although the mens rea under s20 includes where the accused is reckless as to whether his act would cause some harm (see *R v Savage; DPP v Parmenter* [1992] 1 AC 699), this is unlikely to lead to a conviction since *Cunningham* recklessness is required, ie that U subjectively foresaw the risk. Since U mistakenly believed that this kind of incident was impossible he would not have the requisite mens rea for the offence.

Thus it appears that this incident is a true 'accident' for which no criminal liability will be attached.

## QUESTION TWO

Q went to R's house at the invitation of M, R's wife. Q and M were lovers. They had been drinking heavily and having made love were asleep in bed. Q woke up and despite heavy intoxication started again to make love to M who was still asleep. M woke up to find Q on top of her. She protested but Q did not believe that M's protestations were real. M's protestations brought R, who had just entered the house, into the bedroom. He was extremely angry, believing that Q had raped M. R, who was incensed with rage, pulled Q out of the bed. Q raced for the window but, because of his drunken condition, he fell out of the window and broke a leg.

Advise the parties of their criminal liability. What difference, if any, would it make to your advice if Q had died?

University of London LLB Examination
(for External Students) Criminal Law June 1995 Q3

## General Comment

A relatively straightforward question involving a discussion of the actus reus and mens rea of rape, non-fatal offences against the person and manslaughter.

## Skeleton Solution

Q: rape – R: offences against the person?; self defence?; mistake?; causation?; constructive manslaughter.

## Suggested Solution

A charge of rape against Q may be made both on the basis of when he commenced sexual intercourse with M as she was sleeping, and when he continued to so after she woke up.

Rape is defined in s1(2) of the Sexual Offences Act 1956 (as amended by the Criminal Justice and Public Order Act 1994) as the unlawful sexual intercourse with a person without his or her consent. The accused must know or be reckless as to whether the victim is consenting or not.

The issue for a charge of rape based on the sexual intercourse with M when she was asleep is whether a person who is asleep can be said not to consent to the intercourse. Q may argue that since she was asleep she did not positively object to the intercourse. However, it was established in *R v Fletcher* (1859) 8 Cox CC 131 that a person who is asleep or unconscious does not consent to sexual intercourse.

When M awakes she positively objects to the intercourse and so there can be no question of her actual consent. The question now is whether Q has the mens rea for the offence. The accused must know or be reckless as to whether the victim is consenting or not.

It was held in *R v Bashir* (1982) 77 Cr App R 59 that recklessness in the context of rape applies in the subjective sense. Consequently, the prosecution is generally required to prove that the accused is at least aware of the possibility that the victim may not be consenting. An honest, even if unreasonable, belief would entitle the accused to an acquittal. It would appear at this stage therefore, that Q may be acquitted of rape because he did not believe M's protestations. However, this case is complicated by the fact that Q was drunk at the time of the alleged offence. It was held in the case of *R v Woods* (1982) 74 Cr App R 312 that a mistaken belief, due to drunkenness, that the victim was consenting to sexual intercourse will not be accepted. Consequently, if Q's belief that M was really consenting was due to the fact that he was drunk, he will be convicted of rape under the principle stated in *Woods*.

When R pulled Q out of the bed he may have committed an assault (in that he caused Q to apprehend immediate personal violence (*Fagan v Metropolitan Police Commissioner* [1969] 1 QB 439)) or battery (in that he used unlawful force on Q): see *R v Venna* [1975] 3 All ER 788.

When Q broke his leg by falling out of the window R may be guilty of the more serious offences under the Offences Against the Person Act 1861.

The first problem which has to be overcome is whether or not R, in law, caused the broken leg to Q. R may argue that Q is responsible for this injury himself since he fell out of the window whilst drunk. Although it was established in *R v Roberts* [1972] Crim LR 27 that an accused may be responsible for injuries sustained by the victim's efforts at escaping from an attack, this is limited to where the victim's reaction is 'reasonable and not daft'. Arguably, running for the window and then falling out of it when all R did was to pull Q out of bed, is unreasonable. If this is the case then Q's falling out of the window may be seen as a novus actus interveniens which will break the chain of causation and absolve R of any liability for Q's broken leg.

Assuming there has been no break in the chain of causation, R may be charged with an assault occasioning actual bodily harm contrary to s47 of the 1861 Act. An assault, as defined above, would appear to be present, and a broken leg would almost certainly amount to actual bodily harm (which was defined in *R v Chan Fook* [1994] Crim LR 432 as 'any injury which is more than trivial'. By pulling Q from the bed, R may not have intended to cause Q any injury, but it has been held in *R v Savage; R v Parmenter* [1991] 4 All ER 698 that no mens rea is required for the injury; it is sufficient if the accused had the mens rea for the assault.

R could also be charged with causing or inflicting grievous bodily harm contrary to ss18 and 20 of the 1861 Act. A broken leg is likely to amount to grievous bodily harm which was defined as 'really serious harm' in *DPP v Smith* [1960] 3 All ER 161. It is unlikely that R could be charged under s18 of the 1861 Act since this requires the accused to intend to cause the victim a serious injury, of which there is no evidence in this question. However, a charge under s20 may be possible since the mens rea of this offence includes where the accused merely foresaw that his act would cause some harm: see *R v Savage; R v Parmenter*. Of course, it is debatable whether R has the mens rea for this offence.

To all of these offences, R may raise the defence of self-defence because he believed that Q was raping M. As discussed above, it is not sure that Q is guilty of raping M, but even if he is not guilty of rape, under *R v Williams* [1983] 3 All ER 316 an accused who makes a mistake as to the factual circumstances he finds himself in is entitled to have his liability assessed on the basis of the circumstances as he believes them to be. Thus, R may be entitled to the defence of self-defence providing he has acted reasonably and proportionately: *R v Oatridge* [1992] Crim LR 205. It is submitted that merely pulling a man whom you believe to be raping a woman off a bed is a reasonable and proportionate use of force.

If Q had died when he fell out of the window R may be charged with constructive manslaughter. However, the same problem of causation as discussed above arises. Even if the problem of causation can be overcome, it would have to be shown that R killed Q by committing an unlawful criminal act which all reasonable and sober people would inevitably recognise would subject another to the risk of some, albeit not serious, harm: *R v Church* [1966] 1 QB 59. R may argue that he has not committed any unlawful act because he is entitled to the defence of self-defence (as discussed above). Alternatively, he may argue that pulling someone out of bed is not 'dangerous' within the meaning laid down in *Church*, because merely pulling someone out of bed does not inevitably expose them to the risk of any harm.

## QUESTION THREE

Strict liability must be retained. It provides social benefits that would not be obtained through any of the supposed alternatives to it and the injustice caused by it is often exaggerated.

Discuss.

University of London LLB Examination
(for External Students) Criminal Law June 1981 Q9

### General Comment

A very hard question which admits of detailed discussion. Therefore, it is potentially hazardous in that answering essay questions such as this can quickly eat into one's time. Only students who are well disciplined and organised in their examination technique should attempt such a question.

### Skeleton Solution

Strict liability and absolute liability compared and contrasted – social benefits of no-fault liability at criminal law – negligence aspect – drawbacks of such liability and apparent inequity thereof.

### Suggested Solution

A crime of strict liability is one where mens rea (intention, recklessness or even negligence) is not required as to one or more elements in the actus reus. By contrast crimes of absolute liability are those where no mens rea at all is required.

Crimes of strict liability are generally the creation of statute. Under the common law it was, on the whole, accepted that every crime required mens rea of some kind. However, with the industrial revolution, Parliament began to legislate in such matters as safety in factories, selling impure food and the regulation of economic activities of all types. When it did so, it frequently laid down in detail what the prohibited act consisted of, but failed to specify any mental element. It therefore fell to the courts to decide whether this omission was intended to mean that strict liability was to be imposed or, alternatively, whether such statutes were to be interpreted in accordance with the general principles of criminal law where there is a presumption in favour of mens rea.

On the whole, the courts have taken the first view and almost invariably have imposed strict liability when Parliament has omitted words like 'wilfully' or 'knowingly'. Occasionally, the courts have even interpreted an offence as one of strict liability where such words have been present.

It is necessary to examine exactly what social benefits arise from imposition of criminal liability without fault before it can be considered whether or not strict liability must be retained. It has been argued particularly by Baroness Barbara Wootton, a social scientist, that one of the main aims of criminal law must be to protect society from harmful acts. Acts to be prevented are those that would be harmful, whether done intentionally, recklessly, negligently or even inadvertently. However, this argument does not apply simply to crimes of strict liability and, if it were a correct approach, it is one which could be applied to all crimes, so that simply performing the actus reus of any offence would amount to a crime.

Indeed, one of the very strong arguments against strict liability is that the influence of strict liability does tend to affect the court's attitude to all crimes and undermine greatly the strength of the presumption in favour of mens rea.

A further argument frequently put forward in support of strict liability is that it is generally applied only to offences of a minor nature, those that could be described as 'regulatory' or 'social' rather than 'real' crimes. Originally there may have been some truth in this argument. The first type of strict liability offences did relate to food and hygiene legislation and other social regulatory offences. However, it is not an argument that is supported when one looks at the present areas where strict liability is applied. Legislation relating to pollution is usually interpreted as giving rise to strict liability: *Alphacell Ltd* v *Woodward* [1972] AC 824. However, the consequences of allowing rivers to become polluted can be extremely serious and it would certainly be wrong to say that such crimes have no moral content.

In *Atkinson* v *Sir Alfred McAlpine & Son Ltd* [1974] Crim LR 668 it was held that the company committed an offence contrary to the Asbestos Regulations 1969 by failing to give written notice that they were going to undertake work involving crocidolite. The company neither knew nor indeed had reason to know that the work did involve crocidolite. However, the court found that where a statute contained an absolute prohibition against the doing of some act, as a general rule, mens rea was not a constituent of that offence. Furthermore, it distinguished the situation from that where the law imposed a duty to act where mens rea was a necessary requirement, for example, failure to report an accident. In such cases the defendant would not be guilty if he was unaware that the accident had occurred: *Harding* v *Price* [1948] 1 KB 695.

A further example of the application of strict liability in pure criminal law may be seen in the legislation concerning dangerous drugs. This has on occasions in recent years been defined as involving crimes of strict liability: *Yeandel* v *Fisher* [1966] 1 QB 440. Here the defendant was found guilty of 'being concerned with the management of premises for the purposes of smoking cannabis', even though he did not know and had no means of knowing that such smoking was taking place. However, this case was overruled by *Sweet* v *Parsley* [1969] 1 All ER 347 where a conviction on similar facts to those in the *Yeandel* v *Fisher* case was quashed by the House of Lords. The Misuse of Drugs Act 1971 has to some extent moved away from imposing pure strict liability by allowing a statutory defence for an accused, where charged with being in possession of prohibited drugs, to show that he neither knew of or suspected nor had reasons to suspect the existence of some fact alleged by the prosecution which it is necessary for the prosecution to prove if he is to be convicted of the offence charged. Thus, if it can be shown that the accused did not know or believe that he has a controlled drug on him, he will have a defence. However, it will not be a defence for the accused to show that he did not know or believe the substance to be the particular controlled drug it in fact was, if he knew or suspected that it was a controlled drug which he was not entitled to have: *R* v *McNamara* (1988) 87 Cr App R 246. Neither will the fact that D 'forgets' he has such a drug absolve him: *R* v *Martindale* [1986] 1 WLR 1042.

A rather better argument in support of strict liability is one founded in practicality. If the courts were to accept that mens rea had to be proved in every case, the prosecutor's task would often be made impossible. Indeed, this aspect was one stressed by Lord Salmon in *Alphacell Ltd* v *Woodward* and by their Lordships in the Court of Appeal decision in *R* v *Bradish* [1990] Crim LR 271 where the appellant had been found in possession of a can of CS gas, a 'prohibited weapon' under s5(1)(b) of the Firearms Act 1968. The Court held that a balance had to be struck between protecting the innocent possessor of such articles and the underlying policy behind legislation that sought to protect the public from such weapons.

In *Alphacell Ltd* v *Woodward* Lord Salmon said:

> 'If it were held to be the law that no conviction could be obtained of the 1951 Act unless the prosecution could discharge the often impossible onus of proving that the pollution was caused intentionally or negligently, a great deal of pollution would go unpunished, and undeterred to the relief of many riparian factory owners. As a result, many rivers which are now filthy, would become filthier still and many rivers which are now clean, would lose their cleanliness.'

This indeed is probably one of the most important historical explanations for the existence of such offences. However, the consequences of such a situation are very grave. If a prosecutor does not have to prove mens rea, it is unlikely that he will go to the bother of doing so. So, when it comes to sentencing, the court will often find it very difficult to distinguish between the worst cases of a deliberate breach of the law and instances of inadvertent failure to comply with the required standard. It is very difficult to impose a sentence in such a situation and generally the court will want to enquire into which category the convicted person falls. Treating the offence as a crime of strict liability simply removes the decision as to these very important facts, from the jury into the hands of the judge.

It has been argued in support of offences of strict liability that the guilty defendant will, in almost every case, at least have been negligent, otherwise the statute would not have been complied with. However, there are cases where the defendant is absolutely blameless – for example, *Alphacell* v *Woodward*; *Atkinson* v *Sir Alfred McAlpine & Son Ltd* – so even in the absence of any fault, liability may still be imposed. This point is sometimes argued in a slightly different way by saying that there is a substantial amount of empirical evidence to show that prosecutions are frequently only brought where the prosecuting agency (eg the factory inspectorate) is sure that some degree of fault is present. If this is so, why does Parliament not specify in detail what degree of fault must be proved for the offence to be committed?

Certainly, therefore, there are some arguments that can be put forward in support of strict liability, although on the whole the arguments have rather shaky foundations. However, before it can be considered whether or not strict liability must be retained, it is necessary to look at the arguments against such offences. There are two main arguments against strict liability, indeed arguments that have been touched on already in considering supporting arguments to strict liability, the first being that it is unnecessary. Strict liability results in the conviction of persons who have been found by the court to have behaved impeccably and who should not be required to alter their conduct in any way. Second, and possibly more importantly, strict liability is unjust. It is no argument to say that strict liability offences are not 'real' crimes. Those convicted of strict liability offences are treated as criminals, they go through a criminal process and the stigma of a criminal conviction attaches to them. Strict liability offences may catch the large number of truly guilty defendants, but they also catch the small number of persons who are absolutely morally innocent.

A conviction in a criminal court in that situation will obviously make the defendant feel rightly aggrieved and have consequences far outside the courts as in *Sweet* v *Parsley*. It is no answer to such an argument to say that where there is no moral guilt, then the penalty imposed by the court will be only nominal. The court's penalty is the least of many penalties that attach to an individual when convicted of an offence. The stigma attached to the conviction may be a much more severe penalty. Where such a sense of injustice arises from a conviction in an offence of strict liability, the aggrieved defendant's attitude to criminal law generally may be affected so that the public respect for the criminal law, which is necessary for its upkeep, is undermined.

A practical argument in favour of strict liability is the most persuasive of all the arguments in support and could possibly outweigh the arguments against strict liability if there were no alternative to such offences. The practical problems of showing mens rea, which is the basis of the argument for strict liability, could to some extent be mitigated by altering the burden of proof in such offences. Indeed, to some extent, this has been seen by the statutory defence contained in the Misuse of Drugs Act as outlined above. However, a simpler approach would be to provide for the imposition of liability for negligence. Thus, a person would be liable if it were shown that they had inadvertently taken an unjustified risk. However, they would be acquitted if it were found that their conduct was faultless. The imposition of liability for negligence does seem to meet the arguments of most of those who are in favour of strict liability. Roscoe

Pound in *The Spirit of the Common Law* writes that the good sense of the courts has introduced the doctrine of acting at one's peril with respect to statutory crimes that express the needs of society. Such crimes are not meant to punish the vicious will, but to put pressure upon the thoughtless and the inefficient to do their whole duty in the interest of public health or safety or morals. The 'thoughtless and inefficient' to which Roscoe Pound refers are obviously those who are negligent. They are certainly not those who have done everything they could possibly do and are in no way to blame for the act, omission or state of affairs that constitutes the actus reus of the offence.

Furthermore, by providing for liability for negligence, the public will be encouraged to do their duty to the highest possible standard and thus avoid a possible criminal conviction. Bearing in mind the alternatives available to strict liability in its present form, it is difficult to support a statement that it must be retained. It is certainly true to present a fairly strong argument that it provides social benefits. Furthermore, these social benefits might not be obtained where mens rea in the sense of intention or recklessness was a necessary requirement of every crime. However, in this social regulatory field, where the aim of the criminal law is to encourage the highest possible standards of care, this may be achieved by the imposition of liability for negligence without the very serious consequence of catching those who are blameless.

### QUESTION FOUR

Fitzgerald, aged 13 years, was playing on an embankment near a highway. He threw stones at passing cars. Gordon, who was driving his car very fast hit a stone. The car crashed into the control barrier and Gordon was severely injured.

Fitzgerald who was not very bright had not realised the danger his stone throwing constituted. He also threw a stone at Dan but it missed him, hitting John.

Advise Fitzgerald.

> University of London LLB Examination
> (for External Students) Criminal Law June 1983 Q3

### General Comment

This question again examines the elements of recklessness, in relation here to criminal damage and offences against the person. Also considered is the doctrine of transferred malice.

### Skeleton Solution

Sections 1(1) and 1(2) Criminal Damage Act 1971 – recklessness – ss20 and 18 Offences Against the Person Act 1861 – recklessness – abolition of doli incapax.

*Suggested Solution*

Fitzgerald should be advised that he may have committed an offence contrary to s1(1) of the Criminal Damage Act 1971 which provides that it is an offence to destroy or damage any property belonging to another, intending to destroy or damage any such property or being reckless as to whether any such property would be destroyed or damaged, without lawful excuse. The mens rea for s1(1) is intention or recklessness as to all the circumstances and consequences that constitute the actus reus of criminal damage under s1(1)(b).

Furthermore, Fitzgerald may have committed the more serious offence contained in s1(2) of the Criminal Damage Act which provides that it will be an offence for a person without lawful excuse to destroy or damage any property, whether belonging to himself or another:

a) intending to destroy or damage any property or being reckless as to whether any property would be destroyed or damaged; and

b) intending by the destruction or damage to endanger the life of another, or being reckless as to whether the life of another would be thereby endangered.

In relation to both of these offences certain aspects need further consideration.

First, the question of causation could be a problem. We are told that Gordon was driving very fast when he hit the stone on the road, and it could be argued that he was the cause of the damage to the property and the consequent injuries because of his excessive driving speeds. Only if the jury is satisfied that Fitzgerald was in law a substantial and operating cause of the consequences that occurred will he be held to be liable. It should be noted that it is unnecessary to show that Fitzgerald is the only cause in law. There may be other causes contributing to the consequence which actually flows. The second point requiring consideration is whether Fitzgerald would be viewed as reckless in relation to the circumstances and consequences contained in the actus reus of s1(1) and (2). In *Commissioner of Police of the Metropolis* v *Caldwell* [1982] AC 341 Lord Diplock considered the meaning of the word in the context of the Criminal Damage Act.

> 'In my opinion, a person charged with an offence under s1(1) of the Criminal Damage Act 1971 is reckless as to whether or not any property would be destroyed or damaged if:
> (a) he does an act which in fact creates an obvious risk that property will be destroyed or damaged;
> (b) when he does the act he either has not given any thought to the possibility of there being any such risk or has recognised that there was some risk involved and has nonetheless gone on to do it.'

This definition of recklessness is a departure from the earlier definitions contained in cases like *R* v *Stephenson* [1979] QB 695 where emphasis was placed on the accused subjectively having appreciated the risk. In Lord Diplock's definition of recklessness many more states of mind would be in decided, ranging from failure to give any thought at all to whether or not there is any risk of those harmful consequences to recognising the existence of the risk and nevertheless deciding to ignore it.

The result of this much wider definition of recklessness is that thoughtless people or people of low intelligence who may not have appreciated a risk that would be obvious to the ordinary person may now be caught within the definition of recklessness and therefore be liable in criminal law: see *Elliott* v *C (A Minor)* [1983] 1 WLR 939.

This 'objective' type of recklessness was confirmed in *R* v *Sangha* [1988] 2 All ER 385 where the Court of Appeal held that in criminal damage cases – here arson of a flat – the test was whether an ordinary and prudent bystander would have perceived an obvious risk that property would be damaged and life endangered thereby.

It could be argued that Fitzgerald has committed an offence contrary to s18 or s20 in the Offences Against the Person Act 1861. Section 18 is the more serious offence and it provides that a person who unlawfully and maliciously wounds or causes any grievous bodily harm to any person with intent to do any grievous bodily harm shall commit an offence.

The actus reus of this offence may well be satisfied providing the jury are satisfied that in law Fitzgerald was the legal 'cause' of the injuries sustained by Gordon. However, the mens rea element of s18 would not be satisfied. There is no 'intention' to cause the grievous bodily harm as Fitzgerald does not desire it nor does he know it is certain to occur.

Under s20 it is an offence for a person unlawfully and maliciously to wound or inflict any grievous bodily harm upon another. The problem on the facts would be whether or not there has been an infliction of grievous bodily harm. In the case of *R* v *Clarence* (1888) 22 QBD 23 it was held that the term 'inflict' implied an assault in the sense of a battery. The House of Lords has more recently confirmed that the term is effectively synonymous with 'causing': see *R* v *Burstow* [1997] 3 WLR 534. In addition it would have to be shown that Fitzgerald acted 'maliciously'. In the case of *R* v *Mowatt* [1968] 1 QB 421 it was stated that the term 'maliciously' imported upon the part of the person who unlawfully inflicts the wound or other grievous bodily harm an awareness that his act may have the consequence of causing some physical harm to some other person. Following *R* v *Savage; R* v *Parmenter* [1991] 3 WLR 914, in order to secure a conviction under s20 the prosecution would need to establish that Fitzgerald intended or foresaw that he might cause some harm to Gordon.

Assuming the events described occurred after September 1998, Fitzgerald's age would not of itself afford any defence. Following the enactment of s34 of the Crime and Disorder Act 1998 the rebuttable presumption that a child between the ages of ten and 14 was doli incapax has been abolished.

When Fitzgerald throws the stone at Dan but hits John the mens rea he has toward Dan is, under the doctrine of transferred malice, transferred to John, provided the actus reus and mens rea are the same: *R* v *Latimer* (1886) 17 QBD 359. Had he intended to hit a car when he threw the stone, his hitting John could not be subject to the doctrine as the actus reus and mens rea would not be the same: *R v Pembliton* (1874) LR 2 CCR 119. Likewise if he had intended to hit Dan but had missed and damaged John's property.

QUESTION FIVE

Mistake operates by considering the position the accused thought he was in and on that assumption examines the legal significance of his acts.

Discuss.

University of London LLB Examination
(for External Students) Criminal Law June 1984 Q3(a)

*General Comment*

Bearing in mind the recent case law and the academic discussion surrounding the defence of mistake and the problems that arise from it this question should be one that a well-prepared student would have been able to answer well and possibly would even have been pleased to see. The fact that it is half essay/half problem in its format may also assist a student because the essay aspect of the question will often help a student to recall clearly and accurately the necessary cases and principles that are to be applied in relation to the problem part of the question.

*Skeleton Solution*

Negation of mens rea – 'honest and reasonable' – recent cases: removal of 'reasonableness' requirement except in certain cases.

*Suggested Solution*

A mistaken belief held by an accused may be as to fact or as to law (either civil or criminal). It is necessary always to distinguish what particular type of mistake an accused may be labouring under as a mistake of law is usually to be regarded as no defence. In *R v Bailey* (1800) Russ & Ry 1, CCR the mistaken belief that conduct was not criminal when in fact it was, was held to be no defence, although it went to mitigation. A mistake of fact may be a defence providing it negates the particular mens rea necessary to prove the crime charged.

A mistake which does not preclude the mens rea cannot provide a defence as it is irrelevant.

The difficulty for many years has been in settling what particular type of mistake of fact should enable an accused to be judged according to the position he thought he was in. Some early case law, for example *R v Rose* (1884) 15 Cox CC 540, suggested that the mistake had to be both honest and reasonable. However, in *DPP v Morgan* [1976] AC

182 a purely subjective approach was adopted. In that case D had invited three friends to have sexual intercourse with his wife. He told them that she would put up a struggle as this would increase her sexual pleasure. The men had intercourse with the wife and were convicted of rape. The men appealed against conviction to the House of Lords on a question of whether an honest though unreasonable belief in consent to intercourse was a defence. The House of Lords held that since rape required intercourse without consent, if an accused honestly (though unreasonably) believed that his victim was consenting the prosecution had failed to prove the necessary mens rea for the crime.

In *B* v *DPP* [2000] 1 All ER 833 the House of Lords confirmed the move away from the 'honest and reasonable' school of thought in relation to mistake towards the subjective approach based on what the defendant believed. Lord Nicholls observed that there had, in the latter part of the twentieth century, been a series of cases where the courts had placed renewed emphasis on the subjective nature of the mental element in criminal offences. As he confirmed, when mens rea is ousted by a mistaken belief it is as well ousted by an unreasonable belief as by a reasonable belief. Where a statute expressly provides that the fault elmement is negligence, there might still be room for a concept of honest and reasonable mistake, but the concept plays no part in common law principles of general application. Mistake, whether reasonable or not, is a defence where it prevents the defendant from having the mens rea which the law requires for the crime with which he is charged.

The same reasoning can be observed where D relies on a defence because he has made a genuine mistake of fact. In *R* v *Kimber* [1983] 1 WLR 1118 it was stated that, on a charge of indecent assault, if an accused honestly believed a victim was consenting then he would be entitled to be acquitted. The question of whether his belief was reasonable or unreasonable was irrelevant save in so far that it might have assisted the jury to decide whether an accused did believe what he said he did. Furthermore in *R* v *Williams (Gladstone)* [1984] Crim LR 163 it was held to be a material misdirection when it was not made clear to the jury that it was for the prosecution to eliminate the possibility that the appellant was acting under a genuine mistake of fact. Once again the Court of Appeal stated that the question of reasonableness of the appellant's mistaken belief was material only to the question of whether or not the belief was in fact held.

In *Beckford* v *R* [1987] 3 WLR 611, where the Privy Council described *Morgan* as 'a landmark decision in the development of the common law', the court approved the decision in *R* v *Williams (Gladstone)* (above). That decision was that, in relation to assaults, 'the mental element necessary … is the intent to apply unlawful force' and that if the accused believed, reasonably or otherwise, in the existence of facts which would justify his using that force in self-defence, then he did not have the required mens rea.

Since *Beckford* v *R* then, the distinction made in *Albert* v *Lavin* [1981] 1 All ER 628 between elements of the offence and these of a defence has been removed.

It is therefore true to say that mistake generally operates by considering the position the accused thought he was in and on that assumption examines the legal significance of his acts. There do appear to be exceptions to this rule, for example in *DPP* v *Morgan* (above) the House of Lords refused to overrule *R* v *Tolson* (1889) 23 QBD 168. In that case the accused had been deserted by her husband for five years and believed him to be dead. She remarried whereupon her first husband reappeared. Her conviction for bigamy was quashed because her belief was not only an honest one but also based upon reasonable grounds. Lord Hailsham stated in *DPP* v *Morgan* that he viewed *R* v *Tolson* as a narrow decision based on the construction of a statute which prima facie seemed to make an absolute statutory offence with a proviso of the statutory defence. In Lord Hailsham's view there was a distinction between *R* v *Tolson* and other cases based on statute and the more general situation in *DPP* v *Morgan*.

This view is supported by *Westminster City Council* v *Croyalgrange* [1986] 2 All ER 353.

However, in *R* v *O'Grady* [1987] 3 WLR 321 it was held that where D, because of self-induced intoxication, formed a mistaken belief that he was using force to defend himself his plea (of self-defence) failed.

Finally, where a crime is one capable of commission by negligence, the requirement of reasonableness in mistake persists as an unreasonably held mistaken belief is itself negligent.

### QUESTION SIX

I was a plain clothes policeman arresting a violent criminal dressed as an old lady. J saw the incident and honestly believed that I was attacking an old lady. J hit I over the head with his bag.

Advise J.

> Adapted from University of London LLB Examination
> (for External Students) Criminal Law June 1984 Q3(b)

### General Comment

A simple test of the application of the principles relating to mistake and justified use of force.

### Skeleton Solution

Assault: s89 Police Act 1996 (replacing s51 Police Act 1964) – prevention of crime s3 CLA 1967 – mistake.

### Suggested Solution

I should be advised that J may have committed a number of serious offences against him. In particular, s89(1) of the Police Act 1996. However, it may be open to J to claim the benefit of s3 of the Criminal Law Act 1967 in conjunction with his genuine mistake of fact.

Under s89(1) of the Police Act 1996 a person who assaults a constable in the execution of his duty shall be guilty of an offence. It is not necessary that an accused knows that it is a constable he is assaulting, provided that the constable is acting in execution of his duty . In order for J to be convicted of an offence contrary to s89(1) it must be shown that the initial arrest being effected by I was lawful: *Riley v DPP* (1989) The Times 13 December. I would seem to be acting in the execution of his duty as his conduct falls within the general scope of preventing crime and catching offenders: *R v Waterfield* [1964] 1 QB 164. J could not be liable under s89(2) for wilfully obstructing a constable in the execution of his duty because on the facts in question he was not acting wilfully as he did not know I was a policeman.

J will wish to claim the defence contained in s3 of the Criminal Law Act 1967 in conjunction with the defence of mistake. The facts in question are very similar to those contained in *R v Williams (Gladstone)* [1984] Crim LR 163. In that case the accused saw M knock a youth to the ground. M said that he was arresting the youth for mugging a woman. The accused did not believe his story and the struggle ensued during which the accused punched M who sustained injuries to his face. The accused was charged under s47 of the Offences Against the Person Act 1861 and put forward the defence that he had honestly believed M was unlawfully assaulting the youth. The trial judge directed that the accused could only rely on his mistake if it was both honest and reasonable. The accused was found guilty and appealed to the Court of Appeal where it was held that there had been a material misdirection in that it had not been made clear to the jury that it was for the prosecution to eliminate the possibility that the appellant was acting under a genuine mistake of fact. The question of whether or not that mistake was reasonable was relevant only in deciding whether the belief was honestly held.

Furthermore, following the Privy Council decision in *Beckford v R* [1988] AC 130 the question to be asked will be did the accused believe, reasonably or not, in the existence of facts which would justify his use of force under the circumstances?

Applying that principle to the facts in question, providing J honestly believed that I was attacking an old lady his criminal liability must be judged on the basis of what he perceived the facts to be.

He would therefore be able to claim the defence contained in s3 of the Criminal Law Act 1967 which provides that a person may use such force as is reasonable in the circumstances in the prevention of crime. This defence will not be available to him if he used excessive force in the light of all the circumstances.

The test of what is 'reasonable' here will be an objective one: *Farrell v Secretary of State for Defence* [1980] 1 All ER 166. However, account will be taken of the 'heat' of the situation and allowances made therefor. J will be judged, in respect of his use of force, by the standards of a reasonable man under those particular circumstances and not by those of a reasonable man who is able to exercise detached reflection in the cold light of day: *R v Whyte* [1987] 3 All ER 416.

# Chapter 3

## Homicide

**3.1**    **Introduction**

**3.2**    **Key points**

**3.3**    **Key cases and statutes**

**3.4**    **Questions and suggested solutions**

## 3.1 Introduction

Criminal law examination papers nearly always include one, if not more, question on homicide. The topic encompasses murder, voluntary manslaughter based on provocation and diminished responsibility, and involuntary manslaughter, whether constructive or based on gross negligence.

## 3.2 Key points

### Basic points

Homicides involve the killing – that is, the acceleration of the death of – a person under the Queen's peace. Until 1996 the common law requirement was that the death had to occur within a year and a day of the defendant's act. Following the enactment of the Law Reform (Year and a Day Rule) Act 1996, the rule has been abolished and replaced with a requirement that, if the death of the victim occurs more than three years after the injury alleged to have caused the death, the consent of the Attorney-General will be required for any prosecution.

### Causation

When considering any homicide problem a candidate should begin the discussion by investigating whether the accused's act or omission is a factual and legal cause of death. The rules of causation and circumstances in which the different rules should be used must be known.

a) The defendant must be the cause in fact of the victim's death – the 'but for' test is applied – as in *R v White* [1910] 2 KB 124 – 'but for the defendant's actions would the victim have died?'

b) If the defendant is a cause in fact of the victim's death – assess whether or not legal causation can be established. Was his act or omission an 'operating and substantial cause of death'? See *R* v *Smith* [1959] 2 QB 35.

c) Consider factors that might amount to a novus actus interveniens and break the chain of causation in law:

   i) The victim refusing treatment – *R* v *Holland* (1841) 2 Mood & R 351 – will not break the chain of causation.

   ii) The 'thin skull' rule – chain of causation not broken by pre-existing physical or mental peculiarities: *R* v *Blaue* (1975) 61 Cr App Rep 271.

   iii) Chain of causation not broken by the victim aggravating the condition caused by D: see *R* v *Wall* (1802) 28 State Tr 51; *R* v *Dear* [1996] Crim LR 595.

   iv) Chain of causation can be broken by a positive supervening voluntary act by the victim: see *R* v *Dalby* [1982] 1 All ER 916; *R* v *Armstrong* [1989] Crim LR 149. *R* v *Roberts* (1971) 56 Cr App Rep 95 – escape can be a novus actus if not reasonably foreseeable.

   v) Chain of causation will not be broken by the reasonably foreseeable intervention of a third party: see *R* v *Pagett* (1983) 76 Cr App Rep 279.

   vi) Chain of causation can be broken by medical treatment if 'palpably wrong' – see *R* v *Jordan* (1956) 40 Cr App Rep 152 – but subsequent cases have limited this to its own facts: see *R* v *Malcherek and Steel* [1981] 2 All ER 422. In *R* v *Cheshire* (1991) 93 Cr App R 251 the Court of Appeal suggested that the negligent treatment would have to be an independent and potent cause of death rendering the actions of D insignificant before it could amount to a novus actus interveniens.

## Murder

If D causes the victim's death with intent to kill or do grievous bodily harm he can be convicted of murder. The intent can be based on proof that it was his purpose to produce either consequence, or on proof that he foresaw either consequence as a virtually certain result of his actions: *R* v *Woollin* [1998] 4 All ER 103. If such evidence of foresight is put before the jury it will be entitled to infer intent therefrom.

## Voluntary manslaughter

Voluntary manslaughter is where the accused commits murder but in circumstances in which what would otherwise be a conviction for murder will be mitigated down to manslaughter on the grounds of provocation or diminished responsibility.

a) Provocation

   The definition of this defence is a combination of statements in *R* v *Duffy* [1949] 1 All ER 932, the Homicide Act 1957, s3 and *R* v *Smith (Morgan)* [2000] 4 All ER 289.

The first stage of the defence is to establish whether or not the accused lost his self-control (a subjective test). This is a question of fact for the jury.

The second stage is to establish that the loss of self-control was 'sudden'. Note that the cases which establish that any time delay between the act or words of provocation and the killing will prevent the successful raising of the defence (such as *R v Hayward* (1833) 6 C & P 157 and *R v Thornton* [1992] 1 All ER 306) must now be read in the light of dicta in *R v Ahluwalia* [1993] Crim LR 63, to the effect that such a delay will not necessarily be fatal to the defence.

Once the evidential basis for provocation has been made out the jury will have to consider whether or not the defendant displayed, what was for him, reasonable self-control. It is no longer appropriate to direct a jury to consider the objective stage by reference to how a reasonable person (with or without attributes of the defendant) would have reacted. The test for provocation should be drawn in terms that give the jury the discretion to act as justice requires. Hence, it would be incorrect for a judge to direct a jury that certain characteristics of the accused were to be disregarded in assessing the degree of self-control to be expected. The emphasis is now on what degree of self-control it is fair and just to expect from a defendant, bearing in mind that certain character traits, such as pugnacity and irritability, are not to be seen as excuses for engaging in violent acts. For these purposes no distinction is to be drawn between the characteristics that explain the gravity of the provocation to the defendant and those that explain why he might have difficulty in controlling his anger. Intoxication and insanity would still be regarded as characteristics to be disregarded for these purposes as they give rise to defences in their own right.

b) Diminished responsibility

The first stage of this defence under s2 of the Homicide Act 1957 is to investigate whether the accused was suffering from an abnormality of mind due to retarded development, inherent causes or disease or injury. Note that an abnormality of mind due to external causes, such as the consumption of drink or drugs, is excluded (see *R v Gittens* [1984] QB 698, although the exceptions to this rule stated in *R v Tandy* [1989] 1 WLR 350 when alcoholism may sustain the defence should be noted).

The second stage (often omitted in candidates' examination scripts) is to investigate whether the abnormality is so great that it has substantially impaired the accused's responsibility. Note that the burden of proof is on the accused to prove this defence on balance of probabilities.

Note that the following have been held to amount to diminished responsibility: abnormal urges (*R v Byrne* [1960] 3 All ER 1); epileptic upset (*R v Bailey* (1977) 66 Cr App R 31); morbid jealousy (*R v Vinagre* (1979) 69 Cr App R 104); depression (*R v Gittens* [1984] QB 698); and the effects of alcoholism (*R v Tandy* [1989] 1 WLR 350).

### Involuntary manslaughter

This is where the accused kills without the mens rea of murder.

a) Unlawful act/constructive manslaughter

This is where D commits a dangerous criminal act that causes death. On the basis of *R* v *Church* [1966] 1 QB 59 and *R* v *Dawson* (1985) 81 Cr App R 150 the unlawful act will be dangerous if it is such as all sober and reasonable people would inevitably recognise must subject the other person to, at least, the risk of some physical harm resulting therefrom, albeit not serious harm.

Note that the unlawful act need not be directed at the victim: *R* v *Goodfellow* (1986) 83 Cr App R 23 and *R* v *Mitchell* [1983] 2 WLR 938.

D need not foresee death in order to be guilty, but must have the mens rea for the unlawful act: see *DPP* v *Newbury* [1977] AC 500 and *R* v *Lamb* [1967] 2 QB 981.

b) Manslaughter by gross negligence

In *R* v *Adomako* [1994] 3 WLR 288 the House of Lords in a landmark decision effectively abolished the offence of reckless manslaughter as defined in *R* v *Lawrence* [1982] AC 510, and replaced it with a newly defined offence of manslaughter by gross negligence. To secure a conviction for this offence the prosecution must prove:

i) that the accused owed the victim a duty of care;

ii) that the duty was breached causing death;

iii) that the accused's act or omission is grossly negligent, which is defined as supremely a question for the jury to decide whether the risk of death was so great as to amount to a criminal act or omission .

Note that this is purely an objective test and manslaughter by gross negligence has now effectively become an offence of strict liability.

c) Causing death by dangerous driving

The offence of causing death by dangerous driving under s1 Road Traffic Act 1988 has replaced the offence of causing death by reckless driving under s1 Road Traffic Act 1972. The offence of causing death by dangerous driving is committed when the accused's driving falls far below the standard expected of the competent and careful driver, and it is obvious to such a driver that driving in that way would be dangerous. Note that the offence is essentially one of strict liability and there is no longer any room for the 'lacuna' argument.

## 3.3 Key cases and statutes

*Causation*

- *R v Blaue* (1975) 61 Cr App R 271
  Refusing medical treatment

- *R v Dear* [1996] Crim LR 595
  Victim aggravating existing condition

- *R v Holland* (1841) 2 Mood & R 351
  Refusing medical treatment

- *R v Jordan* (1956) 40 Cr App R 152
  Medical treatment as a novus actus

- *R v Majoram* [2000] Crim LR 372
  Escape not a novus actus

- *R v Malcherek and Steel* [1981] 2 All ER 422
  Medical treatment not a novus actus

- *R v Pagett* (1983) 76 Cr App R 279
  Actions of third party not a novus actus

- *R v Roberts* (1971) 56 Cr App R 95
  Escape not a novus actus

- *R v Smith* [1959] 2 QB 35
  Medical treatment not a novus actus

- *R v White* [1910] 2 KB 124
  Cause in fact

- *R v Williams* [1992] 2 All ER 183
  Escape not a novus actus

*Murder*

- *R v Woollin* [1998] 4 All ER 103
  Mens rea for murder

- Homicide Act 1957, s1 – abolition of constructive malice

*Voluntary manslaughter*

*Provocation*

- *R v Humphreys* [1995] 4 All ER 1008
  Cumulative provocation

- *R v Ibrams and Gregory* (1981) 74 Cr App R 154
  'Cooling' time between provocation and killing

- *R v Smith (Morgan)* [2000] 4 All ER 289
  Jury direction on provocation

- Homicide Act 1957, s3 – provocation factors

*Diminished responsibility*

- *R v Byrne* [1960] 2 QB 396
  'Abnormality of the mind'

- *R v Tandy* [1989] 1 All ER 267
  Link with intoxication

- Homicide Act 1957, s2(1) – definition

**Involuntary manslaughter**

*Unlawful act manslaughter*

- *DPP* v *Newbury and Jones* [1977] AC 500
  Mens rea for unlawful act manslaughter

- *R v Cato* [1976] 1 WLR 110
  Need for a criminal act

- *R v Dawson* (1985) 81 Cr App R 150
  Test for dangerousness

- *R v Goodfellow* (1986) 83 Cr App R 23
  Not directed at the victim

*Killing by gross negligence*

- *R v Adomako* [1994] 3 WLR 288
  Direction on gross negligence

## 3.4 Questions and suggested solutions

QUESTION ONE

L, aged 13 years, was not very bright. He and his friend, M, aged 14 years, used to absent themselves from school. From X's shop, L used to steal fruit for L and M to eat. L and M climbed into an electricity substation which they used as a den despite the proximity of high-powered electrical equipment. L threw an apple core at a piece of equipment, causing it to short and plunging a sector of the area into darkness. N, who was a claustrophobic, was stuck in a lift for two hours before power was restored and, as a result, he suffered a heart attack. O, who was driving, was involved in a car crash caused by a failure of a local traffic light. P, who used a ventilating machine, died because the power surge had damaged the computer which controlled his machine. M said L was mad to throw the apple core and L pushed M who fell against some equipment and was badly burned.

Advise L and M of their criminal liability, if any.

University of London LLB Examination
(for External Students) Criminal Law June 1998 Q4

### General Comment

This question covers an enormous range of topics – hence each has to be dealt with in a very brief and concise way. The issue of the age of the defendants has to be noted. Doli incapax may have been abolished but age may still be a factor in determining mens rea. A good knowledge of criminal damage is essential here, as is an understanding of the principles of causation.

### Skeleton Solution

General points about doli incapax – L: theft of fruit; is he dishonest? – M: handling stolen goods – L: criminal damage to the equipment; is he reckless? L: any mens rea for the assault on N? – various homicides – consider causation in relation to each – elements of unlawful act manslaughter – residual issues regarding conspiracy and accessorial liability.

### Suggested Solution

The facts state that L is 13 years of age and that M is 14. Section 34 of the Crime and Disorder Act 1998 abolished the rule whereby defendants between the ages of ten and 14 could only be convicted of criminal offences if it could be shown that, in addition to mens rea, they were aware that their actions were seriously wrong. In relation to any defendant over the age of 10, the prosecution now only has to establish mens rea.

L stealing fruit would obviously be an offence contrary to s1(1) of the Theft Act 1968. The only live issue might be dishonesty. Given that he is not very bright, does he realise he does not have the right to take the fruit without paying for it? In taking the fruit he could also be guilty of making off without payment contrary to s3 of the Theft act 1978. If entered the shop intending to steal the fruit he would have done so as a trespasser with intention to steal, thereby committing an offence contrary to s9(1)(a) of the Theft Act 1968. M, in being given the fruit by L, could be guilty of handling stolen goods contrary to s22 of the Theft Act 1968, provided he knows or believes the fruit to be stolen. The facts indicate this to be the case.

When L throws the apple causing the electrical machinery to short circuit he may have committed the offence of criminal damage. The Criminal Damage Act 1971, s1(1) provides that an offence is committed where a person, without lawful excuse, destroys or damages any property belonging to another intending to destroy or damage any such property or being reckless as to whether any such property would be destroyed or damaged. The equipment is clearly property belonging to another and L has damaged it by interfering with its operation. It may not have been L's intention to damage the property but the section makes it clear that recklessness will suffice. The recklessness here is as defined by the House of Lords in *R v Caldwell* [1982] AC 341 – did L create an obvious risk of harm; if so did he realise such and take the risk, or did he fail to give any thought to the risk? Either way L will be regarded as reckless for the purposes of the offence. The fact that he is young and not very bright will not avail him. In *Elliot v C* [1983] 1 WLR 939 the Divisional Court confirmed that the obviousness of the risk is to be determined by the standards of the reasonable prudent adult bystander. On the facts it is submitted that the basic offence of criminal damage will be made out.

The 1971 Act also provides for an aggravated offence where the defendant causes criminal damage intending by the destruction or damage to endanger the life of another or being reckless as to whether the life of another would be thereby endangered. L may also be guilty of this offence in the light of the consequences of his action. Again *Caldwell* recklessness (*Commissioner of Police of the Metropolis v Caldwell* [1982] AC 341) will suffice. Note that no lives actually have to be put in danger by his criminal damage, he merely has to be reckless as to whether or not this could be a consequence of his actions. *R v Steer* [1987] 2 All ER 833 makes clear that the mens rea must relate to the actual criminal damage – hence L will only be guilty if he was reckless as to whether the damage to the electrical installation would endanger life.

N's heart attack could constitute grievous bodily harm caused by L's actions. The problem for the prosecution would be in establishing that L had the mens rea for the harm. Section 18 of the Offences Against the Person Act 1861 requires proof of intent – not apparent on the facts. Section 20 requires proof that L was malicious. According to *R v Mowatt* [1968] 1 QB 421 this involves proof that L foresaw that some physical harm to some person, albeit of a minor character, might result from his actions. Of course L may have had no such foresight – he is after all not very bright. Failing this a charge under s47 of the 1861 Act would have to be considered – he causes actual bodily harm – but there would have to be proof that he was at least reckless as to assault. He does not have to have any mens rea as regards the causing of the actual bodily harm. Again on the facts proving mens rea looks difficult.

O suffers unspecified injuries and damage to his car. Again assault charges could be brought but would fail due to lack of mens rea. Criminal damage could be charged as outlined above.

L causes P's death in fact. As regards causation in law, the fact that P was a hospital patient would not break the chain of causation. L must take his victim as he finds him: *R v Blaue* [1975] 1 WLR 1411. Mens rea for a homicide charge would be problematic. There is no evidence of the mens rea for murder – ie intention to kill or cause grievous bodily harm. The prosecution could charge unlawful act manslaughter – the unlawful act being the criminal damage outlined above. The unlawful act must be 'dangerous'. On the basis of *R v Church* [1965] 2 All ER 72 and *R v Dawson* (1985) 81 Cr App R 150 the unlawful act must be such as all sober and reasonable people would inevitably recognise must subject another person to, at least, the risk of some physical harm resulting therefrom. For these purposes the objective test for dangerousness is undertaken upon the basis of the knowledge gained by a sober and reasonable man as though he were present at the scene, watching the unlawful act being performed, with the same knowledge as the man committing the unlawful act. It is this last point that is problematic. L is not very bright – hence what harm does he foresee?

The mens rea for unlawful act manslaughter would be the mens rea for the unlawful act, as to which see above. On the facts a charge of killing by gross negligence looks inept in the absence of a clear duty of care owed by L to the ultimate consumers of the electricity.

L causes M to become badly burnt. This suggests grievous bodily harm. As outlined above charges under s18 and s20 of the 1861 Act are possible, dependant on the mens rea that can be established on the part of L. One would assume that L was at least malicious as defined in *Mowatt*. If nothing else there would be liability under s47 for assault occasioning actual bodily harm. L would have no obvious defences, anger providing no legal basis for any defence.

### QUESTION TWO

Jane has a jealous temperament and was quick tempered. She suspected that her boyfriend, Keith, was having an affair with Lucy. This was not true. Jane found Keith and Lucy sitting close together on a park bench and Lucy seemed to be crying. In fact, Keith was looking for a dust speck in Lucy's eye which Lucy had asked him to remove. Jane suspecting the worst went up to them and aimed a blow with her heavy handbag at Lucy. Lucy saw it coming and ducked. Instead, Keith was hit on the head and died two hours later from a brain haemorrhage, because unknown to everyone, he had a thin skull. Lucy lost her eye which had been accidentally poked out by Keith as Lucy ducked.

Advise Jane. What difference, if any, would it make to your advice if Jane thought that Lucy was attacking Keith?

University of London LLB Examination
(for External Students) Criminal Law June 1997 Q4

### General Comment

Once the issue of transferred malice has been dealt with, this is a fairly standard question on homicide, non-fatal offences against the person, defences and some straightforward causation points.

### Skeleton Solution

Whether Jane caused Keith's death – murder – transferred malice – provocation –

unlawful act manslaughter – attempted actual bodily harm – non-fatal offences against Lucy – self defence.

## Suggested Solution

Jane may be charged with Keith's murder. The actus reus of murder is the factual and legal causation of another person's death. Under the 'but for' test (see *R v White* [1910] 2 KB 124) Keith would not have died but for Jane's actions, and Jane is therefore a cause of Keith's death. The fact that the average person might have survived Jane's attack and that Keith may have died only because he had a thin skull will not break the chain of causation, since it has been established that the accused must 'take his victim as he finds him': *R v Hayward* (1908) 21 Cox CC 692 and *R v Blaue* [1975] 1 WLR 1411. This means that the existing medical or psychological vulnerabilities of the victim which exacerbate the effects of the accused's attack will not constitute a novus actus interveniens.

In order to secure a conviction for murder the prosecution will have to prove that Jane had the mens rea for murder, which has been defined in *R v Vickers* [1957] 2 QB 664 as an intention to kill or cause grievous bodily harm. An apparent problem on the facts is that Jane intends to hit Lucy and the handbag striking Keith appears to be an accident. This problem can be overcome by the doctrine of transferred malice under which the mens rea directed at the intended victim may be transferred to the actual victim: see *R v Latimer* (1886) 17 QBD 359. Consequently, Jane may be convicted of Keith's murder if it can be demonstrated that she intended to kill or cause serious harm to Lucy. In the absence of a confession to this effect it is unlikely that the prosecution would be able to prove that Jane intended to kill Lucy by attempting to hit her with a heavy handbag (although to cause serious harm is more likely). If such an intention could be proven, this would be transferred to Keith, and Jane could then be convicted of Keith's murder.

Jane may be entitled to the defence of provocation which, if successful, would have the effect of reducing what would otherwise be a conviction for murder (attracting a mandatory life sentence) to manslaughter (attracting a sentence at the discretion of the judge). Following the decision in *R v Duffy* [1949] 1 All ER 932, as amended by s3 Homicide Act 1957, and *R v Smith (Morgan)* [2000] 4 All ER 289, Jane would be entitled to this defence if she suffered a 'sudden loss of self control' and the jury was satisfied that she had displayed what was, for her, a reasonable level of self-control. Jane would be entitled to the defence if she suffered a 'sudden' loss of self-control in the sense that she was immediately provoked by what she saw (or thought she saw) Lucy and Keith doing: *R v Duffy* (above). If Jane had planned to go out, find Lucy and attack her this would make her guilty of a premeditated attack and be inconsistent with the defence of provocation.

Was the degree of self-control she displayed such as was reasonable to expect from her? The jury can take into account all factors other than insanity and intoxication (which would found defences in their own right). It should be noted, however, that Lord Hoffmann in *R v Smith (Morgan)* observed that a person who flies into a murderous rage when he or she is crossed, thwarted or disappointed in the vicissitudes of life should not be able to rely upon his or her anti-social propensities as even a partial excuse for killing. He added that a tendency to violent rages or childish tantrums is a defect in character rather than an excuse. It is highly questionable, therefore, as to whether Lucy's bad temper would be a factor attracting much weight.

It is important to note that even though Jane's belief that Keith and Lucy are having an affair is erroneous and her belief that they are 'up to the worst' when she sees them is wrong, following *R v Williams* [1968] Crim LR 678 her liability will be judged from the perspective of what she believed.

If the prosecution were unable to prove that Jane intended to kill or cause serious harm to Lucy and therefore unable to secure a conviction for Keith's murder, Jane may still be liable for unlawful act manslaughter. Unlawful act manslaughter was defined in *R v Church* [1966] 1 QB 59 as where the accused caused the death of another by an unlawful act 'which all sober and reasonable people would inevitably recognise must subject the other person to the risk of some harm, albeit not serious harm'. Attempting to hit Lucy with a handbag is clearly an unlawful act (an attempted actual bodily harm, or at least an assault) and hitting someone with a heavy handbag clearly exposes them to the risk of some harm. Although Jane's unlawful act was directed at Lucy and not Keith, it was established in *R v Goodfellow* (1986) 83 Cr App R 23 (reinterpreting *R v Dalby* [1982] 1 WLR 425) that the unlawful act need not be directed at the deceased.

Jane may also be liable for non-fatal offences against the person arising from the loss of Lucy's eye such as an assault occasioning actual bodily harm contrary to s47 Offences Against the Person Act 1861. The loss of an eye would clearly constitute actual bodily harm (defined in *R v Chan Fook* [1994] 1 WLR 689 as any injury which is more than trivial). Jane may be said to be the cause of the injury even though it may have been caused by Lucy ducking to avoid the handbag, since it was established in *R v Roberts* (1971) 56 Cr App R 95 that an accused is responsible for injuries sustained by the victim's reasonable efforts at escaping the accused's attack. The assault, an essential element of this offence, is also present even though Jane missed Lucy, since an assault merely requires that the victim to apprehend personal violence: *Fagan v Metropolitan Police Commissioner* [1969] 1 QB 439. It has been held in *R v Savage*; *R v Parmenter* [1991] 3 WLR 914 that the only mens rea required for the offence under s47 is that required for the assault. No mens rea is required as to the harm caused, and Jane would therefore appear to have the mens rea for this offence even if she did not intend to injure Lucy.

The loss of an eye would almost certainly constitute 'grievous bodily harm' (essentially a jury question and defined rather vaguely in *DPP v Smith* [1961] AC 290 as 'really serious injury') for the purposes of a charge under ss18 or 20 Offences Against the Person Act 1861. It is submitted that it is unlikely that the prosecution would secure a conviction under s18 because it would be difficult to prove that Jane intended to cause Lucy serious harm. A conviction would be more likely under s20 where the prosecution need only prove that Jane intended (or even foresaw) that her act would cause Lucy some harm: *R v Savage*; *R v Parmenter* (above).

If Jane thought that Lucy was attacking Keith, she may be entitled to raise the defence of self-defence, provided the force she was used was reasonable. Whether striking at Lucy with a heavy handbag was reasonable will be measured by the standards of the objective reasonable person (*R v Owino* [1996] Cr App R 128), although the fact that she may have acted in the heat of the moment will be taken into consideration: *Attorney-General's Reference for Northern Ireland (No 1 of 1975)* [1977] AC 105. She may be entitled to the defence of self-defence even if Lucy was not attacking Keith, since following *R v Williams* (above) her liability will be judged on the basis of the facts as she believed them to be.

QUESTION THREE

A and B were on a walking holiday in a remote part of Wales and were three days walk to the nearest point of assistance. B fell down a ravine and injured his throat. A, who had received some first aid training, realised that B was having considerable difficulty breathing, so he gave B artificial respiration but this did severe damage to B's lungs. A realised that B needed a tracheotomy (opening up B's throat to allow him to breathe). A used his penknife to cut open B's windpipe but, as a result, B died from a severed artery. Medical experts agreed that a successful completed tracheotomy would have extended B's life by only three hours.

Advise A of his criminal liability.

> University of London LLB Examination
> (for External Students) Criminal Law June 1996 Q1

*General Comment*

A fairly straightforward question including a discussion of non-fatal offences against the person and homicide and the defence of necessity. The main area of difficulty is the issue of causation – whether the tracheotomy breaks the chain of causation with respect to the initial damage A caused to B's lungs or amounts to an independent cause of death.

*Skeleton Solution*

A's liability for non-fatal offences against the person – causation – homicide – defence of necessity.

*Suggested Solution*

When A administered artificial respiration to B he may have committed a number of non-fatal offences against the person.

It is unlikely that A has committed an assault. An assault is defined as where the accused intentionally or recklessly causes the victim to apprehend immediate physical violence: *Fagan v Metropolitan Police Commissioner* [1969] 1 QB 439. It is unlikely that even an incompetent effort at artificial respiration would create an apprehension of violence and therefore it would appear that the actus reus of this offence is absent. It is also unlikely that A could be convicted of battery which requires the accused to intentionally or recklessly make unlawful physical contact with the victim: *R v Venna* [1976] 1 QB 421. However, it will be a defence to a charge of battery to show that the accused had the victim's express or implied consent: *Collins v Wilcock* [1984] 1 WLR 1172. In this case the courts are likely to take the view that anyone in need of artificial respiration will have impliedly consented to such treatment being given.

It is also unlikely that A could be convicted under s47 Offences Against the Person Act (OAPA) 1861 with an assault occasioning actual bodily harm. Actual bodily harm was defined in *R v Chan Fook* [1994] Crim LR 432 as any injury which is more than trivial. This would clearly include 'severe damage to B's lungs'. A may argue that he neither intended nor was reckless as to whether his efforts at artificial respiration would injure B. However, it has been established in *R v Savage; DPP v Parmenter* [1992] 1 AC 699 that under s4 OAPA 1861 no mens rea is required as to the injury, it being sufficient for the prosecution to show that the accused assaulted or battered the victim and that as a matter of fact this caused actual bodily harm. However, it is an essential ingredient of the s47 offence that the accused assaulted or battered the victim. If the conclusion reached under the above discussion is correct and A has not battered or assaulted B, then there can be no successful prosecution under s47 OAPA 1861.

A may be charged under s20 OAPA 1861 with wounding or inflicting grievous bodily harm. Grievous bodily harm was defined in *DPP v Smith* [1961] AC 290 as a 'really serious injury', which is likely to encompass the harm caused to B's lungs. Section 20, unlike s47, does not require an assault: *R v Wilson* [1984] AC 242. However, the prosecution must establish that the accused intended or was reckless as to whether he caused some harm to the victim: *R v Savage; DPP v Parmenter*. A clearly did not intend harm and it is unlikely that the prosecution could show that he was *Cunningham* reckless (*R v Cunningham* [1957] 2 QB 396), since this would require the prosecution to prove that A actually foresaw that his efforts at artificial respiration may cause some harm to B. A charge under s18 OAPA 1861 is unlikely as there is no evidence that A intended to cause B serious harm.

The next issue is to discuss A's liability for the possible homicide of B. A could be liable for the homicide of B either because of the severe damage caused to B's lungs or because of the negligently performed tracheotomy. It could be argued that had A performed the subsequent tracheotomy properly, B would have lived for another three hours and therefore that the tracheotomy broke the chain of causation with respect to the initial injuries A caused to B's lungs. However, it has been established in the case of *R v Smith* [1959] 2 QB 35 that negligent medical treatment will not break the chain of causation so long as the original wound is still an operating and substantial cause of death. Following *R v Cheshire* (1991) 93 Cr App R 251, since the tracheotomy was performed in the course of treating the injuries to B's lungs it is likely that the injury to B's lungs will still be regarded as a legal cause of death even if the immediate medical cause of death is the tracheotomy.

Alternatively, the prosecution may allege that death was caused by the tracheotomy which severed B's artery. In this case we are told that a successful tracheotomy would have extended B's life by only three hours. However, it is established that the actus reus of homicide is committed if the accused accelerates death by any period of time. Since we are told that B died from a severed artery, it follows that in fact and law, the improperly performed tracheotomy can be regarded as a cause of death.

Consequently, both the injuries caused to B's lungs by A's efforts at artificial respiration and the tracheotomy may be regarded as factual and legal causes of death which may form the basis of a charge of homicide.

It is unlikely that A can be charged with murder. The men rea for murder is explained in *R v Woollin* [1998] 4 All ER 103 as existing where the accused intends to kill or cause grievous bodily harm. There is no evidence on the facts that A has such an intent. It is unlikely that A can be charged with constructive manslaughter since this requires the accused to kill the victim in the course of committing a criminal unlawful act: *R v Church* [1966] 1 QB 59. A may, however, be charged with manslaughter by gross negligence. This was defined in the case of *R v Adomako* [1994] 3 WLR 288 as where the accused owes a duty to the accused and breaches the duty causing death and breaches the duty in a manner the jury considers is grossly negligent. It was held by the House of Lords in *Adomako* that everyone owes everyone else a duty not to cause harm and therefore there will be little difficulty establishing that A owed B such a duty. However, it would also have to be established that A was in breach of this duty to B. This would require the prosecution to establish that A was in some way negligent in performing the tracheotomy with the skills that he had. The courts will not judge an amateur in A's position by the standards of a qualified surgeon. In addition, it would be insufficient to sustain a criminal charge of manslaughter by gross negligence to establish that A was merely negligent. The prosecution must go further and establish that he was grossly negligent sufficient that a jury would consider A deserving a criminal punishment.

To a charge of homicide, A may raise the defence of necessity. It was thought at one time that English law did not recognise the defence of necessity. It was held specifically in the case of *R v Dudley and Stephens* (1884) 14 QBD 273 that the defence of necessity was not available to an accused charged with murder. However, the harshness of this principle seems to have been ameliorated by cases such as *R v Willer* (1986) 83 Cr App R 225 and *R v Conway* [1989] QB 290 which have established that necessity may be available as a defence to charges of careless or reckless driving. There is some authority in the case of *R v Cole* [1994] Crim LR 582 that necessity may be available to offences other than traffic offences. In *R v Cole* the Court of Appeal stated (obiter) that necessity may be a defence to a charge of robbery. It should be noted, however, that this statement was obiter and even if it is followed it does not necessarily mean that necessity will be recognised as a defence to a charge of manslaughter or offences against the person. The important factor that distinguishes the present case from *R v Dudley and Stephens* is that A is not choosing to take another's life to save his own. Lord Brooke in

*Re A (Children) (Conjoined Twins: Surgical Separation)* [2000] 4 All ER 961 expressed the view that the defence of necessity could be available on a murder charge where the defendant kills in an effort to save a life other than his own, provided: (i) the act of the defendant is needed to avoid inevitable and irreparable evil; (ii) the defendant does no more than is reasonably necessary for the purpose to be achieved; and (iii) the evil inflicted by the defendant is not be disproportionate to the evil avoided. On this basis the defence of necessity might well be open to A.

## QUESTION FOUR

M was a keen gardener. He had spent a good deal of money employing a garden designer and planting bushes, flowers and installing garden furniture. On several occasions intruders had removed plants and furniture valued at £2,500. M had decided to wait in the garden shed to catch the intruders. He had with him a shotgun and a rake because he had reason to believe that the intruders would be violent. M was disturbed by noises outside and shouted, 'Who's there?' N, O and P were in the garden. N shouted, 'Stay in there or we will do for you. We only want your property.' Nevertheless M emerged with his rake. N, O and P laughed at him. Enraged at their reaction M returned inside the shed and brought out the shotgun. He pointed it at P who said, 'We are taking your property whether you like it or not!' M shot at N, O and P who were standing close together. P and N were killed.

Advise M and O of their criminal liability.

University of London LLB Examination
(for External Students) Criminal Law June 1995 Q5

### General Comment

A fairly straightforward question mainly on homicide and self-defence. A sound knowledge of the mens rea of murder is required.

### Skeleton Solution

O: burglary?; conspiracy?; attempted theft – M: murder?; provocation?; constructive manslaughter?; self-defence.

### Suggested Solution

It should be noted at the outset that O cannot be convicted of burglary contrary to s9 of the Theft Act 1968. Under s9, burglary is defined as the unlawful entry of a building as a trespasser with the intention to commit a number of specified offences including theft. However, in *Stevens v Gourley* (1859) 7 CBNS 99, a building was defined as a structure of considerable size and, thus, a garden would not fall under this definition.

It is likely that O could be charged with a conspiracy to commit theft. A conspiracy is defined in s1 of the Criminal Law Act 1977 as an agreement to carry out a course of conduct which will lead to the commission of an offence. The actus reus of the offence is committed the moment the agreement to commit the offence is made and thus O may be convicted of a conspiracy even though his co-conspirators are deceased.

It was clearly O's intention to steal from M and therefore O may be guilty of attempted theft contrary to s1 of the Criminal Attempts Act 1981, which defines an attempt as where the accused does an act which is more than more than merely preparatory towards the commission of an offence. O may argue that, although he was in M's garden, he had not yet had the chance to try to steal anything before being confronted by M, and therefore has not done an act which is more than merely preparatory. Under s4(3) of the 1981 Act, whether an act is more than merely preparatory is a mixed question of law (for the judge) and fact (for the jury). In *R v Gullefer* [1990] 3 All ER 882, it was held that an act would be more than merely preparatory when the accused 'embarked on the crime proper'. It is submitted that by entering the garden O has embarked on the crime proper and could successfully be charged with attempted theft.

When M emerged from the shed with a rake he may have committed an assault which is defined in *Fagan v Metropolitan Police Commissioner* [1969] 1 QB 439 as where the accused intentionally or recklessly causes the victim to apprehend immediate physical violence. Although P, N and O did not appear to be particularly frightened by M's threat, it is sufficient if they apprehend or expect an attack.

By shooting and killing P and N, M may be guilty of murder. He has clearly committed the actus rea of the offence in that he has killed a human being who has died within a year and a day of the unlawful act.

The issue here is whether M has the mens rea for murder. It was stated in *R v Moloney* [1985] 1 All ER 1025 that the mens rea of murder is an intention to kill or cause grievous bodily harm. In firing a shotgun at P, N and O it is quite possible that a jury would conclude that M intended to kill them. However, this is not certain and may depend on such evidential issues as how far M was standing from the deceased when he fired and what type of ammunition he used.

It is important to note that there are two mens rea to murder: either an intention to kill, or an intention to cause grievous bodily harm. If the prosecution finds it difficult to prove that M had a specific intention to kill, it may be easier to secure a conviction by proving that he at least intended to cause grievous bodily harm.

In circumstances where it is unclear whether the accused intended to kill or cause grievous bodily harm, the judge may direct the jury that they may infer that the accused so intended if they are satisfied that he foresaw that his act would lead to death or serious bodily harm: see *R v Hancock and Shankland* [1986] 1 All ER 641. However in *R v Nedrick* [1986] 1 WLR 1025 it was held foresight could only be used as evidence of intention if the accused foresaw death as a 'virtual certainty'. This latter view is endorsed by the House of Lords in *R v Woollin* [1998] 4 All ER 103.

If M has the mens rea of murder he may attempt to raise the defence of provocation. Under s3 of the Homicide Act 1957 and *R v Duffy* [1949] 1 All ER 932 it would have to be established that M suffered a 'sudden loss of self-control'. There would also have to be evidence to satisfy the jury that he had displayed the degree of self-control that it was reasonable to expect from him: *R v Smith (Morgan)* [2000] 4 All ER 289.

Although M may argue that he was enraged by the deceased's reaction in laughing at him, and thus satisfy the first test, it is questionable as to whether he could convince a jury that he nevertheless exercised reasonable self-control by his standards. The jury could have regard to his passion for gardening and his anger at previous attacks, but these may not carry a great deal of weight.

If the prosecution fails to prove that M had the mens rea of murder, a charge of constructive manslaughter may be brought. This offence was defined in the case of *R v Church* [1966] 1 QB 59 as where the accused caused death by an unlawful and dangerous act which all sober and reasonable people would inevitably recognise would expose another person to the risk of harm, albeit not serious harm.

It is clear that firing at P, N and O with a shotgun exposes them to the risk of harm. It is submitted that the only way M may avoid a conviction for this offence is to show that his use of force was not 'unlawful' because he was acting in self-defence; M may raise the defence of self-defence at common law. Although P, N and O made it clear that they had no intention of harming M providing he did not interfere with their theft, self-defence is available for the protection of property, as well as a threat to the person: *R v Hussey* (1924) 18 Cr App R 160. The fact that M had armed himself in advance would not necessarily prevent him from successfully raising this defence, since it was held in *Beckford v R* [1988] AC 130 that one does not have to wait for an attack to occur before making preparations to repel such an attack. However, it must be shown that the degree of force used was commensurate with the level of the threat (*R v Oatridge* (1991) 94 Cr App R 397) and it is submitted that using lethal force to protect one's garden is an unreasonable use of force and is not commensurate with the threat.

Alternatively, M may seek to rely on the defence under s3 of the Criminal Law Act 1967 which provides that reasonable force may be used in the prevention of crime. Clearly P, N and O were in the course of committing a crime when they were in M's garden. However, M is likely to be defeated by the same point made above, that the force he used was not reasonable.

## QUESTION FIVE

U, who was 22 years but with a mental age of ten years, had a terrible temper, which he did his best to control. Also, because of a motoring accident he had only one leg. He was in the park when a neighbour, V, abusively called him, Pegleg. U lost his temper and pushed V to the ground. V, who had a thin skull, was concussed by the fall. X, who was U's best friend, tried to pull U away from V whom U was trying to kick. Released U ran and kicked V on the ground.

Advise the parties of their criminal liability on the basis that V had died as a result of concussion and internal injuries.

Adapted from University of London LLB Examination
(for External Students) Criminal Law June 1987 Q7

### General Comment

A good question to tackle. Core elements of the syllabus were examined and all the main aspects were easily recognisable on the facts.

### Skeleton Solution

U: assault – s47, s20 Offences Against the Person Act 1861; causation; murder; diminished responsibility; constructive manslaughter – X: battery; lack of mens rea; accomplice role; s3 Criminal Law Act 1967.

### Suggested Solution

When U, having lost his temper, pushes V to the ground he may commit a number of assaults contrary to the Offences Against the Person Act (OAPA) 1861.

Section 47 OAPA 1861 provides that it will be an offence to assault occasioning actual bodily harm. Actual bodily harm was defined in *R v Chan Fook* [1994] Crim LR 432 as any injury which is more than trivial . Following *R v Savage; R v Parmenter* [1991] 3 WLR 914 it need only be proven that the accused had the mens rea for the assault or battery, there being no mens rea necessary as to the actual bodily harm.

Section 20 OAPA 1861 provides that it is an offence to unlawfully wound or inflict grievous bodily harm. Grievous bodily harm means really serious bodily harm. The term 'inflict' can be established by evidence of direct or indirect harm: see *R v Martin* (1881) 8 QBD 54. Increasingly the courts seem to be wiling to regard this requirement as having been satisfied if there is proof of causation: see *R v Burstow* [1997] 3 WLR 534. Undoubtedly this is satisfied in the facts in question as U uses direct force on V. For s20 the prosecution must establish that the defendant acted maliciously. In *R v Cunningham* [1957] 2 QB 396 this was explained as requiring proof of intention or recklessness in the subjective sense. In *R v Mowatt* [1968] 1 QB 421 Diplock LJ explained this further by stating that the defendant had to be proved to have foreseen the risk of some physical harm albeit slight, an interpretation subsequently approved by the House of Lords in *R v Savage; R v Parmenter* (above). This would seem to be made out on the facts.

Both s47 and s20 are result crimes , that is crimes where a consequence must be shown as part of the actus reus.

V who had a thin skull was concussed by the fall. In order to establish the actus reus of either s47 or 20 it must be shown that U is the legal cause of the injury sustained by V. However U must take his victim as he finds him *R v Blaue* [1975] 1 WLR 1411, and therefore the chain of causation will not be broken because of the victim's special characteristic of a thin skull.

When U later returns to kicking V he will commit further assaults within s47 or s20 depending on his state of mind. If he has the necessary foresight he may be liable under s20. If he lacks this he will be liable under s47.

The victim dies as a result of concussion and internal injuries. V's possible liability for murder must be considered. In order to established this very serious offence it must be shown that U is the legal cause of V's death. Furthermore it must be shown that U had the necessary mens rea for murder at the time of the actus reus. The mens rea for murder is very high. The prosecution would have to establish that U killed V intending to kill or intending to do grievous bodily harm. Intention includes both desiring to kill or do grievous bodily harm (direct intent) or foreseeing that death or grievous bodily harm is certain or virtually certain to occur (oblique intent). Where the prosecution rely on oblique intent it is not sufficient to establish the accused foresaw the result as highly probable. While this may be useful as evidence it is no more than that. Foresight is not to be equated with intention. A jury should be directed that they are not entitled to infer the necessary intention unless they are satisfied that death or grievous bodily harm was virtually certain as a result of the defendant's actions and the defendant appreciated that this was the case: *R v Woollin* [1998] 4 All ER 103.

On the facts in question there seems little doubt that U is the legal cause of death. If he has intention to kill or intention to do grievous bodily harm at any time when the actus reus is continuing he may be liable for murder.

The offence of murder carries a mandatory life sentence. Provocation is a limited defence available to murder which, if successful, will reduce murder to voluntary manslaughter thus avoiding the mandatory life sentence. Provocation is a common law defence available to a charge of murder where by words or acts an accused is so provoked by the victim or a third party that he suffers a sudden and temporary loss of self-control. Prior to the decision in *R v Smith (Morgan)* [2000] 4 All ER 289 it was the case that the provocation had to have been such as would have caused a reasonable man to lose his self-control and so act as the accused did: see *R v Duffy* [1949] 1 All ER 932, as amended by s3 Homicide Act 1957.

Following *R v Smith (Morgan)*, however, the question is now one of whether or not the jury believes the accused displayed, what was for him, a reasonable level of self-control. In this case U having only one leg is a factor relevant to the provocation, as is his mental age. On the other hand U's bad temper is likely to be irrelevant. As Lord Hoffmann in *R v Smith (Morgan)* observed, a person who flies into a murderous rage when he or she is crossed, thwarted or disappointed in the vicissitudes of life should not be able to rely upon his or her anti-social propensities as even a partial excuse for killing. He added that a tendency to violent rages or childish tantrums is a defect in character rather than an excuse. It is highly questionable, therefore, as to whether U's bad temper would be a factor attracting much weight, unless there is medical evidence that it is symptomatic of a psychiatric illness. .

The fact that shouting abuse may not of itself be u■
amounting to provocation provided it would have provoke■
U's characteristics to lose self-control: *R v Doughty* [1986] Cri■

There was a time lapse between the provocation and the ultima■
longer the time lapse the more difficult it is to establish provoca■
accused will have had opportunity to recover control: *R v Ibrams and*■
Crim LR 229. However on the facts the period of time involved is not ■
discount provocation as a defence.

In addition to the defence of provocation, the statutory defence of dimin■
responsibility under s2 Homicide Act 1957 may be available. Section 2 provides t■
where a person kills he shall not be convicted of murder if he was suffering from such
abnormality of mind (whether arising from arrested or retarded development or any
inherent causes or induced by disease or injury) as substantially impaired his
responsibility. Thus murder will be reduced to voluntary manslaughter. On the facts
in question this may well be available.

If U lacked mens rea for murder he could be liable for constructive manslaughter. This
is established where a person kills as a result of an unlawful act in this case one of the
assaults. Furthermore in addition to an intention to do the unlawful act it must be
shown that a reasonable man would foresee the possibility of at least a little harm from
the act: *DPP v Newbury* [1977] AC 500

X has no criminal responsibility on the facts as given. Undoubtedly he uses force
against U when pulling him away and this could amount to a common law battery – a
direct use of force, intentionally or recklessly committed. However, under s3 Criminal
Law Act 1967, a person may use reasonable force in the prevention of a crime. It must
be established that X was acting defensively and not aggressively: *R v Shannon* (1980) 71
Cr App R 192. The question of whether the force used was reasonable must be
considered objectively by reference to the circumstances the accused found himself in:
*R v Palmer* [1971] AC 814; *R v Whyte* [1987] 3 All ER 416. There seems little doubt on
the facts that this would be available to X as a defence.

It is traditional to separate the various offences against the person into those of non-fatal offences against the person, sexual offences and homicide.

The offences ranging from threats to injure, through to grievous bodily harm, form the basis of many examination questions and it is vital that students are familiar with the requirements for each type of 'assault'.

## 4.2 Key points

a) Assault and battery

i) Assault

*Fagan* v *Metropolitan Police Commissioner* [1969] 1 QB 439 – 'where the accused intentionally or possibly recklessly causes another person to apprehend immediate and unlawful personal violence'. (See also *R* v *Lamb* [1967] 2 All ER 1282; *Logdon* v *DPP* [1976] Crim LR 121; *R* v *Wilson* [1955] 1 All ER 744.) Note that the threat of violence must be immediate: *Tuberville* v *Savage* (1669) 1 Mod Rep 3. Words can now amount to an assault: see *R* v *Ireland* [1997] 4 All ER 225.

ii) Battery

*R* v *Venna* [1975] 3 All ER 788 – 'In our view the element of mens rea in the offence of battery is satisfied by proof that the defendant intentionally applied force to the person of another'. (Note the defence of consent discussed below and that a battery can be inflicted indirectly: *Scott* v *Shepherd* (1773) Wm Bl 892.)

b) The Offences Against the Person Act 1861

The offences under this Act must be known thoroughly, especially the differences between the actus reus and mens rea of the main offences.

i)   Actual bodily harm (s47)

   *R v Chan Fook* [1994] Crim LR 432 held that for the purposes of a charge under s47 of the Offences Against the Person Act 1861 'harm' has the same meaning as injury and 'actual' indicates that the injury must not be so trivial as to be wholly insignificant. The court pointed out that, generally, an injury must be caused and an assault which merely interferes with the victim's health or comfort is not sufficient, although the court accepted that psychological illness due to an assault may amount to actual bodily harm providing:

   • it amounts to more than mere emotional distress;

   • it constitutes an 'identifiable clinical condition'; and

   • it is supported by expert evidence.

   This has been confirmed by the House of Lords in *R v Ireland* [1997] 4 All ER 225.

   The House of Lords in *R v Savage; R v Parmenter* [1991] 3 WLR 914 clarified the mens rea of the s47 offence by holding that the accused need have no intention or recklessness as to the injury caused (although of course he must have the mens rea for the assault). Thus a person who only intends to put another in fear of violence but actually caused injury may be convicted of this offence.

ii)  Maliciously wounding or inflicting grievous bodily harm (s20)

   Note that there are two alternative actus reus to this offence: 'wounding' (*JJC (A Minor) v Eisenhower* [1984] QB 331 which is defined as an injury in which both layers of the skin have been broken) and 'grievous bodily harm' (which is a more general term defined as 'really serious harm': *DPP v Smith* [1960] 3 All ER 161). 'Inflict' here can be equated with 'causing': see *R v Burstow* [1997] 4 All ER 225.

   The mens rea of the offence was established in *R v Savage; R v Parmenter* (above) – it being sufficient that the accused intended or foresaw that his act would cause some harm (note that the accused need not intend or foresee serious harm).

iii) Intentionally wounding or causing grievous bodily harm (s18)

   The definitions of 'wounding' and 'grievous bodily harm' are the same as that given above for s20. The accused must cause the wounding or grievous bodily harm and intend to do some grievous bodily harm.

c)  The provisions of s89(1) of the Police Act 1996 should be known, together with the question of 'in the execution of his duty'. Also, the defence under s3 of the Criminal Law Act 1967.

d)  Students should be aware of the offences of kidnapping and false imprisonment which occasionally feature in OAPA questions.

Child destruction under the Infant Life (Preservation) Act 1929 should be known, together with the corresponding provisions of the Abortion Act 1967 and s58 of the Offences Against the Person Act 1861. See *Rance* v *Mid-Downs Health Authority* [1991] 1 All ER 801.

e) Administering poison

Under ss23 and 24 of the 1861 Act it is an offence to administer or cause another person to take a poison, destructive or noxious thing.

Note the wide definition given to 'administer' in *R* v *Gillard* (1988) 87 Cr App R 189 to include spraying someone with a poison or noxious substance.

Note that the meaning of 'poison' or 'noxious thing' may be wider in s24 than in s23. *R* v *Cato* [1976] 1 All ER 260 held that with respect to s23 the substance administered must be inherently dangerous. *R* v *Marcus* [1981] 2 All ER 833 indicated that for s24 any substance could be 'noxious' if administered with the intention to injure, aggrieve or annoy.

Note that s23 is the more serious offence, subject to a maximum punishment of ten years, because the administration of the poison or noxious substance must actually endanger life or cause grievous bodily harm. Under s24 no effects need actually be caused to the victim, it being sufficient that the substance was administered with the intention to injure, aggrieve or annoy.

## 4.3 Key cases and statutes

* *JJC (A Minor)* v *Eisenhower* [1983] 3 WLR 537
  Wounding defined

* *R* v *Ireland; R* v *Burstow* [1998] AC 147
  Infliction, assault by words and psychological harm

* *R* v *Miller* [1954] 2 QB 282
  Actual bodily harm defined

* *R* v *Mowatt* [1967] 3 All ER 47
  Maliciously defined

* *R* v *Saunders* [1985] Crim LR 230
  Grievous bodily harm defined

* *R* v *Savage; R* v *Parmenter* [1992] 1 AC 699
  *Mowatt* confirmed by House of Lords

* *Smith* v *Superintendent of Woking Police Station* (1983) 76 Cr App R 234
  Nature of assault

* Crime and Disorder Act 1998, s29 – introduces aggravated forms of the offences

under ss47 and 20 of the Offences Against the Person Act 1861 where the accused's acts are racially motivated.

- Offences Against the Person Act 1861, s18 – grievous bodily harm
- Offences Against the Person Act 1861, s20 – wounding
- Offences Against the Person Act 1861, s47 – actual bodily harm
- Offences Against the Person Act 1861, ss23 and 24 – poisoning
- Protection from Harassment Act 1997 – creates stalking offence

## 4.4 Questions and suggested solutions

QUESTION ONE

U, who had been receiving treatment for clinical depression, was drinking fruit juice in a pub when V came in. U, who was jealous of V's success with U's girlfriend, W, picked a fight with V. They agreed to go outside to fight. There U beat up V very badly causing him to be blinded in one eye. Elated, U went home and at W's request U beat her up and knocked two nails through each hand.

Advise U, V and W of their criminal liability, if any. What difference, if any, would it have made to your advice if W developed blood poisoning, refused treatment and died?

University of London LLB Examination
(for External Students) Criminal Law June 1998 Q6

*General Comment*

This is a question that covers a narrower range of topics than is the case with some others, hence a little more depth is required. The issue of consent runs through various parts of the question and candidates need to be alive to the way in which the application of the rules on consent can vary with circumstances. The question also requires quite a detailed knowledge of the novus actus interveniens case law.

*Skeleton Solution*

U blinds V; gbh; mens rea evident; consider defence of consent; is there a mental illness defence? – U beats W; consider the ss18, 20 and 47 offences; availability of consent; mental illness defence? – V commits non-specific assaults on U; again consider consent – W could be inciting offences, but she is the victim – what difference if W dies – consider causation issue; self-neglect cases; what type of homicide would it be?

## Suggested Solution

The facts indicate that U attacks V causing V to be blinded in one eye. This type of injury would constitute grievous bodily harm in the sense that it is 'serious' harm; see *R v Saunders* [1985] Crim LR 230. U could be charged with causing grievous bodily harm with intent to do some grievous bodily harm contrary to s18 of the Offences Against the Person Act 1861. The prosecution would have to prove that U intended the harm in the sense that there was at least evidence that he foresaw such harm as a virtually certain consequence of his actions; see *R v Woollin* [1998] 4 All ER 103. If this intent cannot be established U could be charged under s20 Offences Against the Person Act 1861 in that he maliciously inflicted grievous bodily harm on V. For these purposes U will have acted maliciously if, on the basis of *R v Mowatt* [1967] 3 All ER 47, he foresaw that some physical harm to some person, albeit of a minor character, might result from his actions. It is submitted that this at least could be established on the facts.

U is suffering from clinical depression. This could only form the basis of a defence to the s20 or s18 charges if he was able to put is forward as evidence of insanity. According to *McNaghten's Case* (1843) 10 Cl & F 200, there would have to be evidence that at the time of the committing of the act, U was labouring under a defect of reason, from disease of the mind, as not to know the nature and quality of the act he was doing; or, if he did know it, that he did not know he was doing what was wrong. Even if one accepts for the moment that U was suffering from a disease of the mind, there is no evidence to suggest that U was unaware of his actions. He might contend that he did not know they were wrong – but according to *R v Windle* [1952] 2 QB 826 'wrong' in this context mens legally wrong. U would have to show that he did not realise that blinding another man was against the law. Highly unlikely on the facts.

U might argue that he had been acting in self-defence but the authorities are clear that the defence is not available to one who picks a fight, or one who acts in anger to seek revenge. In *R v Julien* [1969] 1 WLR 839, Widgery LJ observed that the defendant seeking recourse to self-defence must demonstrate by his actions that he does not want to fight, that he is prepared to temporise and disengage and perhaps to make some physical withdrawal. In any event U would only be permitted to use reasonable force, and he appears to have exceeded the scope of this.

U's strongest argument is that he acted in the belief that V consented to the fight and that this constituted a defence. The court in *R v Donovan* [1934] 2 KB 498 held that consent could be a defence to physical harm provided the harm caused did not amount to actual bodily harm or worse. Clearly the harm here exceeds that. The common law has, however, recognised a number of exceptions to this rule where consent can be raised as a defence where more serious harm is caused, such as during sporting activities. The Court of Appeal has made it clear, however, that this exception does not arise simply because two persons agree to settle their differences by resorting to violence, and thereby consent to the harm that will be caused by fighting: see *Attorney-General's Reference (No 6 of 1980)* [1981] QB 715. There is a further exception made in respect of 'horseplay', but it is submitted that deliberate violence such as that evidenced in the facts would fall outside this exception: see *R v Aitken* [1992] 1 WLR 1066.

When U beats up W he commits various non-specified assaults. The facts do not indicate the harm done; hence it is impossible to be specific as to the likely charges. There would at least be assault and battery as physical contact is made. A charge under s47 of the Offences Against the Person Act 1861 of assault occasioning actual bodily harm may have been committed. There would have to be evidence of actual bodily harm. This was defined in *R v Miller* [1954] 2 QB 282 as involving any hurt or injury calculated to interfere with the health or comfort of the victim. Shock could be enough. The mens rea for this offence seems evident on the facts as U deliberately attacks W.

The insertion of nails through W's hands would amount to grievous bodily harm, as defined above, and wounding as defined in *JJC (A Minor) v Eisenhower* [1983] 3 WLR 537. Again charges under s18 and s20 would be possibilities. The 'wounding' formulation of s18 provides that it is an offence to wound with intent. to do some grievous bodily harm to any person. Under s20 the offence is simply malicious wounding. There is no doubt that U causes the actus reus of both crimes. His actions are deliberate, hence the mens rea for the offences, as outlined above, seems evident.

What defences might U raise? As indicated above insanity is a possibility – particularly if he asserts that he did not realise his actions were wrong in law because he believed the victim's consent made the actions lawful. It is doubtful whether U would want to raise insanity, however, for fear of being detained in a secure prison hospital for an indeterminate period of time following the special verdict of 'not guilty by reason of insanity'.

U is much more likely to rely on W's consent. If W 'only' suffers minor harm when U beats her, her consent may be a valid defence. If the harm exceeds what the common law would normally permit the victim to validly consent to, it will not be available. U will have to argue that the case comes within the exceptions. The House of Lords in *R v Brown* [1993] 2 All ER 75 held, by a majority, that the defence of consent was not available to defendants who derived pleasure from inflicting pain on their victims. Lord Jauncey observed that it would not be in the public interest for the deliberate infliction of actual bodily harm during the course of homosexual sado-masochistic activities to be held to be lawful. U could argue that this case involves heterosexual behaviour, hence a distinction should be made. There is dicta in *R v Boyea* [1992] Crim LR 574 to support the view that a more robust view is taken of what is permitted in terms of consensual harm during heterosexual 'loveplay'. U could contend, on the basis of *R v Wilson* [1996] 3 WLR 125, that the nails in W's hands amounted to an 'adornment' hence coming within the tattooing exception identified by the House of Lords in *R v Brown*.

Russell LJ in *R v Wilson* took the view that the defendant's act in branding his initials on his wife's buttocks at her behest could be covered by the defence of consent because: she had instigated the activity; there was no aggressive intent on the part of the defendant; and because consensual activity between husband and wife in the privacy of the matrimonial home was not a matter for criminal investigation. The issue for the court in U's case will be whether or not the harm caused goes too far beyond that in *R v Wilson* to be allowed within the scope of consent.

V could be charged with various assaults offences arising out of his fight with U. The facts do not indicate the nature of the harm caused by V, hence it is not possible to specify appropriate offences, beyond an assumption that there will have been an assault and battery. Again the points made above regarding the availability of the defence of consent in relation to U apply here. V may have a better case in terms of self-defence, however, as he appears to have got the worst of the encounter.

W is unlikely to be charged with any offence. Technically she incites the commission of the offences that may have been committed against her by U. If W has the defence of consent there may be no offences committed, to the extent that consent nullifies the criminal nature of the activity.

What difference would it have made if W had died from her wounds? U could be charged with some form of homicide. He would have caused her death in fact – but for the wounds she would not have died: see *R v White* [1910] 2 KB 124. W refusing treatment would not operate as a novus actus interveniens so as to break the chain of causation in law: see *R v Blaue* (1975) 61 Cr App R 271. Even if she aggravated the condition the chain of causation would not be broken: see *R v Dear* [1996] Crim LR 595. U could be charged with murder on the basis that he intended to do W some grievous bodily harm. *R v Woollin* (above) provides that if there is evidence that he saw this consequence as virtually certain the jury can infer that he intended it. This seems possible on the facts. If U is charged with murder he may raise the defence of diminished responsibility under the Homicide Act 1957, s2(1). He would argue that his clinical depression is an abnormality of mind that substantially impaired his mental responsibility for his acts. He would need expert evidence to establish this on the balance of probabilities.

W's consent could not be raised as a defence to murder.

If the mens rea for murder cannot be established U could be charged with unlawful act manslaughter. The problem for the prosecution might be in establishing an unlawful act. It depends what view the court takes as to the effect of W's consent. If consent is not accepted as a defence at all in relation to the nailing of the hands, there is no problem. If U would have been able to raise consent as a defence the court would then have decide whether consent actually removes the unlawfulness from the action (ie no actus reus), or whether consent simply operates to provide U with an excuse for what he has done (ie there is still an actus reus). The law is far from clear on this point.

If there is an unlawful act there should be no difficulty in making out the elements of unlawful act manslaughter. The nailing of the hands was dangerous (see *R v Dawson* (1985) 81 Cr App Rep 150), and U had the mens rea for the act. The alternative charge would be killing by gross negligence although this does not look like the usual type of 'duty' situation where liability for this type of homicide is imposed.

## QUESTION TWO

A, aged 13 years, sustained a blow to the head when he fell over a heap of stones left by B, a builder, on the pavement outside C's house where B had been working. B left the stones on the pavement because B considered there was no prospect that they would cause harm to anyone. As a result, A became unconscious because of the fall and was rushed to hospital. When D, A's father, heard what had occurred, he telephoned C saying, "I am coming round to sort you out!" C was annoyed but, as an ex boxer, C was not frightened by the threat. D went to C's house and C's wife, E, opened the door. Unaware of D's threat, she admitted D into the house. D pushed her out of the way but D had no intention of harming her. Inside, D hit C over the head with a poker and C was concussed.

Advise the parties of their criminal liability. What difference, if any, would it make to your advice if A had died?

University of London LLB Examination
(for External Students) Criminal Law June 1999 Q1

### General Comment

This is a relatively straightforward question that requires a good knowledge of the basic aspects of the assault offences, in particular the extent to which assault can be verbal, and the mens rea for assault. Note the burglary possibilities where the defendant commits harm whilst trespassing. An examination of killing by gross negligence will also be required. The fact that B is a builder will be relevant here in terms of the duty of care.

### Skeleton Solution

B causes injury; abh/gbh; but no mens rea – D commits a verbal assault on C; consider attempt; can D attempt to commit a summary offence – D enters C's house as a trespasser; does he have an ulterior intent – D assaults/batters E when he pushes her out of the way – D does hit C; abh/gbh; consider s9(1)(b) burglary – if A had died consider killing by gross negligence; note duty of care point; is risk created sufficient?

### Suggested Solution

In falling over the stones A suffers a blow to the head and is knocked unconscious. The facts state that he was 'rushed' to hospital, indicating that those attending him considered that assistance was urgently needed. It is possible, therefore that A may have suffered grievous bodily harm – defined in *R v Saunders* [1985] Crim LR 230 as

ıarm. A may have also sustained a wound – defined in *JJC (A Minor)* v
 [1983] 3 WLR 537 as involving a break in the surface of the skin, beyond a
 .e.

Under s18 of the Offences Against the Person Act 1861 the prosecution would have to
prove that B caused this harm. As regards causation in fact, but for his leaving the
stones on the pavement A would not have fallen over them: *R v White* [1910] 2 KB 124.
Regarding causation in law there does not appear to be anything that would constitute
a novus actus interveniens so as to break the chain of causation. The fact that A is 13,
failed to look where he was walking, or has any weakness that renders the injury more
serious would be encompassed by the 'take your victim as you find him' rule embodied
in *R v Blaue* [1975] 1 WLR 1411. The problem with a charge under s18 would lie in
establishing intent. Assuming that the approach adopted in *R v Woollin* [1998] 4 All
ER 103 applies here, a jury would not be entitled to return a verdict of guilty under
s18 unless sure beyond all reasonable doubt that B had foreseen grievous bodily harm
as virtually certain to result from his leaving the stones on the pavement. This seems
most unlikely on the facts.

The less serious offence would be that contrary to s20 Offences Against the Person Act
1861, malicious wounding, or maliciously inflicting grievous bodily harm. Wounding
would be as defined above – again it is not clear from the facts if there is a wound.
Grievous bodily harm would be as defined above, but note that under s20 the
defendant must be shown to have inflicted the grievous bodily harm, as opposed to
simply having caused it. Does this make any difference? In *R v Martin* (1881) 8 QBD 54
the defendant was convicted of inflicting grievous bodily harm where he has caused the
victims to be crushed against locked doors, whilst they were trying to escape from what
wrongly believed to be a burning building. On the given facts B is causing A to collide
with the ground by leaving the stones out for him to fall over. The answer now lies in
the House of Lord's decision in *R v Ireland; R v Burstow* [1998] AC 147, where it was
held that 'cause' and 'inflict' should now be regarded as largely synonymous. For B to
be found to be malicious it must be proved that, in leaving the stones on the pavement,
he foresaw that some physical harm to some person, albeit of a minor character, might
result: see *R v Mowatt* [1967] 3 All ER 47. Again there could be difficulties here given B's
evidence that he did not think any harm would occur to anyone.

This lack of mens rea would probably also prevent any liability arising in respect of
lesser offences such as Assault occasioning actual bodily harm, contrary to s47 of the
1861 Act, or common assault and battery. These offences still require proof that B
foresaw at least the risk of another person apprehending immediate physical violence
or unlawful physical contact: see *R v Savage; R v Parmenter* [1992] 1 AC 699.

Consideration needs to be given to whether or not, when D makes threats to C, he
commits an assault. That an assault can be verbal has now been made clear by the
House of Lords in *R v Ireland; R v Burstow*. The difficulty for the prosecution is that C
was annoyed but not frightened by the threat. There is no apprehension of immediate
personal violence by C. A further problem for the prosecution is that if he is charged

with attempted assault D will rely on s1(4) of the Criminal Attempts Act 1981 which provides that a defendant cannot be charged with attempting to commit a 'summary trial only' offence.

When D enters C's house he may commit the offence of burglary. Under s9(1)(a) of the Theft Act 1968 a person is guilty of burglary if he enters any building or part of a building as a trespasser with intent to inflict on any person therein any grievous bodily harm. D obviously enters a building, but does he do so as a trespasser? E gives him permission to enter. There is no doubt she can validly do so even if she is not the legal owner of the property (it is the matrimonial home). In *R v Collins* [1973] QB 100 Edmund Davies LJ expressly rejected the proposition that such an occupier could not extend an effective invitation to enter. D could nevertheless be a trespasser because he is entering for a purpose in excess the express of implied permission granted by E. This can be tested by asking whether, had she known D's true purpose in entering the property, she would still have given him permission to enter? The answer must be 'no'. Authority for the proposition that such an entry can be trespassory is to be found in *R v Jones and Smith* [1976] 3 All ER 54, where one of the defendants was found to have been a trespasser in his father's house because he had entered it intending to steal his father's television set. That D has the ulterior intent to do some grievous bodily harm seems evident on the facts.

When D pushes E out of the way he commits a common battery. There is an unlawful touching caused by D and he clearly intends to make physical contact: see *Cole v Turner* (1705) 6 Mod Rep 149. If E was caused to apprehend immediate physical violence as a result of D's actions then he will also have committed a common assault. The mens rea requirement will be that he at least foresaw the risk that E would apprehend immediate physical violence.

In hitting C with the poker and causing him to become concussed it is likely that D has committed grievous bodily harm as described above. The possibilities are charges under ss18 and 20 of the 1861 Act, depending on the degree of mens rea found to be present. More significantly, if the harm is found to fall within the definition of grievous bodily harm, D could be charged with burglary contrary to s9(1)(b) of the Theft Act 1968 on the basis that, having entered a building as a trespasser he inflicted on a person therein grievous bodily harm. On the basis of *R v Wilson; R v Jenkins* [1984] AC 242 D can incur liability under s9(1)(b) even though he did not intend to do any grievous bodily harm.

If A had died from falling over the stones B might have incurred liability for killing by gross negligence. This type of liability for homicide does not require proof of any unlawful act by B, and can be based on omission – B's failure to clear the hazard: see *R v Miller* [1983] 2 AC 161.

The prosecution will have to establish that B owed A a duty of care, but as B is a builder this should not be too difficult. For example, in *R v Singh (Gurpal)* [1999] Crim LR 582, the court held that a gas fitter owed a duty of care to tenants killed by fumes escaping from badly fitted gas fires. Once a duty of care is made out the court will have to assess whether or not B's negligence is 'gross'. The fact that B did not foresee harm will not be decisive. On the basis of *R v Adomako* [1994] 3 WLR 288, the test will be whether B's conduct departed from the proper standard of care incumbent upon him. B must be shown to have created a risk of death. If, on this basis, the negligence is so bad it deserves to be labelled criminal, the jury can convict.

On the facts, it is submitted that the prosecution would have difficulties establishing the necessary risk of death.

## QUESTION THREE

At H's party, F laced G's fruit juice with a sedative drug. When G became somnolent, H took her upstairs and placed her on his bed. Later, J entered the bedroom and, detecting no resistance to his advances, had sex with G. H gave evidence that G was distracted but otherwise conscious when he had left her on the bed. J protested that he would not have had sex with G unless he thought that she was consenting. When K, G's boyfriend, learned what had happened, he hit H. As a result, H lost the sight of one eye, suffered a nervous breakdown and was in hospital for six weeks.

Advise the parties of their criminal liability. What difference, if any, would it make to your advice if G had become HIV positive from the intercourse?

University of London LLB Examination
(for External Students) Criminal Law June 1999 Q2

### General Comment

This question requires a good knowledge of the 'poisoning' offences under ss23 and 24 of the Offences Against the Person Act 1861 and their relationship with the more mainstream assaults. In addition candidates need to be well versed in the law relating to the mens rea of rape and the effect of mistake. The range of harm caused by the assaults extends to psychiatric harm and this needs to be considered in full.

### Skeleton Solution

F's liability under ss23 and 24 of the 1861 Act for administering drug – battery in carrying G upstairs – J's liability for rape; mens rea is problematic – consider whether elements of burglary made out – H may be an accomplice to the offences committed by J – K causes gbh/abh to H; consider what the psychiatric harm might be – J renders G HIV positive; consider the range of assault-based offences; did J know of his condition?

### Suggested Solution

F's actions in lacing G's drink with a sedative drug could well result in liability under ss23 and/or 24 of the Offences Against the Person Act 1861. Under s23 it is an offence to unlawfully and maliciously administer to another person any poison or other destructive or noxious thing, so as to thereby endanger the life of such person, or so as thereby to inflict upon such person grievous bodily harm. Under s24 it is an offence to unlawfully and maliciously administer to any other person any poison or other destructive or noxious thing, with intent to injure, aggrieve, or annoy such person. Placing the drug in G's drink would constitute administration: see *R v Gillard* (1988) 87 Cr App R 189 – administration simply meaning cause to be taken. The drug would be a noxious substance. In *R v Cato* [1976] 1 All ER 260 a noxious substance was held to be anything that was likely to injure in common use. On the basis of *R v Marcus* [1981] 1 WLR 774, if it is a substance not likely to injure in common use regard should be had to the quantity, quality and recipient. Under s23 there can be no liability unless G's life was endangered by the administration of the drug or she suffered grievous bodily harm. G may feel that the sexual intercourse with J amounts to grievous bodily harm but, it is submitted, liability under s23 would depend on the drug itself causing such harm. Merely causing her to become somnolent would not suffice. A charge under s24 therefore looks more likely. Assuming there has been the administration of a noxious substance as defined above, the issue would be as to whether or not F acted with the required degree of mens rea. The administration must be malicious. In the context of s23 this requires proof that F was at least aware of the risk that G might suffer the harm specified in the section, ie that she would be injured, aggrieved, or annoyed: see *R v Cunningham* [1957] 2 QB 396. On the facts it should not be difficult to establish that F at least foresaw the risk that G would be annoyed by what he had done, although the House of Lord's decision in *R v Hill* (1986) 83 Cr App R 386 suggests that regard ought to be had to F's ulterior purpose. Why did F administer the drug? Was his motive a worthy one or not?

In moving G to the bedroom by carrying her H inevitably commits a battery. On the basis of *Cole v Turner* (1705) 6 Mod Rep 149, and *Coward v Baddeley* (1859) 28 LJ Ex 260 the merest touching will be enough. H clearly has the intention to have physical contact. The offence would be charged as common battery contrary to s39 of the Criminal Justice Act 1988. There is no evidence to suggest that his touching of G is indecent.

There is no evidence of what was in H's mind when he placed her on his bed. If he intended to have sexual intercourse with her whilst she was under the influence of the drug he may have committed attempted rape, but there is insufficient evidence to advise on this point.

J may have committed the offence of rape in having sexual intercourse with G. Section 1(1) of the Sexual Offences Act 1956, as amended by the Sexual Offences (Amendment) Act 1976, and s142 of the Criminal Justice and Public Order Act 1994, provides that a man commits rape if he has sexual intercourse with a person who at the time of the intercourse does not consent to it and, at the time, he knows that the person does not consent to the intercourse or is reckless as to whether that person consents to it.

There is no doubt that sexual intercourse takes place. If G was asleep she cannot have validly consented. Attention therefore focuses on J's state of mind. As he detected no resistance he may have believed G was consenting. As the House of Lords made clear in *DPP* v *Morgan* [1975] 2 All ER 347, the mental element is the intention to commit that act of sexual intercourse or the equivalent intention of having intercourse willy-nilly not caring whether the victim consents or no. If J honestly believed G was consenting he cannot be guilty of rape. There is no requirement that this belief be reasonably held, in the sense that the reasonable person would also have made the mistake. Everything depends on what J honestly believed. Even if the prosecution allege 'reckless rape' J cannot be convicted unless he was at least aware of the risk that G was not consenting: see *R* v *Satnam*; *R* v *Kewal* (1983) 78 Cr App R 149. Section 1(2) of the Sexual Offences (Amendment) Act 1976 provides that in considering whether a man believed that a woman was consenting to sexual intercourse, the presence or absence of reasonable grounds for such a belief is a matter to which the jury is to have regard, in conjunction with any other relevant matters, in considering whether he did so believe. All this is saying, however, is that circumstantial evidence can be taken into account in determining whether or not there was mens rea. It does not alter the basic position that the test is subjective – what was J thinking?

Given that these events take place at a party it may be the case that J, as a guest, has no right to enter the bedroom, thus making him a trespasser. If this is the case one would have to consider whether there might be liability for burglary contrary to s9(1)(a) of the Theft Act 1968 on the basis that he entered part of a building as a trespasser with intent to rape. Everything depends on whether or not he had the intention to rape at the time he entered the room. Why was he going into the room? If J entered the bedroom for some innocent purpose and, seeing G on the bed, then decided to have sexual intercourse with her, regardless of her consent, he would not have entered as a trespasser with the requisite intent. Further, if, subject to the points made above, he did rape G, he could be charged with burglary under s9(1)(b) of the 1968 Act. The further offences relevant to s9(1)(b) are restricted to theft and the infliction of grievous bodily harm, but it could be argued that the rape constituted the infliction of grievous bodily harm. In *R* v *Saunders* [1985] Crim LR 230 it is defined as simply 'serious' harm.

The prosecution may consider charging F as an accomplice to J on the basis that he procured the offence of rape and or burglary. The Court of Appeal in *Attorney-General's Reference (No 1 of 1975)* [1975] 3 WLR 11 held that to procure meant to 'produce by endeavour'. F would procure the rape and burglary by setting out to see that it happened and taking the appropriate steps to produce that event. There must also be a causal link, between the drug being placed in the drink by F and the commission of the offence of rape (and hence burglary). On these facts it could be argued that 'but for' the drug G would not have been raped. In terms of mens rea the Court of Appeal in *Attorney-General's Reference (No 1 of 1975)* (above) appears to support a narrow approach, Lord Widgery commenting that to procure meant setting out to see that the desired consequence happens and taking the appropriate steps to produce that happening. His words are suggestive of more than mere contemplation of a consequence on the part of the procurer, perhaps requiring proof of something closer to intention: see further *Blakely and Others* v *DPP* [1991] Crim LR 763, where the Court of

Appeal suggested that a procurer had to been shown to have intended the commission of the offence by the principal offender. On the facts, there is no clear evidence that H has the necessary intent. If intent was established, the fact that J might be acquitted of rape on the basis that he lacked mens rea would not absolve H of liability for procuring: see *R v Cogan and Leak* (1975) 61 Cr App R 217.

H suffers the loss of sight in one eye and psychiatric harm as a result of the attack by K. It is beyond doubt that the loss of sight in one eye would constitute grievous bodily harm, see *R v Saunders* (above). Under s18 of the Offences Against the Person Act 1861 the prosecution would have to prove that K caused this harm – there are no novus actus interveniens problems here. Assuming that the approach adopted in *R v Woollin* [1998] 4 All ER 103 applies here, a jury would not be entitled to return a verdict of guilty under s18 unless sure beyond all reasonable doubt that K had foreseen grievous bodily harm as virtually certain to result from his attack. If this mens rea cannot be established the less serious offence would be that contrary to s20 Offences Against the Person Act 1861, ie malicious wounding, or maliciously inflicting grievous bodily harm. Grievous bodily harm would be as defined above. For K to be found to be malicious it must be proved that, in attacking H, he foresaw that some physical harm to H, albeit of a minor character, might result: see *R v Mowatt* [1967] 3 All ER 47. There is no clear evidence as to his mens rea, but it is submitted that if he hit H hard enough to cause this harm, establishing that he was malicious should not be a problem. Psychiatric harm can be charged as grievous bodily harm contrary to s18 or s20 of the 1861 Act, or actual bodily harm contrary to s47 of that Act – it depends on the severity of the harm. In *R v Ireland*; *R v Burstow* [1998] AC 147 Lord Steyn explained that neuroses must be distinguished from simple states of fear, or problems in coping with every day life. A nervous breakdown would suffice for at least s47 provided there was medical evidence to support the prosecution case. Causation is evident. If K were charged with inflicting grievous bodily harm contrary to s20 in respect of the nervous breakdown he might contend that such harm cannot be inflicted as a direct assault is required: see *R v Clarence* (1888) 22 QBD 23. *R v Ireland*; *R v Burstow* (above) makes it clear that inflict and cause are essentially the same thing. The facts do not indicate any obvious defences available to K.

If G had become HIV positive as a result of having sexual intercourse with J, he may have committed a number of assault-based offences. For the purposes of s23 or s24 of the 1861 Act (as explained above) the sexual intercourse could be the administration, and the HIV the noxious substance. Much would depend upon proof of mens rea. Did J know he was HIV positive? Was he at least aware of the risk that he might be? In the absence of evidence to this effect a prosecution would not succeed. Being made HIV positive would undoubtedly constitute grievous bodily harm, thus opening up the possibility of charges under s18 or s20, but again mens rea would be problematic if J was unaware of his condition. On the basis of *R v Clarence* (above) J would argue that he cannot be guilty under s20 as there was no direct assault upon G. Whilst *R v Ireland*; *R v Burstow* (above) suggests that this should be no bar to liability, *R v Clarence* has, strictly speaking, not been overruled on this point.

## QUESTION FOUR

C, a doctor, knew that he had contracted a dangerous contagious disease which proved fatal in 90 per cent of persons catching it. He went home and did not tell his wife, D, about his condition or that he was exposing her and their children to the risk of the disease. He did this because their relationship was going through difficulties and C knew that D would not be sympathetic. D and one of the children contracted the disease. Subsequently, the child died but D recovered. When D's condition was diagnosed, steps were taken to apprehend C, who by this time had fled into neighbouring mountains to hide. There, E's sheep contracted the disease as a result. Four died from the disease and the rest had to be destroyed. This was the first time that sheep has succumbed to this contagion.

Advise C of his criminal liability.

University of London LLB Examination
(for External Students) Criminal Law June 1996 Q2

### General Comment

A question which at first glance may appear unusual and difficult. In fact the question involves a straightforward discussion of homicide and non-fatal offences against the person, albeit in the unusual context of the transmission of a contagious disease.

### Skeleton Solution

Battery – assault occasioning actual bodily harm – grievous bodily harm – unlawful act manslaughter – manslaughter by gross negligence – criminal damage.

### Suggested Solution

By passing on the disease to D, C may be guilty of a number of offences against the person. It is unclear how the disease is passed on – whether through physical contact or by some other method. The prosecution may charge C with battery on the basis that he made physical contact with D and his child. The actus reus of battery requires the making of unlawful physical contact by the accused on the victim: *Collins* v *Wilcock* [1984] 3 All ER 374. Physical contact between family members will not usually constitute an offence since everyone is taken to give implied consent to touching which is ordinary and usual in daily life: *Collins* v *Wilcock*. The prosecution may allege that C's failure to disclose to his family that he had this disease may 'vitiate' his family's consent to such ordinary physical contact. Such an argument was advanced in *R* v *Clarence* (1888) 22 QBD 23 but was rejected by the court, which held that the failure to disclose that one has a communicable disease does not invalidate the consent given to physical contact. It would appear, therefore, that D's and the child's implied consent to ordinary physical contact will be valid and no charge of battery can be sustained.

Could C be liable for an assault occasioning actual bodily harm contrary to s47 Offences

Against the Person Act (OAPA) 1861? It is likely that the illness D suffered from contracting the disease would constitute actual bodily harm, which was defined in *R v Chan Fook* [1994] Crim LR 432 as any injury which is more than trivial. In addition, it has been established in *R v Savage; R v Parmenter* [1991] 3 WLR 914 that the accused need not intend or even foresee that he will cause any injury. However, it is essential that the actual bodily harm is caused by the accused's assault or battery of the victim. Since there is no evidence that C passed the disease on by assaulting or battering D there could be no successful prosecution under s47.

Could C be liable for wounding or inflicting grievous bodily harm on D contrary to s20 OAPA 1861? Grievous bodily harm was defined as 'really serious harm' in *DPP v Smith* [1961] AC 290, therefore, if D became seriously ill before she recovered, C will have committed the actus reus of this offence. On the basis of *R v Burstow* [1997] 3 WLR 534 C can 'inflict' harm by causing it to occur to another – this seems wide enough to cover infection, notwithstanding *R v Clarence* (above).

The mens rea for the s20 offence requires that the accused either intends or foresees that his act will cause some harm: *R v Savage; R v Parmenter*. Since C is a doctor he is likely to be aware of the consequences of contracting the disease and consequently could have foreseen that he might cause harm to his family.

An interesting question is whether C could be convicted of wounding or causing grievous bodily harm contrary to s18 OAPA 1861. The actus reus is similar to that discussed with respect to s20 above. However, the mens rea is stricter, requiring that the accused actually intends to cause grievous bodily harm. On the assumption that C knew he would pass on the disease and that it was 90 per cent fatal, the question is whether this 'knowledge' can be equated with 'intention'. It was held in *R v Hancock and Shankland* [1986] AC 455 that foreseeing a consequence is not the same as intending it. Although it was held in *R v Nedrick* [1986] 1 WLR 1025, and confirmed in *R v Woollin* [1998] 4 All ER 103, that the jury may infer that the accused intended a consequence if he knew it was virtually certain, it appears quite clear that C did not intend to cause serious harm to his wife and would therefore be acquitted of the charge under s18 OAPA 1861.

Passing on a contagious disease could also result in liability under s23 or s24 of the Offences Against the Person Act 1861, namely maliciously administering a noxious substance so as to endanger life, or inflict grievous bodily harm (s23), or maliciously administering a noxious substance, with intent to injure, aggrieve, or annoy the victim: s24. It is submitted that the offence under s23 would be the most appropriate, given the life threatening nature of the disease. C would be malicious in the sense that he was aware of the risk of the disease being passed on and of the risk of physical harm arising to others who contracted it: see *R v Mowatt* [1967] 3 All ER 47.

Could C be charged with the murder of his daughter? It appears clear that he has caused her death by passing on the disease. The mens rea required is that the accused intends to kill or cause grievous bodily harm: *R v Woollin* (above). The prosecution would have to produce evidence that he at least foresaw death or grievous bodily harm as 'virtually certain' – only then could the jury infer that he intended either consequence.

D may be liable for the offence of unlawful act of manslaughter, which was defined in the case of *R v Church* [1965] 2 All ER 72 as where the accused causes death by an unlawful act which all sober and reasonable people would inevitably recognise would subject the other person to the risk of some physical harm, albeit not serious harm. The unlawful criminal act may be present in the form of the s20 offence discussed above. No mens rea is actually required as to the death of the victim, it being sufficient that the accused had the mens rea for the unlawful act: *DPP v Newbury and Jones* [1977] AC 500.

However, the most likely charge to be brought against C for causing his child's death is that of manslaughter by gross negligence which was defined in *R v Adomako* [1994] 3 WLR 288 as where the accused breaches his duty to the victim causing death and is regarded by a jury as sufficiently negligent to amount to a criminal act. It was held in *Adomako* that everyone owes a duty to everyone else not to cause injury. Consequently if the jury regards C's act of exposing his family to the risk of contamination with a disease which is 90 per cent fatal as sufficiently negligent, he will be convicted of this offence.

The final issue is whether C could be liable for criminal damage to the sheep, contrary to s1 Criminal Damage Act (CDA) 1971. Under s10(1)(a) CDA 1971 property is defined to include wild animals which have been reduced into possession and not lost or abandoned. If the sheep belong to a farmer and are not 'wild' they will fall under the definition of property contained in s10. However, it is unlikely that C has the mens rea for this offence since he does not intend to damage the sheep and, since it is stated that 'this is the first time that sheep had succumbed to this contagion', is unlikely that the reasonable person would regard this possibility as being 'obvious' for the purposes of the *Caldwell* test for recklessness.

## QUESTION FIVE

J and K went into a jeweller's shop in order to have their ears pierced. The 16-year-old assistant, L, employed by M, the owner of the shop, failed to sterilise the needle before piercing J's ears and between piercing J and K's ears. J developed blood poisoning as a result of the ear piercing and was seriously ill for three months. Subsequently, K, after a blood test, was found to have become HIV positive. J had known that she, J, was HIV positive when she went into the shop.

Advise L and M of their criminal liability. What difference, if any, would it make to your advice if J had died?

University of London LLB Examination
(for External Students) Criminal Law June 1995 Q2

## General Comment

An interesting question raising the issues relating to the criminal liability for passing on the HIV virus. Although the transmission of the HIV virus may seem unfamiliar territory to the student of criminal law, it really only involves a straightforward discussion of the main offences against the person. The complications lie not with the discussion of HIV, but with the liability of M which (unusually) raises the issue of vicarious liability and also liability for omissions.

## Skeleton Solution

L: offences against the person for the poisoning of J and the possible transmission of the HIV virus to K – J: offences against the person for the possible transmission of the HIV virus to K – M: vicarious liability and liability by omission; homicide.

## Suggested Solution

When L pierced J's ears without sterilising the needle and gave her blood poisoning, L may have committed a number of offences against the person.

It is unlikely that L has committed an assault on J, since J was not put in apprehension of immediate physical violence: see *Fagan* v *Metropolitan Police Commissioner* [1969] 1 QB 439. It is also unlikely that L has committed a battery since J consented to the procedure. Although it may be argued that J would not have consented if she knew that the needle had not been sterilised, it is established law that ignorance of a relevant fact, or even fraud, will not vitiate consent: see *R* v *Clarence* (1888) 22 QBD 23.

Although such poisoning would almost certainly amount to actual bodily harm for the purposes of a charge under s47 of the Offences Against the Person Act 1861 (actual bodily harm being defined in *R* v *Chan Fook* [1994] Crim LR 432 as any injury which is more than trivial), it is unlikely that such a charge would succeed because this offence requires either an assault or battery to occasion the harm. If the submissions above are correct, there is no assault or battery.

Serious poisoning causing someone to be ill for three months would almost certainly amount to grievous bodily harm for the purposes of a charge under ss18 or 20 of the 1861 Act. Neither of these offences require the prosecution to prove an assault and therefore the problems discussed above do not arise: see *R* v *Wilson* [1983] 1 All ER 993. Grievous bodily harm was defined in *DPP* v *Smith* [1960] 3 All ER 161 as 'really serious harm'. It is unlikely that L could be charged under s18 as this requires the specific intention to cause serious harm of which there is no evidence. However, under s20 it is sufficient if L was reckless in that she foresaw that some harm would result from her actions: *R* v *Savage*; *R* v *Parmenter* [1991] 4 All ER 698. It would appear that a conviction would seem unlikely under s20 because there is no evidence that L actually foresaw that some harm would be caused.

It is possible that L could be charged with maliciously administering a poison or noxious substance which inflicts grievous bodily harm contrary to s23 of the 1861 Act. One could argue that L has 'maliciously' administered the poison or contamination on the needle in the sense that failing to clean the needle is reckless. The problem again, however, is that to maliciously administer a noxious substance the accused must foresee the possibility that the substance will be administered to the victim: see *R v Cunningham* [1957] 2 QB 396. It may be the case that the possibility of infecting a client had never crossed L's mind.

It may be possible to charge L with a number of offences against the person because of her use of the same needles between J and K, and K's subsequent contraction of the HIV virus.

The first (and one of the most difficult) problems for the prosecution to overcome is to prove that K contracted the HIV virus from J at the jeweller's shop. It is possible that K contracted the virus from another source, such as sexual intercourse or intravenous drug use. It must be remembered that the burden of proving causation is on the prosecution.

Assuming that the problem of causation can be overcome, it may be possible to charge L with maliciously inflicting grievous bodily harm contrary to s20 of the 1861 Act. Such a charge would be breaking new legal ground and, although possible, is fraught with difficulties. The first problem to overcome is to prove that the HIV virus, before it causes AIDS to develop, constitutes 'grievous bodily harm' at all. The defence may argue that since a person who is HIV positive is virtually symptomless until the onset of AIDS, no charge involving grievous bodily harm can be brought. Even if this problem can be overcome, it would still have to be established that L maliciously inflicted grievous bodily harm on K. As discussed above, this requires the prosecution to prove that the accused was *Cunningham* reckless as to whether he or she would cause some harm ie that the causing of harm was foreseen. L is only 16 years old and may not be aware of the methods by which the HIV virus can be transmitted.

L could also possibly be charged with the offence of administering a noxious substance contrary to s23 of the 1861 Act if the use of a contaminated needle did indeed pass the HIV virus on to K. The problems with this charge are similar to those discussed above. It would have to be shown that L maliciously administered or caused to be taken a noxious substance. Malice would require the prosecution to prove that L knew that the HIV virus may be transmitted by using the same needle on J and K.

M could be charged under ss20 or 23 with the poisoning of J or the transmission of the HIV virus to K by failing to ensure the safety of his clients. It may be argued that such an omission may give rise to liability because of the contractual duty owed by M to his clients. However, even if such an argument were to succeed the prosecution would still need to prove that M had the mens rea for these offences which, as discussed above, generally requires the awareness that harm would be caused. It is insufficient to prove that the accused should have been so aware.

It is unlikely that M could be charged with an offence under ss20 or 23 of the 1861 Act under the doctrine of vicarious liability because of the courts' reluctance to use this doctrine against an employer, unless the employer as well as the employee has the mens rea for the offence: see *James & Son Ltd* v *Smee* [1955] 1 QB 78.

If J had died, then a charge of manslaughter by gross negligence could be brought against L and M.

Manslaughter by gross negligence is defined in the case of *R* v *Adomako* [1994] 3 WLR 288 as requiring the prosecution to prove that: (a) the accused owed the victim a duty of care; (b) that the duty was breached causing death; and (c) the the negligence of the accused is so great that it amounts to a criminal act or omission. It would probably be fair to assume that L and M owe a duty of care to their clients, either on the basis of general principles of negligence or because of the contractual relationship between the clients and the jeweller's shop. It is submitted that in failing to sterilise the needle L has breached her duty, which has caused J's death. However, it is doubtful whether a jury would accept that her negligence goes beyond the civil law and deserves criminal punishment (especially in view of her relatively young age).

It is more likely that M could be convicted of manslaughter by gross negligence, since a stricter duty should be imposed on him as the owner to ensure that his staff are adequately trained to perform this potentially dangerous task. Again, it is questionable whether a jury would accept that even this negligence deserves criminal rather than civil sanction.

# Chapter 5

## Sexual Offences and Consent

5.1     Introduction

5.2     Key points

5.3     Key cases and statutes

5.4     Questions and suggested solutions

## 5.1 Introduction

The sexual offences covered on most mainstream criminal law syllabuses comprise rape, indecent assault, indecency with children and offences related to rape under the Sexual Offences Act 1956. The topic of consent falls naturally to be considered here, given that it can normally be raised as a defence of offences such as indecent assault, or its absence is an element of the offence that has to be established by the prosecution, as is the case with rape. It should be borne in mind, however, that the general common law rules applicable to consent are equally relevant to the non-sexual offences covered in Chapter 4.

## 5.2 Key points

### *Indecent assault*

a) The relevant statutory provision is the Sexual Offences Act 1956: s14 (indecent assault on a woman); s15 (indecent assault on a man). The age of consent is 16.

b) In most cases the assault will involve physical contact (ie a battery). In *Faulkner* v *Talbot* [1981] 3 All ER 468 Lord Lane CJ observed that this contact need not necessarily be hostile or rude or aggressive.

c) It is possible to have an indecent assault without physical contact provided P apprehends immediate physical violence: see *R* v *Sargeant* [1997] Crim LR 50.

d) For these purposes *R* v *Court* [1989] AC 28 defines indeceny as activity that contravenes standards of decent behaviour in regard 'to sexual modesty or privacy'. Objectively decent acts cannot become indecent simply because D has an indecent motive: see *R* v *George* [1956] Crim LR 52. Obviously indecent acts will be regarded as indecent in the absence of some excuse, explanation or justification. Where an activity is ambiguous, evidence of D's secret indecent motive will be admissible to help the jury conclude whether or not there was indecency: see *R* v *Court* (above).

e) D can escape liability even where P is under the age of 16 if D honestly believes P to be over the age of 16, and either P is consenting or D honestly believes P to be consenting.

f) An alternative charge where P is under 16 is that of indecency with children contrary to s1(1) of the Indecency with Children Act 1960, which provides that any person who commits an act of gross indecency with or towards a child under the age of 16 commits an offence: see further *R* v *Speck* (1977) 65 Cr App R 161 and *B* v *DPP* [2000] 1 All ER 833.

## Rape

a) Under s1 of the Sexual Offences Act 1956 , as amended by s142 of the Criminal Justice and Public Order Act 1994, a man commits rape if he has sexual intercourse with a person (whether vaginal or anal) who at the time of the intercourse does not consent to it; and at the time he knows that the person does not consent to the intercourse or is reckless as to whether that person consents to it.

b) Whether or not P was consenting to the sexual intercourse will be a question of fact to be determined by the jury: see *R* v *Olugboja* (1981) 73 Cr App R 344. This issue is especially problematic where P submits to sexual intercourse without being physically overpowered by D.

c) P's consent may be vitiated where D deceives P into consenting to intercourse: see s1(3) Sexual Offences Act 1956 – a man commits rape if he induces a married woman to have sexual intercourse with him by impersonating her husband. Impersonation of a long standing partner may also vitiate consent: see *R* v *Elbekkay* [1995] Crim LR 163. Consent will also be void if D deceives P as to the nature of the act he is performing: see *R* v *Williams* [1923] 1 KB 340.

d) To be guilty of rape the prosecution must prove that D intended to have sexual intercourse and either knew that P was not consenting or was reckless, in the subjective sense, as to whether or not P was consenting. This means that D must be acquitted if he honestly, albeit unreasonably, believed that P was consenting to the sexual intercourse: see *R* v *Morgan* [1975] 2 All ER 347and s1(2) Sexual Offences (Amendment) Act 1976.

## Other offences involving sexual intercourse

a) Sexual Offences Act 1956, s5 – it is an offence for a man to have unlawful sexual intercourse with a girl under the age of 13. Sexual Offences Act 1956, s6 – it is an offence for a man to have unlawful sexual intercourse with a girl under the age of 16. The s5 offence carries the possibility of life imprisonment. Under the s6 offence a man may escape liability if he is under the age of 24 and has not previously been charged with a like offence, and he believes P to be of the age of 16 or over and has reasonable cause for the belief.

b) The 1956 Act creates other offences based around sexual intercourse: s2(1) ('It is an offence for a person to procure a woman, by threats or intimidation, to have sexual intercourse in any part of the world.'); s3(1) ('It is an offence for a person to procure a woman, by false pretences or false representations, to have sexual intercourse in any part of the world.'); s4(1) ('It is an offence for a person to apply or administer to, or cause to be taken by, a woman any drug, matter or thing with intent to stupefy or overpower her so as thereby to enable any man to have unlawful sexual intercourse with her.')

c) The Sexual Offences (Amendment) Act 2000 makes it an offence for D (who must be 18 or older) to have sexual intercourse (whether vaginal or anal) with P who is under the age of 18, or to engage in any other sexual activity with or directed towards P, in circumstances where D can be said to have occupied a position of trust in relation to P. The offences carries the possibility of five years' imprisonment in the event of conviction. The section is aimed at adults working in institutions such as care homes, colleges and hospitals with young people, who take advantage of young people for sexual gratification. Note that the offence is made out even where P is over the age of 16 and P consents.

## Consent to harm

a) P can consent to harm provided he is of sound mind, over the age of 16, and the harm inquestion does not amount to actual bodily harm or worse: see *R* v *Donovan* [1934] 2 KB 498 and *Attorney-General's Reference (No 6 of 1980)* [1981] QB 715.

b) This basic common law rule is subject to many exceptions based on public policy, notably consent to reasonable surgical interference and consent to harm in the course of games, sport and 'horseplay': see *R* v *Billinghurst* [1978] Crim LR 553 and *R* v *Aitken* [1992] 1 WLR 1066.

c) Other exceptions include dangerous exhibitions, male circumcision and tattooing: see *R* v *Wilson* [1996] 3 WLR 125. The law does not recognise consent to actual bodily harm, or worse, simply to gratify a particular sexual craving of P: see *R* v *Brown* [1993] 2 All ER 75.

d) Where D honestly believes that P is consenting D will be judged on the facts as he believes them to be: see *R* v *Kimber* [1983] 1 WLR 1118. The law is unclear as regards the effect of a deception by D on the apparent consent given by P. *R* v *Richardson* [1998] 2 Cr App R 200 suggests that it might merely render the consent voidable, but *R* v *Tabassum* [2000] Crim LR 686 suggests that deception might render consent void where the act done is of a different nature to the act consented to.

## 5.3  Key cases and statutes

*Indecent assault*

- *R v Court* [1989] AC 28
  Meaning of indecent

- *R v George* [1956] Crim LR 52
  Secret intent irrelevant

- *R v K* [2001] 3 All ER 897
  Mistake as to consent to indecency

- *R v Sargeant* [1997] Crim LR 50
  Indecent assault without contact

- *R v Tabassum* [2000] Crim LR 686
  Deception and consent to indecency

- Sexual Offences Act 1956, s14 and s15 – indecent assault offences

*Rape*

- *DPP v Morgan* [1975] 2 All ER 347
  Honest belief in consent

- *R v Kaitamaki* [1985] AC 147
  Intercourse as a continuing act

- *R v Olugboja* (1981) 73 Cr App R 344
  Direction on consent

- *R v Satnam; R v Kewal* (1983) 78 Cr App R 149
  Reckless rape

- Criminal Justice and Public Order Act 1994, s142 – extension to male rape

- Sexual Offences Act 1956 – basic offence of rape

- Sexual Offences Act 1956, s5 – sex with a girl below 13

- Sexual Offences Act 1956, s6 – sex with a girl between 13 and 16

- Sexual Offences (Amendment) Act 1976 – direction on honest belief

- Sexual Offences (Amendment) Act 2000 – abuse of trust

*Consent*

- *Attorney-General's Reference (No 6 of 1980)* [1981] QB 715
  Consent no defence to street fighting

- *R v Aitken* [1992] 1 WLR 1066
  Consent to rough play

- *R* v *Billinghurst* [1978] Crim LR 553
  Consent to sports injuries

- *R* v *Brown* [1993] 2 All ER 75
  Consent no defence to sado-masochism

- *R* v *Donovan* [1934] 2 KB 498
  Consent valid up to actual bodily harm

- *R* v *Emmett* (1999) The Times 15 October
  Consent no defence to sado-masochism

- *R* v *Richardson* [1998] 2 Cr App R 200
  Effect of mistake on consent

- *R* v *Richardson and Irwin* [1999] Crim LR 494
  Intoxication and mistake as to consent

- *R* v *Wilson* [1996] 3 WLR 125
  Tattooing and consent

## 5.4 Questions and suggested solutions

QUESTION ONE

Q, who was a total abstainer, was at R's birthday party. S, another guest, laced Q's orange juice with a drug to which Q proved allergic. 'The drug caused Q to go berserk, running about the room tearing at her own and other people's clothes, before falling down and breaking an arm. Q, who was in a semi-conscious state, was placed on R's bed while everyone waited for the ambulance to arrive. T had sexual intercourse with Q who did not resist T's advances and T thought that she was consenting. Q was found to be HIV positive as a result of the intercourse.

Advise S and T of their criminal liability, if any.

University of London LLB Examination
(for External Students) Criminal Law June 1999 Q5

*General Comment*

A varied question that requires a good knowledge of defences affecting mens rea. The issue of intoxication requires careful coverage as does its relationship with automatism. Note the accessorial liability points that arise in the course of the question – some of these are quite complex. Candidates also need to have a good knowledge of both assaults and sexual offences. The range of issues covered is a salutary warning against question spotting.

## Skeleton Solution

Indecency assault by Q; criminal damage to clothes; defences of automatism and involuntary intoxication – also consider disinhibition – S causes Q to break her arm; gbh; s18/s20 – S procures various offences; but only if it was his purpose; note allergy point; consider poisoning offences – innocent agency also an issue – T has sex with Q; is it rape; was consent genuine – HIV issue; s23/24; s18/20; mens rea a problem.

## Suggested Solution

When Q tears clothes off various party guests she may be committing a number of offences. First, criminal damage to the clothes. Section 1(1) of the Criminal Damage Act 1971 provides that Q commits an offence if she intentionally or recklessly, without lawful excuse, damages or destroys property belonging to another. Clearly she had committed that actus reus of the offence and has no obvious lawful excuse. The issue of mens rea must be looked at in the light of possible defences considered below. The second possible offence is that of indecent assault. The Sexual Offences Act 1956, ss14(1) (assault on a woman) and 15(1) (assault on a man) create the offences. There is clearly an assault, on the given facts, leaving the issue of indecency. According to the House of Lords in *R* v *Court* [1989] AC 28 this involves a contravention of standards of decent behaviour in regard 'to sexual modesty or privacy'. This would appear to be made out. Strictly speaking the only mens rea required for the offence is the intention to assault, or recklessness. Again this has to be looked at in the context of the defences available to Q.

Regarding defences, much depends on how seriously the drug affects Q's consciousness. Q could raise the defence of automatism. As Lord Denning explained in *Bratty* v *Attorney-General for Northern Ireland* [1963] AC 386 no act is punishable if it is done involuntarily in the sense that the defendant was unconscious at the time and did not know what he was doing. How involuntary must Q's acts be to qualify as automatism? On the basis of *Attorney-General's Reference (No 2 of 1992)* [1993] 3 WLR 982 Q would have to provide medical evidence that laid a proper evidential foundation for the defence. The defence of automatism requires that there was a total destruction of voluntary control on Q's part. Impaired, reduced or partial control is not enough.

On the facts it is submitted that Q should succeed with this defence and be acquitted on both charges of criminal damage and indecent assault.

Alternatively, the defence of involuntary intoxication could be raised, if the lack of awareness required for automatism cannot be made out. Q would have to show that she did not form the necessary intent because of the effect of the drug. The problem for Q is that both of the offences referred to are basic intent crimes – ie they can be committed recklessly. On the basis of *DPP* v *Majewski* [1977] AC 443 a defendant charged with a basic intent crime cannot succeed with a defence of intoxication. The rationale for this is that consuming the drugs is a reckless course of conduct. This recklessness prior to committing the actus reus provides the 'fault' element for the offence with which the defendant is actually charged. The rule is clearly one based on public policy rather than any logic. Q should argue that, as her consumption of the drug was involuntary, she did not display any prior recklessness in consuming it, hence the case can be distinguished from *Majewski*. It is submitted that this argument would result in an acquittal. If Q was not even intoxicated but merely had her inhibitions reduced by the drug she has no defence. Such is made clear by the House of Lords' decision in *R v Kingston* [1994] 3 WLR 519. In that case the defendant committed an indecent assault after his coffee was 'spiked' with a drug. The evidence was that he would not have committed the offence but for the effects of the drug. Unfortunately the evidence was that he nevertheless still had the mens rea for the offence. The House of Lords ruled that there was no defence of 'disinhibition' and that the evidence of the drug only went to mitigation.

Q breaks her arm. This constitutes 'serious harm', ie grievous bodily harm. S could be regarded as having caused this harm by administering the drug. S must take Q as s/he finds her – *R v Blaue* [1975] 1 WLR 1411 – and this includes the allergic reaction to the drug. Establishing mens rea for a charge under s18 of the Offences Against the Person Act 1861 could be difficult. S must be proved to have intended to cause grievous bodily harm. This seems unlikely on the facts. A better charge might be maliciously inflicting grievous bodily harm contrary to s20 of the 1861 Act. Infliction for these purposes can now be regarded as simply requiring proof of causation: see *R v Burstow* [1997] 3 WLR 534. S must be shown to have been malicious which, on the basis of *R v Mowatt* [1968] 1 QB 421, requires proof that S foresaw the possibility of some physical harm occurring (to Q) albeit slight. There should be no problem establishing this on the given facts.

S could be charged with procuring the acts of criminal damage and indecent assault committed by Q. The *Attorney-General's Reference (No 1 of 1975)* [1975] 3 WLR 11 provides that to procure means to produce by endeavour. The problem for the prosecution is that the ruling also indicates that S cannot be guilty of procuring unless it can be shown that she/he intended the commission of the offences by Q, in the sense that it was his/her purpose.

By placing the drug in Q's drink S may have committed offences contrary to ss23 and 24 of the 1861 Act. Section 23 of the 1861 Act creates the offence of 'maliciously administering a noxious substance so as to endanger life, or inflict grievous bodily harm'. Section 24 also involves the malicious administering of a noxious substance: but requires a further intent, namely that this should 'injure, aggrieve, or annoy' the victim. Both ss23 and 24 require the administering of a noxious substance satisfied here by placing the drug in the drink. The drug would clearly be a noxious substance *R v Marcus* [1981] 1 WLR 774. Both offences require proof of the defendant acting maliciously, as to which see above, but note particularly that the defendant in *R v Cunningham* [1957] 2 QB 396 was charged under s23 – hence S must be aware of the risk of the harm specified in either s23 or s24. If S was unaware of the allergy, this might be more difficult to establish.

An alternative tactic for the prosecution would be to charge S with committing the offences of criminal damage and indecent assault as the principal offender on the basis that Q was an 'innocent agent'. This would be particularly appropriate if Q was to succeed with the defence of automatism in respect of those charges: see *R* v *Michael* (1840) 9 C & P 356.

T has sexual intercourse with Q. He will, therefore, have committed the actus reus of rape as defined in s1(1) of the Sexual Offences Act 1956 as amended by s142 of the Criminal Justice and Public Order Act 1994 if Q was not consenting at the time or was not capable of consenting. In terms of mens rea T must be shown to have known that Q was not consenting or to have been reckless as to whether she was. If T honestly but mistakenly believed Q was consenting to the sexual intercourse he will not be guilty of rape, as he will lack the requisite mens rea. *DPP* v *Morgan* [1976] AC 182 makes it clear that T must be judged on the facts, as he honestly believed them to be. Hence if he honestly believed Q was consenting he must be acquitted.

Q becoming HIV positive following the intercourse could involve T in liability for offences contrary to ss18, 20, 23 or 24 of the Offences Against the Persons Act 1861 as outlined above. For the purposes of s23 or s24 the sexual intercourse could be the administration, and the HIV the noxious substance. Much would depend upon proof of mens rea. Did T know he was HIV positive? Was he at least aware of the risk that he might be? In the absence of evidence to this effect a prosecution would not succeed.

## QUESTION TWO

'Consent prevents criminal liability from arising. It is not a defence. In this connection there is no distinction between property offences and offences against the person.'

Discuss.

University of London LLB Examination
(for External Students) Criminal Law June 1998 Q8

### General Comment

This is a very specific question that should only be attempted by candidates who have thoroughly prepared the topic. It is important to look at consent in the context of a range of criminal offences – not just offences against the person. The question actually raises a subtle and difficult point concerning the difference between consent as an element of an offence and consent as a substantive defence. Does consent prevent a crime being committed at all – in the sense that the action is not unlawful, or does it provide a defence when the actus reus and mens rea are made out?

### Skeleton Solution

Explain the effect of consent on criminal liability; the need for certainty; the problem of granting the victim autonomy – use rape as an illustration of consent as part of the crime – show how consent can negative the actus reus of property offences – consider the operation of consent as a factor external to the elements of the offence – judicial discretion in permitting a certain scope to consent – conclude with reference to *R* v *Brown* and the evidential significance of the element/defence dichotomy.

### Suggested Solution

The issue of consent presents difficulties for the criminal law. The consent in question will be that of the victim. The proposition is that this consent can prevent the defendant being convicted of an offence. This is problematic because the criminal law is meant to be known, certain and sure. It is meant to apply consistently. By looking at the definition of a crime the defendant should be able to tell whether or not his actions will be criminal. Such certainty is, of course, rarely attained in criminal justice systems. Some discretion always remains. Usually that discretion will be vested in the agents of law enforcement. A police officer has discretion to arrest. More significantly the Crown Prosecution Service has discretion as to whether or not it should prosecute. The problem with consent is that it leaves it to the victim to determine whether or not an offence has been committed. Historically the common law has been wary of this notion and has sought to restrict the victim's autonomy by seeking to delineate the contours of consent – laying down rules on when consent is and is not a valid consideration. The result is very much a 'patchwork quilt' of common law and statutory provisions from which it is not easy to pick out a coherent line of reasoning.

As the quotation under consideration indicates there are situations where consent operates to prevent any criminal offence being committed – in effect it prevents an actus reus from occurring. The most significant example of this is the offence of rape. The Sexual Offences Act 1956, s1(1) as amended provides that the offence of rape occurs where a man has sexual intercourse with another person who is not consenting and at the time he knows that the other person is not consenting or is reckless as to whether there is consent.

The key point here is that the absence of consent is part of the actus reus that the prosecution must prove beyond all reasonable doubt. If it is not established liability for rape cannot arise. It would be inept in such cases to refer to an alleged rapist raising the 'defence' of consent (although many commit this solecism out of bad habits). In such cases there is no room for judicial discretion about the relevance of consent. The statute makes it clear that if there is consent there is no crime.

Elsewhere consent operates, to a lesser or greater extent as a substantive defence. This means that the prosecution must establish the actus reus and mens rea of the crime and invite the defendant to introduce evidence of consent. Sometime this evidence will actually have the effect of negativing, by necessary implication, an element of the actus reus – thus causing a situation where there is no crime. In others the consent will be offered up as a justification or excuse for the defendant's actions.

As regards property offences the courts appear to be willing to give the owner of the property almost complete autonomy in respect of the disposition of the property. Some examples will illustrate. P can allow (ie consent) D to take his property away and keep it for good. P's consent effectively prevents D's actions from amounting to theft. It is true that post *R* v *Gomez* [1993] AC 442 P's consent cannot prevent D's actions from amounting to an appropriation of the property, but D's knowledge that P consented would certainly prevent D from being held to have been dishonest. Hence the elements of the offence are not made out. To talk of a defence of consent in such cases would not be appropriate. The same reasoning would apply to criminal damage. If P asks D to destroy property belonging to P, D would not be charged with criminal damage contrary to s1(1) of the Criminal Damage Act 1971. D would have a lawful excuse – hence an element of the offence would not be made out and liability would not arise. Lastly, take the example of burglary contrary to s9(1)(a) of the Theft Act 1968. To commit the offence D must enter P's building as a trespasser. If, however, P has given D permission to enter he cannot, per se, be a trespasser. Here again P's consent to D's actions prevents an element of the offence being made out, thus preventing liability from arising.

It is the issue of physical autonomy, however, that has given rise to the most difficulty. Sexual intercourse is governed by the offence of rape, as considered above. Not surprisingly the statute recognises that adults have the power to consent to sexual intercourse. Public policy dictates it is not an activity that the state should regulate more than is necessary. What of other activities involving some violation of the victim's physical integrity?

Take an offence such as battery. The common law definition requires proof that D had physical contact with P. If one implies into this definition that the touching must be non-consensual then proof of consent will destroy the evidence of actus reus. An alternative view, however, is that the actus reus simply requires proof of physical contact. Hence bumping into a fellow passenger on the train would constitute a battery. If charged with the offence D would be at liberty to raise the defence of consent once the actus reus and mens rea had been established. This in turn creates an opening for the exercise of judicial discretion. The judge will have a view as to whether the victim can consent to such harm. In the example given it is assumed that the judge would recognise the concept of implied consent. Everyone using public transport at busy times impliedly consents to reasonable physical contact with fellow passengers because the system is overcrowded at such times. In essence the law is saying: ' You can travel at busy times if you want to, and you can consent to reasonable physical contact with fellow passengers at such times.' Clearly any other position would be impracticable.

What the courts have done, however, is to draw a line in terms of the harm to which a victim can validly consent. *R* v *Donovan* [1934] 2 KB 498 draws that line at the point of actual bodily harm. Subject to a number of exceptions P's consent to such harm or worse becomes irrelevant.

The exceptions are well known. They include sports, horseplay, tattooing, dangerous exhibitions and so on. Where these exceptions arise, what is the effect of consent? If the defendant's actions are 'justified' because of the consent it could be argued that they are not, therefore, unlawful. If they are not unlawful it follows that there is no actus reus (literally no unlawful activity). As the quotation suggests, no criminal liability arises. If, on the other hand, consent is an excuse, then the offence is made out, but because of the defendant's excuse he escapes the full, or any, punishment. If P is consenting to the harm in question it seems odd to think in terms of D therefore having an 'excuse'. Excusatory defences tend to arise where the defendant's plea is, effectively, 'I couldn't help it' (provocation), or 'I was forced to do it' (duress). Justificatory defences on the other hand tend to involve the defendant who says 'I had to do it, it was the right thing to do'. It is but a small step from this to the defendant saying 'I did it because P wanted me to'.

At present the law on this issue remains unclear. Consent can be relied upon by a defendant who causes physical harm provided there are good public policy reasons for his activities (ie the exceptions). This would hold true even if death resulted, as has been the case in some sporting events. It is not regarded as being good public policy to encourage mercy killing – hence consent is not a defence to murder simply because P asked to be killed. In *R v Brown* [1993] 2 All ER 75 conflicting dicta can be found on the issue of whether consent is a defence or whether the absence of consent is part of the actus reus to be proved. In practice the only difference it makes is as regards the burden of proof. If it is part of the offence the prosecution must prove it beyond all reasonable doubt. If it is a substantive offence there is an evidential burden on the defendant to provide some basis for the defence that can be put before the jury.

## QUESTION THREE

'No one can licence another to commit a crime. That is why consent is irrelevant to criminal liability.'

Discuss.

University of London LLB Examination
(for External Students) Criminal Law June 1999 Q7

### General Comment

This is a question on a rather specific topic that should only be attempted by candidates who are well versed in the arguments. Although the thrust of the quotation is a little different it is effectively the same question that was set in the 1998 paper. It is important to look at consent in the context of a range of criminal offences – not just offences against the person. The statement is a sweeping one that invites the candidate to challenge it. You should be prepared to do so. Be aware, however, that a good answer will require an examination of some of the more subtle and arcane aspects of the defence of consent. A basic run through the authorities will not suffice.

## Skeleton Solution

Consider the way in which consent empowers the victim – look at the property offences to see how consent does and does not nullify the actus reus – illustrate the actus reus/defence point by looking at rape – note the comments on this issue in *R* v *Brown* – open up the essay to look at the wider range of assault based offences and explore the exculpatory/justificatory dichotomy – conclusion.

## Suggested Solution

The quotation under discussion holds that consent is irrelevant to criminal liability. Whilst this statement is clearly wrong, it does invite an examination of the role played by the consent of the victim in respect of the defendant's criminal liability.

Why does consent cause difficulties for the criminal law? There are a number of reasons. The first is that the consent in question will be that of the victim – his attitude can prevent the defendant being convicted of an offence. This means that the application of the law can become uncertain. It is meant to apply consistently. If the victim can become the one who determines whether or not activity is criminal the law is no longer a known quantity.

Elsewhere consent operates, to a lesser or greater extent as a substantive defence. This means that the prosecution must establish the actus reus and mens rea of the crime and invite the defendant to introduce evidence of consent. Sometime this evidence will actually have the effect of negativing, by necessary implication, an element of the actus reus – thus causing a situation where there is no crime. In others the consent will be offered up as a justification or excuse for the defendant's actions.

Is it true that consent is irrelevant? Let us look first at some property offences to test this proposition.

P can allow (ie consent) D to take his property away and keep it for good – this is one of the obvious legal consequences of owning property. Interestingly, according to *R* v *Gomez* [1993] AC 442, P's consent cannot prevent D's actions from amounting to an appropriation of the property for the purposes of s1(1) of the Theft Act 1968. This would lend support to the view that no one can license another to commit crime. On the other hand D's knowledge that P consented would certainly prevent D from being held to have been dishonest. Hence the elements of the offence are not made out. The same reasoning would apply to criminal damage. If P asks D to destroy property belonging to P, D would not be charged with criminal damage contrary to s1(1) of the Criminal Damage Act 1971. D would have a lawful excuse – hence an element of the offence would not be made out and liability would not arise. Lastly, take the example of burglary contrary to s9(1)(a) of the Theft Act 1968. To commit the offence D must enter P's building as a trespasser. If, however, P has given D permission to enter he cannot, per se, be a trespasser. Here again P's consent to D's actions prevents an element of the offence from being made out, thus preventing liability from arising.

These examples, therefore, suggest that P's consent is a vital factor in determining liability. Does this mean the quotation under discussion is, therefore, entirely wrong? Not quite. If P consents to D destroying P's property there is no crime. But why is there no crime? The answer lies in the failure of the prosecution to establish the complete actus reus. To talk of a 'defence' of consent in such cases would not be appropriate. Defences are irrelevant where the elements of the charge are not made out. To that extent the quotation is correct in suggesting consent (as a substantive defence) is irrelevant to criminal liability.

The use of the phrase ' No one can licence another to commit crime' in the context of a debate about consent is misleading. By consenting to the activity P is not 'allowing ' a crime to be committed. By consenting to the activity P is ensuring that there is no crime because the actus reus is not made out. There is, therefore, no 'crime' to 'licence'.

This argument is graphically illustrated by he offence of rape. The Sexual Offences Act 1956, s1(1) as amended provides that the offence of rape occurs where a man has sexual intercourse with another person who is not consenting and at the time he knows that the other person is not consenting or is reckless as to whether there is consent.

The essential point here is that the absence of consent is part of the actus reus that the prosecution must prove beyond all reasonable doubt. If it is not established liability for rape cannot arise. It is not for the defendant to prove that the victim was consenting. It would be inept in such cases to refer to an alleged rapist raising the 'defence' of consent (although many commit this solecism out of bad habits). In such cases there is no room for judicial discretion about the relevance of consent. The statute makes it clear that if there is consent there is no crime. As explained above, it would be very odd to describe a woman having consensual sexual intercourse with a man as having given him a licence to commit a crime. Her consent means that there is no crime in the first place.

With most other offences against the person consent is either regarded as a substantive defence to be raised by the defendant once the actus reus and mens rea have been established by the prosecution, or the absence of consent is regarded as an implied part of the actus reus that has to be proved beyond all reasonable doubt by the prosecution. In *R v Brown* [1993] 2 All ER 75 conflicting dicta can be found on the issue of whether consent is a defence or whether the absence of consent is part of the actus reus to be proved. In practice the only difference it makes is as regards the burden of proof. If it is part of the offence the prosecution must prove it beyond all reasonable doubt. If it is a substantive offence there is an evidential burden on the defendant to provide some basis for the defence that can be put before the jury.

Take an offence such as battery. The common law definition requires proof that D had physical contact with P. If one implies into this definition that the touching must be non-consensual then proof of consent will destroy the evidence of actus reus. An alternative view, however, is that the actus reus simply requires proof of physical contact. Hence bumping into a fellow passenger on the train would constitute a battery.

If charged with the offence D would be at liberty to raise the defence of consent once the actus reus and mens rea had been established. This in turn creates an opening for the exercise of judicial discretion. The judge will have a view as to whether the victim can consent to such harm. In the example given it is assumed that the judge would recognise the concept of implied consent. Everyone using public transport at busy times impliedly consents to reasonable physical contact with fellow passengers because the system is overcrowded at such times. In essence the law is saying: ' You can travel at busy times if you want to, and you can consent to reasonable physical contact with fellow passengers at such times.' Clearly any other position would be impracticable. To describe the passenger consenting to contact as giving his other passengers a licence to commit crime sounds ludicrous because it is ludicrous.

What the Parliament and the courts have done, however, is to draw a line in terms of the 'harm' to which a victim can validly consent. This means that there are situations where, notwithstanding that P consents, the actus reus of the offence will be made out because P is not competent to consent. A person under the age of 16 cannot validly consent to sexual intercourse or indecent assault; it is not regarded as being good public policy to encourage mercy killing – hence consent is not a defence to murder simply because P asked to be killed. In terms of non-fatal harm, *R v Donovan* [1934] 2 KB 498 draws the line at the point of actual bodily harm. Subject to a number of exceptions P's consent to such harm or worse becomes irrelevant.

There are many well known exceptions to the general rule identified in *R v Donovan*, however. They include sports, horseplay, tattooing, dangerous exhibitions and so on. Where these exceptions arise, what is the effect of consent? If the defendant's actions are 'justified' because of the consent it could be argued that they are not, therefore, unlawful. If they are not unlawful it follows that there is no actus reus (literally no unlawful activity). As the quotation suggests, no criminal liability arises. If, on the other hand, consent is an excuse, then the offence is made out, but because of the defendant's excuse he escapes the full, or any, punishment. If P is consenting to the harm in question it seems odd to think in terms of him therefore having an excuse. Excusatory defences tend to arise where the defendant's plea is, effectively, 'I couldn't help it' (provocation), or 'I was forced to do it' (duress). Justificatory defences on the other hand tend to involve the defendant who says 'I had to do it, it was the right thing to do'. It is but a small step from this to the defendant saying 'I did it because P wanted me to'.

In conclusion, therefore, it can be said that the relevance of consent as a defence must depend to a large extent on the view taken as to whether or not the absence of consent is an implied part of the actus reus of offences. Even if it is regarded as irrelevant in that sense, it would still be wrong to take the view that a 'victim' who consents is licensing another to commit a crime'.

## QUESTION FOUR

Lemon, aged 18 years, was at a party when Mick laced his juice with a hallucinogenic drug. Lemon felt strange, but because he had been strictly brought up and was a total abstainer from drugs and alcohol, he did not put these feelings down to the effect of the drug. Lemon began to sing loudly. Noah, the host, asked him to desist. Lemon pushed Noah over a low coffee table causing him to sustain concussion. Lemon then started to remove his clothes in time with the music which was playing. In this he was encouraged by the other party goers. After Lemon has disrobed completely he was ushered into a bedroom by Owen who behaved indecently with Lemon. Owen mistakenly believed Lemon had consented to these acts though Lemon thought he was merely undergoing a medical examination. The police were called and all those at the party were arrested.

Advise the parties about their criminal liability, if any.

University of London LLB Examination
(for External Students) Criminal Law June 1997 Q5

### General Comment

A rather unusual question in that it involves a discussion of sexual offences other than rape which is rare for the London University examination paper.

### Skeleton Solution

Lemon: non-fatal offences against the person; indecent exposure; involuntary intoxication; other partygoers; accessory to Lemon's indecent exposure – Mick: administering a poison or noxious substance – Owen: indecent assault.

### Suggested Solution

By pushing Noah over a coffee table causing him concussion, Lemon may have committed a number of non-fatal offences against the person.

An assault was defined in *Fagan* v *Metropolitan Police Commissioner* [1969] 1 QB 439 as where the accused intentionally or recklessly causes the victim to apprehend immediate personal violence. Lemon's push would almost certainly have caused Noah to apprehend immediate personal violence and appears to have been done deliberately.

By pushing Noah, Lemon would also have committed a battery which was defined in *Fagan* (above) as 'the actual intended use of unlawful force to another person without his consent.'

Lemon may also be convicted of an assault occasioning actual bodily harm contrary to s47 Offences Against the Person Act (OAPA) 1861. An assault has clearly been committed (see above) and since it was held in *R* v *Savage*; *R* v *Parmenter* [1991] 3 WLR 914 that the accused need only have the mens rea for the assault and that no mens rea is required as the harm caused, the only question is whether concussion would constitute actual bodily harm. Actual bodily harm was defined in *R v Chan Fook* [1994] 1 WLR 689 as 'any injury which is more than trivial'. It is submitted that even if Noah recovers from his concussion without any lasting ill effects, the concussion would still constitute a more than trivial injury.

It is submitted that Lemon is unlikely to be charged with wounding or causing grievous bodily harm contrary to ss18 or 20 OAPA 1861 since a wound requires both layers of the skin to be broken (*JJC (A Minor) v Eisenhower* [1984] QB 331), and mere concussion, without any further injury, is unlikely to constitute grievous bodily harm (defined as a 'really serious injury' in *DPP v Smith* [1961] AC 290, although this is ultimately a jury question).

When Lemon removed his clothes he may have committed the common law offence of indecent exposure. A person commits this offence if he does an act which outrages public decency in public and in such a way that at least more than one person sees the act or is able to see the act: *R v Walker* [1996] 1 Cr App R 111. It is arguable whether Noah's party would constitute a public place. The fact that it may have been held on private premises does not necessarily preclude its categorisation as a public place since it was held in *R v Wellard* (1884) 14 QBD 63 that a public place could include private property if the public had access to it (whether by right or not). Further, it was held in *R v Bunyan and Morgan* (1844) 1 Cox CC 74 that an indecent act would have occurred in a public place if a member of the public passing on the street could have seen the act through a window. It is irrelevant whether anyone (such as the partygoers) thought the act to be indecent. The question is whether the jury considers the act to have transgressed the generally accepted bounds of decency and tends to gravely offend the average person: *Moloney v Mercer* [1971] 2 NSWLR 207. It is debatable whether a striptease at a party would fall within this definition of indecent.

By encouraging Lemon to remove his clothes the other partygoers may become accessories to Lemon's indecent exposure (contrary to s8 Accessories and Abettors Act 1861).

To the above charges Lemon may raise the defence of involuntary intoxication, which is a defence to offences of specific and basic mens rea provided the effect of the intoxication is such as to prevent the accused from forming the mens rea of the offence charged. Therefore if Lemon did not form the mens rea for any of the above offences due the drug which Mick secretly administered to him, he would be entitled to an acquittal. The problem is that, on the facts, Lemon merely 'feels strange' – perhaps implying that he still knows what he is doing. If this is the case, he would be convicted of the above offences. It was held in *R v Kingston* [1994] 3 WLR 519 that it would be no defence for an accused to plead that he would never have committed the offence if he were sober if he nonetheless formed the requisite mens rea for the offence.

By lacing Lemon's drink with an hallucinogenic drug, Mick has committed the offence of maliciously administering a poison or noxious thing with the intention to injure aggrieve or annoy contrary to s24 OAPA 1861. An hallucinogenic drug would fall within the definition of a poison or noxious substance (something likely to cause harm: *R v Cato* [1976] 1 WLR 110) or, for the purposes of a charge under s24, anything administered with a malevolent intent: *R v Marcus* [1981] 1 WLR 774.

When Owen behaved indecently with Lemon, Owen may have committed indecent assault contrary to s15 Sexual Offences Act 1956. The facts state that Owen has committed an act of indecency towards Lemon and therefore the only issues are consent and mens rea. It is a well-established principle of English law that consent to an act is only vitiated if the consent is induced by force, fraud as to the nature of the act or, possibly, the identity of the accused: see *R v Clarence* (1888) 22 QBD 23, *R v Bulduc and Bird* [1967] 3 CCC 294 and *R v Linekar* [1995] 3 All ER 69. Consequently, Owen is not guilty of the s15 offence since Lemon's consent to the physical act perpetrated by Owen is valid despite Lemon's belief that it occurred in the context of a medical examination. Although there is no authority directly on the mens rea of the s15 offence with respect to the issue of the victim's consent, it is likely that subjective recklessness as to the victim's consent would be required (this was so held with respect to rape in *R v Satnam and Kewal* (1983) 78 Cr App R 149). Since Owen mistakenly believes that Lemon consented to the act, it is unlikely that he has the mens rea for the s15 offence.

## QUESTION FIVE

'Consent is a defence to all crimes.'

Discuss.

University of London LLB Examination
(for External Students) Criminal Law June 1996 Q6

### General Comment

A fairly predictable question given the recent spate of cases on consent. However, good marks could only be earned by those who knew the relevant case law well.

### Skeleton Solution

Consent and the public interest – implied consent – sport – fighting outside the context of sport – lawful correction – sexual gratification – consent to the accidental infliction of harm – consent as an element of the offence – fraud and consent.

### Suggested Solution

The extent to which the law should and does recognise the victim's consent as a defence to a crime involves the difficult task of balancing individual freedom with imposing legitimate restrictions on the extremes of behaviour in which some individuals in society may engage.

In the *Attorney-General's Reference (No 6 of 1980)* [1981] QB 715 the House of Lords recognised this delicate balancing exercise by holding that the extent to which the consent of a 'victim' of a crime would constitute a defence would depend on whether this was in the court's perception of whether it was in the 'public interest'. It was held in this case that the victim's consent to assault or battery would be a defence providing no injury was caused? thus preventing a successful prosecution in cases of minor scuffles. However, it would not be in the public interest to allow such a defence to fighting (whether in public or in private) which resulted in injury, unless it arose in the context of 'manly pursuits' such as boxing or wrestling.

In *Collins* v *Wilcock* [1984] 1 WLR 1172 it was held that everyone gives implied consent to bodily contact which is necessary or customary in ordinary daily life. Therefore, routine bodily contact between people in a crowded lift or train would not give rise to a charge of battery. However, it is debatable whether the theoretical basis of this is because such consent amounts to a defence to a charge of battery or whether the absence of the victim's consent is an essential ingredient of the actus reus which would therefore not be proven in such cases.

*R* v *Coney* (1882) 8 QBD 534 established that the participants in a sporting activity give implied consent to the risk of injury by acts which are within the rules of the sport. Consequently, injuries caused by contact outside the rules of the game, ie fouls or the deliberate infliction of injury (see *R* v *Billinghurst* [1978] Crim LR 553), can give rise to a charge under the Offences Against the Person Act 1861 or even homicide.

Parents will have a defence to a charge of battery arising from the chastisement of their children providing it is not excessive: *R* v *Hopley* (1860) 2 F & F 202. It should be noted that the common law 'right' of teachers in state schools to administer corporal punishment has now been removed by s47 Education Act 1986. Such punishment may now only be administered with parental consent.

In a controversial judgment the House of Lords held in *R* v *Brown* [1993] 2 WLR 556 that consent would provide no defence to injuries inflicted in the course of sado-masochistic activities, but that tattooing and ear piercing were lawful. In *R* v *Wilson* [1996] 3 WLR 125 it was held that a wife's consent to having her husband's initials branded on her buttocks was a defence since no serious injury was caused and this was a private sphere of morality in which the law should not interfere. In what may be seen as a movement away from the decision in *Brown* (or at least a restrictive interpretation of it), the court in *R* v *Slingsby* [1995] Crim LR 570 held that the victim's consent to an unusual and potentially dangerous sexual practice may provide a defence to the accidental infliction of injury or even death.

In addition to the circumstances discussed above in which consent may or may not provide a defence to a charge, it should be remembered that the absence of the victim's consent is an essential element which the prosecution must prove to secure a conviction for many offences such as criminal damage, taking a vehicle without the owner's consent and rape. Indeed, for many of these offences merely the defendant's honest belief in the consent of the owner of the property or the victim, or that they would have consented, may be sufficient to prevent a conviction. See, for example, s5 Criminal Damage Act 1971, s2(1)(b) Theft Act 1968 and *DPP* v *Morgan* [1976] AC 182 (in the context of rape).

In conclusion, it can be seen that consent is not a defence to all crimes but will only constitute a defence in limited circumstances, depending mainly on the nebulous concept of the court's perception of what is in the public interest. The consent of the victim will, however, often lead to an acquittal for offences where the absence of the victim's consent is defined as an essential ingredient of the actus reus of the crime, rather than a defence to it.

# Chapter 6
## Theft

6.1    Introduction

6.2    Key points

6.3    Key cases and statutes

6.4    Questions and suggested solutions

## 6.1  Introduction

This area is of crucial importance in understanding the criminal law and makes up a large part of the syllabus.

Students will be examined closely on the different elements of the Theft Acts of 1968 and 1978 and a clear understanding of each individual offence and its relationship to other and crimes of 'dishonesty' is required.

## 6.2  Key points

### Theft

#### Property

Note that under the definition in s4(1) of the 1968 Act although intangible property is included, information is not: *Oxford* v *Moss* [1979] Crim LR 119. Note also the circumstances in which plants and animals may fall within the definition.

#### Appropriation

Property can be appropriated even if the accused is acting with the owner's consent: *Lawrence* v *Metropolitan Police Commissioner* [1972] 2 All ER 1253; *R* v *Morris* [1983] 3 All ER 288; *R* v *Gomez* [1993] 1 All ER 1 HL. Following *R* v *Hinks* [2000] 4 ALL ER 833, D can even be guilty of theft where P validly transfer title to D, provided D is dishonest at the time of the transfer.

#### Belonging to another (s5(1) Theft Act 1968)

The property must belong to someone: *R* v *Woodman* [1974] 2 All ER 955; *Williams* v *Phillips* (1957) 41 Cr App R 5. Ownership may not pass to the receiver if it is given for a particular purpose: s5(3); *DPP* v *Huskinson* [1988] Crim LR 620; *R* v *Hall* [1972] 3 WLR

381. Ownership may not pass to the receiver where it was given by mistake and the recipient is under an obligation to make restoration: s5(4); *Attorney-General's Reference (No 1 of 1983)* [1984] 3 All ER 369.

### Dishonesty

Students should always consider dishonesty as a two-part test: the three statutory circumstances under s2(1)(a), (b) and (c) Theft Act 1968 in which the accused cannot be dishonest and the main definition contained in *R v Ghosh* [1982] Crim LR 608.

Note that the dishonest intent must be formed while the goods still belong to another: *R v Stewart* (1982) The Times 14 December; *Edwards v Ddin* [1976] 1 WLR 942.

### Intention to permanently deprive

On borrowing money see: *R v Velumyl* [1989] Crim LR 299. On borrowing generally see: s6(1) Theft Act 1968; *R v Lloyd and Ali* [1985] 3 WLR 30. Note that in *DPP v Lavender* [1994] Crim LR 297 it was held that an accused may have an intention equivalent to an intention to permanently deprive under s6(1) of the 1968 Act if it is 'his intention to treat the thing as his own regardless of the other's rights' even if this is not equivalent to an outright taking or disposal.

### Making off without payment (s3 1978 Act)

This offence is especially useful where the accused has formed a dishonest intent after obtaining goods and therefore cannot be charged with theft or deception.

'Make off' – the accused must have left the premises (*R v McDavitt* [1981] Crim LR 843); 'without having paid' – payment with an invalid cheque does not constitute this offence as it amounts to conditional payment (*R v Hammond* [1982] Crim LR 611); the accused must know that payment is expected of him (*R v Brooks and Brooks* [1983] Crim LR 188); payment must be contractually due (*Troughton v Metropolitan Police Commissioner* [1987] Crim LR 138); the accused must intend to permanently avoid payment (*R v Allen* [1985] 3 WLR 107).

## 6.3 Key cases and statutes

- *Lawrence v Metropolitan Police Commissioner* [1972] AC 626
  Theft with the owner's consent

- *Low v Blease* (1975) 119 SJ 695
  Electricity not property

- *Oxford v Moss* (1978) 68 Cr App R 183
  Information not property

- *R v Allen* [1985] 2 All ER 641
  Intention to avoid payment under s3 Theft Act 1978

- *R* v *Ghosh* [1982] QB 1053
  Dishonesty at common law

- *R* v *Gomez* [1993] 1 All ER 1
  Theft with the owner's consent

- *R* v *Hinks* [2000] 4 All ER 833
  Theft with the owner's consent

- *R* v *Kelly* [1998] 3 All ER 741
  Theft of body parts

- *R* v *Lloyd and Ali* [1985] QB 829
  Theft and borrowing

- *R* v *McDavitt* [1981] Crim LR 843
  Nature of making off

- *R* v *Marshall*; *R* v *Coombes*; *R* v *Eren* [1998] 2 Cr App R 282
  Theft of property returned to P

- *R* v *Morris* [1983] 3 All ER 288
  Appropriation any assumption of any right of the owner

- *R* v *Turner (No 2)* [1971] 1 WLR 901
  D can steal his own property

- *R* v *Vincent* [2001] Crim LR 488
  Making off following deception

- *Williams* v *Phillips* (1957) 41 Cr App R 5
  Lost and abandoned property

- Theft Act 1968, s2 – dishonesty

- Theft Act 1968, s3 – appropriation

- Theft Act 1968, s4 – property

- Theft Act 1968, s5 – belonging to another

- Theft Act 1968, s6 – intention to permanently deprive

- Theft Act 1968, s13 – dishonestly abstracting electricity

- Theft Act 1978, s3 – making off without payment

## 6.4 Questions and suggested solutions

QUESTION ONE

E went into a store to see if they stocked Allbrand chocolates. He found a large variety of Allbrand chocolates. Seeing no one about, he put a bar of the chocolate into his pocket. On the way out of the store he realised that he might have been caught on camera and returned the bar of chocolate to the display. E found a tin of biscuits which had been underpriced. It was £4 cheaper than all the similar tins. He took it to the checkout where the assistant charged the marked price. Outside the store, E drove his car to the exit intending to use a foreign coin to operate the barrier. In fact, the mechanism was not working and E was waved through by an attendant. At the petrol station, E filled his car with petrol and went to pay, and, by mistake, the attendant asked for a lower sum than was required to be paid for the petrol.

Advise E of his criminal liability.

University of London LLB Examination<br>(for External Students) Criminal Law June 1998 Q2

### General Comment

A question that covers key aspects of theft and deception (deception is dealt with in Chapter 7). Every candidate should be prepared to tackle a question of this nature when attempting the criminal law examination. Care must be taken to consider theft and deception charges arising out of the same fact situation. Burglary also arises as a peripheral issue. Many points resolve around making off without payment. Note that the examiner may set problem questions where, in part at least, no liability arises. Candidates have to explain why there may be no liability.

### Skeleton Solution

Theft of the chocolate: returns the chocolate; makes no difference if he had mens rea – assume E is of age – any deception offence regarding the biscuits? – consider theft instead – overreaching all of this: if E commits theft has he also committed burglary in the store?

Use of the coin: consider deception offences – must operate on a human mind – making off without payment instead.

Petrol: theft is a problem – does he deceive anyone – consider making off as a residual offence.

### Suggested Solution

When E puts the bar of chocolate in his pocket he may have committed theft contrary to s1(1) of the Theft Act 1968. The chocolate is obviously property as defined by s4 and is property belonging to another (the store) as against E: see s5(1). By taking the chocolate and putting it in his pocket he undoubtedly appropriates it. According to s3(1) Theft Act 1968 any assumption by a person of the rights of an owner amounts to an appropriation. Lord Roskill in *R* v *Morris* [1983] 3 All ER 288 added that any assumption of any right of the owner amounted to an appropriation. Even if the owner consents there will be an appropriation: see *R* v *Gomez* [1993] 1 All ER 1. To be guilty of theft E will have to have mens rea. Was his appropriation dishonest? On the facts it clearly appears to be. Under s2(1) Theft Act 1968 he could escape liability if he could show that he appropriated the property in the belief that he had in law the right to deprive the other of it. There is no evidence to support this, or any belief that he thought the owner would consent. The only remaining issue could be age. There could be no liability if E was under the age of 10 at the time of the taking – but there is evidence here suggesting he is old enough to drive, hence the problem does not arise.

What of the fact that E returns the chocolate when he realises he might have been caught on camera? The prosecution must establish that he had intention to permanently deprive the owner of the chocolate and E will argue that his returning of the chocolate is evidence that he had no such intent. The key is to look at E's intention at the time of the appropriation. If at that time he intended to permanently deprive then theft will be made out. The fact that he subsequently changed his mind will only go to mitigation. Once all five elements of theft come together the offence is committed. The problem for the prosecution is an evidential one in establishing that he had intention to permanently deprive at the time of the taking.

The facts also throw up the possibility of burglary contrary to s9 of the 1968 Act. If E entered the store intending to steal he would have done so as a trespasser as he would have been entering the store for a purpose in excess of his implied permission to do so: see *R v Jones and Smith* [1976] 3 All ER 54. If he had the intention to steal, liability under s9(1)(a) of the 1968 Act could be made out. Indeed, if he entered as a trespasser and then stole the chocolate there could also be liability under s9(1)(b). No liability for burglary can arise if he entered as an honest shopper and then decided to steal the chocolate – he would not have entered the store as a trespasser.

Does he commit any offence in purchasing the biscuits for £4 less than the usual price? Consider first his liability when he selects the item. The biscuits at that stage are property belonging to another. Does E appropriate them by picking them up? This problem was considered by the Divisional Court in *Dip Kaur v Chief Constable for Hampshire* [1981] 1 WLR 578, where Lord Lane CJ held that there could be no theft until the defendant committed some act that only the owner would be allowed to perform, such as taking the shoes from the store. A few years later, however, the Lord Chief Justice was to change his views on this matter. When *Morris* (above) came before him in the Court of Appeal, he expressed the view that, on reflection, *Dip Kaur* (above) had been wrongly decided. It was (by then) his Lordship's view that the defendant had appropriated the shoes when she had selected them. In the House of Lords, Lord Roskill stated that he was disposed to agree with the learned Lord Chief Justice on this point. Assuming then that the selection of the biscuits could be an appropriation of property belonging to another everything at that stage would depend on mens rea. Intention to permanently deprive would be evident, leaving the issue of dishonesty. E would argue that he honestly believed he had the right in law to offer to buy the biscuits at the marked price (see s2(1)(a)) and hence was not dishonest. It is submitted that liability for theft at this stage would be difficult to make out. Most shoppers would try to but the biscuits at the lower price: see further *R v Ghosh* [1982] QB 1053 considered below.

Does E commit theft when he leaves the store with the biscuits? Again this matter was considered by the Divisional Court in *Dip Kaur* v *Chief Constable for Hampshire* (above). The Lord Chief Justice was of the view that by the time the shopper had paid for the underpriced item property in the goods had passed to the shopper. The transaction would have been vitiated by the cashier's mistake as to price, but in his Lordship's view the mistake could only render the contract voidable – hence when the shopper leaves the store he is leaving with goods that, for the time being, belong to him. Even if the store still retained some right or interest in the biscuits after the sale there would again be problems in establishing dishonesty on the part of E. Section 2(1)(a) would be relevant, see above.

As an alternative the prosecution might consider charging E with obtaining the biscuits by deception contrary to s15 of the 1968 Act, but it is hard to see how E makes any representation as to price that could be a deception. He does not underprice the goods.

An alternative charge could be making off without payment in respect of the biscuits – see s3 of the Theft Act 1978. E has not paid the correct price, but he will contend that he did pay as required and expected – he paid the marked price. In any event he will contend that in making off with the biscuits he was not dishonest. Dishonesty for these purposes would be determined by the jury following a *Ghosh* direction. The prosecution has to prove that the E was acting dishonestly according to the ordinary standards of reasonable and honest people, and that E realised that what he was doing was by those standards dishonest.

In leaving the car park without paying E may commit no offence. Not paying for his parking could be an offence of making off without payment contrary to s3 of the 1978 Act, but no offence will be committed if payment is not required or expected. The fact that the attendant was waving drivers through indicates that the right to claim payment was being waived. Had E used the foreign coin he would not have committed a deception offence as a deception must operate on a human mind: see *Davies* v *Flackett* (1972) 116 SJ 526. Hence, the most that E could be charged with is attempting to make off without payment by using the foreign coin. In theory the elements of the offence exist. Under s1(1) of the Criminal Attempts Act 1981 he takes steps more than merely preparatory to the commission of the offence and intends to commit the offence. The fact that is becomes impossible would be no bar to liability: see further ss1(2) and 1(3). In reality, unless E confesses, there would be no evidence upon which to base a prosecution.

When E puts the petrol in his petrol tank he appears to be honest and intending to pay. No liability arises in relation to deception offences at this stage. He does not exercise any deception to induce the cashier to charge the lower sum, hence no liability arises in respect of evading a liability contrary to s2(1) of the Theft Act 1978. When E drives away with the petrol in his petrol tank he cannot be charged with theft of the petrol because property in the petrol has passed to him. The only realistic charge is one of making off without payment under s3 of the Theft Act 1978. The prosecution will contend that E did not pay as required and expected. E will argue that he paid what he was asked to pay. Ultimately it will depend upon whether or not E is regarded as dishonest in not pointing out the mistake. The test for dishonesty will be as in *Ghosh* outlined above.

## QUESTION TWO

'Many of the Theft Act offences are now dangerously uncertain. Both dishonesty and appropriation have to be understandable to the ordinary man and should mean the same thing in all parts of England and Wales if there is to be a uniform standard of behaviour expected from everyone.'

Discuss.

University of London LLB Examination
(for External Students) Criminal Law June 1999 Q6

### General Comment

A question that offers an opportunity to range across a number of Theft Act offences. It should be noted that it is not only concerned with theft – the element of dishonesty is relevant to other offences such as burglary, deception and handling. The examiner is not looking for candidates to simply write all they know about dishonesty and appropriation. The points you make must be targeted at the inconsistencies and shortcomings of the law.

### Skeleton Solution

Explain appropriation – when does it occur? – how many times? – the role played by consent – the continuing uncertainty – appropriation where there is a valid transfer of property.

Dishonesty – concept explained – the negative definition – why any other concept needed – the problems with the *Ghosh* test – the danger of inconsistent verdicts.

### Suggested Solution

Section 1(1) of the Theft Act 1968 defines theft as occurring where a person dishonestly appropriates property belonging to another with the intention of permanently depriving the other of it. As the quotation suggests, the twin elements of appropriation and dishonesty have given rise to considerable debate and uncertainty since that definition became part of English law.

Appropriation is defined under s3(1) as any assumption by a person of the rights of an owner. The word was specifically chosen because it was thought to be easily intelligible for the average juror. Experience has shown that it has proved to be anything but that.

First, what assumption and what rights? A defendant obviously appropriates another's property when he takes it, sells it, destroys it, pledges it or gives it away. But what if he simply picks it up to look at it? Following the obiter dictum of Lord Roskill in *R v Morris* [1983] 3 All ER 288, it would appear that any assumption of any right of the owner could now amount to an appropriation. Hence an honest shopper selecting items in the supermarket commits the actus reus of theft – by picking an item up he appropriates it, and the item is property belonging to another. Whether or not he is guilty of theft depends entirely on proof of mens rea. It is doubtful that Parliament intended such a state of affairs when the 1968 Act was passed.

Second, there is the issue of whether or not a defendant can appropriate property even though the owner consents to his taking it. Common sense would suggest that this cannot be theft. If the owner really does give genuine informed consent why should the criminal law intervene? If the owner has been tricked into consenting the appropriate charge would be one of obtaining the property contrary to s15 of the 1968 Act.

The courts seem to think otherwise. In *R v Hinks* [2000] 4 All ER 833 the appellant befriended P, a 53-year-old man of limited intelligence. P had inherited money that was deposited in a building society account. Over a period of time the appellant persuaded P to transfer sums totalling £60,000 from the building society account to her own account. She was charged with theft of this money and made a submission of 'no case' on the basis that the sums involved had been gifts from P and hence could not be the subject of a theft charge. The submission was rejected and the appellant convicted. Her appeal was dismissed. The House of Lords held that a defendant could appropriate property notwithstanding that the donor consented to his receiving it, and notwithstanding the fact that the transfer took the form of a valid gift. Belief that the owner consented to the transfer might be relevant to dishonesty, but had no bearing on appropriation. The decision is alarming as it means that D can be guilty of theft in circumstances where, as regards civil law, he is the lawful owner of the property because he is the recipient of a valid gift.

Even where the owner is tricked into consenting the House of Lords is still insistent that theft can be charged on the basis that there can be an appropriation despite the fact that the owner consents. This approach first emerged in *Lawrence v Metropolitan Police Commissioner* [1972] AC 626, and has since been re-affirmed in *R v Gomez* [1993] 1 All ER 1, Lord Keith expressing the view that consent to or authorisation by the owner of the taking by D is irrelevant, and he accepts that there is an overlap with s15(1) of the Act.

The result is that every case of obtaining property by deception could, instead be charged as theft. The owner's apparent consent being no obstacle to the establishment of an appropriation. Given that s15 carries a higher maximum term of imprisonment than s1(1) theft, this is a strange state of affairs.

Third, there is still uncertainty over the issue of when an appropriation occurs, how long it lasts for, and how many times D can appropriate property. Suppose D steals P's silver teapot. He clearly appropriates it when he first takes it. If he bumps into P as he is walking home with it is he still appropriating it? If he is, and he uses force to exclude P from the property, does D commit robbery? If so is this robbery in addition to the original theft or does it replace it? If D takes the teapot home and uses it every day for a week to make a pot of tea does he commit a fresh theft every day? In *R v Atakpu* [1993] 3 WLR 812 Ward J attempted to clarify the matter by explaining that theft can occur in an instant by a single appropriation but it can also involve a course of dealing with property lasting longer and involving several appropriations before the transaction is complete. At what point the transaction is complete is a matter for the jury to decide upon the facts of each case. Hence, the result could vary from one jury to another. It would appear to be the case, however, that the successive use of the teapot would not amount to successive instances of theft. As he further observed no case suggests that there can be successive thefts of the same property, assuming of course that possession is constant and not lost or abandoned, later to be assumed again.

The issue of dishonesty has also thrown up a number of problems. Where the charge is one of theft, the first point to consider in relation to dishonesty is the 'negative' definition provided by s2(1) of the Theft Act 1968. This provides for three situations where D's appropriation of property belonging to another is not to be regarded as dishonest. First, where D appropriates the property in the belief that he has in law the right to deprive the other of it. Second, where D appropriates the property in the belief that he would have the other's consent if the other knew of the appropriation and the circumstances of it. Third, where D appropriates the property in the belief that the person to whom the property belongs cannot be discovered by taking reasonable steps.

Section 2(2) adds, for the avoidance of doubt, that D's appropriation of property belonging to another may be dishonest notwithstanding that he is willing to pay for the property.

It might well be asked, if a defendant cannot bring himself within the scope of one of the three negative definitions, why should the court have any discretion to find that he has not been dishonest. The answer, presumably, is that there might still be cases where, despite the absence of a s2(1) escape route, the jury would still be reluctant to convict D – perhaps because, viewed in the round, they still do not regard his actions as dishonest. That might explain why such a defendant might still benefit from a 'Ghosh' direct, as explained below.

If a defendant is charged with any other Theft Act offence (other than theft) requiring proof of dishonesty, s2(1) of the 1968 Act has no application. The courts will fall back on the common law concept of dishonesty as currently embodied in the case of *R v Ghosh* [1982] QB 1053. The jury would be directed to consider whether D's conduct was dishonest according to the ordinary standards of reasonable and honest people. If the answer is affirmative, the second question for the jury is to consider whether or not D realised his actions were dishonest by those standards.

The direction is an attempt to avoid fixing on any definition of dishonesty, in favour of an instruction to the jury as to how they should arrive at their conclusion. It seeks to carve a path between the subjective approach whereby D would only be dishonest if he thought he was dishonest – clearly unworkable in practice – and the objective approach based solely on the views of the reasonable person – which could result in injustice. The problems arise where D insists that he thought he was doing the right thing. The direction attempts to head this off by adding that it is dishonest for D to act in a way which he knows ordinary people consider to be dishonest, even if he asserts or genuinely believes that he is morally justified in acting as he did. Examples are given of Robin Hood or ardent anti-vivisectionists who remove animals from vivisection laboratories. The Court of Appeal seems to believe that such people are acting dishonestly, even though they may consider themselves to be morally justified in doing what they do, because they know that ordinary people would consider these actions to be dishonest. It does not deal with D who is so committed to his cause he cannot believe that others would think he was wrong. Also, what would the courts make of a defendant who claimed that he had given no though to what ordinary people might have thought of his actions?

Beyond these criticisms the overriding problem with the common law approach to dishonesty is that it leaves virtually total discretion in the hand of the jury – hence D who takes £50 from his employer's cash register on Monday leaving an IOU may be regarded as dishonest by one jury, but on the same facts be acquitted by another. It turns justice into something of a lottery.

## QUESTION THREE

Evan, aged 13 years, was a compulsive thief. He would frequently return the items later when his conduct was brought to his attention by his parents. From Fred's shop he removed a chocolate bar which later he gave to his friend, Gareth, at school. Fred never ate chocolate. From Harry's store he took his mother's favourite perfume which he put on her dressing table. When she realised what had happened she made Evan take it back to the shop. From Harry's garage Evan took some flowers returning them some four days later when they began to fade. From Ian's house he took some cigarettes. Ian knew that Evan did this but he had made an arrangement with Evan's mother that he would not stop Evan and she would pay for them each week. Gareth threatened Evan that if he did not regularly bring him chocolate he would tell their fellow pupils that he was a homosexual. Gareth knew this was not true. Evan continued taking chocolate from various shops and handing it over to Gareth because he was afraid of what Gareth might say.

Advise the parties about their criminal liability, if any.

University of London LLB Examination<br>(for External Students) Criminal Law June 1997 Q3

### General Comment

A rather straightforward question on a range of offences of dishonesty and defences, the only difficulty being the reference to the fact that the owner of the shop from which the bar of chocolate was stolen never ate chocolate, the relevance of which seems obscure.

### Skeleton Solution

Evan: theft of the chocolate, perfume and flowers – Gareth: incitement to commit theft, blackmail – Evan: defences of infancy and duress.

### Suggested Solution

When Evan took the bar of chocolate from Fred's shop he would have committed theft contrary to s1 Theft Act (TA) 1968. He has clearly appropriated the bar by assuming the owner's right of possession contrary to s3 of the 1968 Act. He is almost certainly dishonest in not paying for the bar and, by giving the bar to Gareth, would appear to intend to permanently deprive Fred of the bar.

Evan has appropriated the perfume which he removed from Harry's store, assuming the owner's rights of possession. It is irrelevant that none of the perfume appears to have been used before it is returned to the store since it was held in *R v Morris* [1984] AC 320 that an appropriation under s3 TA 1968 occurs when any of the owner's rights are assumed, it being unnecessary for the prosecution to demonstrate that all of the owner's rights have been assumed. The fact that Evan eventually returned the perfume at the insistence of his mother is irrelevant as the prosecution needs only to prove that the accused intended to permanently deprive the owner of his property at the time of the appropriation.

With respect to the flowers, the question does not state whether Evan took flowers which Harry's garage had purchased or which were growing on land owned by the garage. If the former is the case then the flowers would clearly constitute the property of Harry's garage (under s4 TA 1968) which Evan has appropriated. However, s4 excludes from the definition of property flowers growing wild on any land. Consequently Evan would not have committed theft if he took such wild flowers. Since Evan returned the flowers four days later it would appear (assuming that he had this intention to return them when he took them) that an essential element in the definition of theft is missing – the intention to permanently deprive. However, it should be noted that under s6(1) TA 1968, an intention to treat the thing taken as one's own regardless of the owner's rights may be equivalent to an intention to permanently deprive if the taking is equivalent to an outright taking or disposal. The traditional analysis of s6(1) is that an accused may be said to have an intention equivalent to an intention to permanently deprive if, but only if, the thing taken is physically returned in circumstances in which its value or usefulness has been exhausted: see for example *R v Lloyd* [1985] QB 829 and *R v Warner* (1970) 55 Cr App R 93. Since the flowers have only begun to fade it is arguable whether their value has been completely exhausted. However, in *DPP v Lavender* [1994] Crim LR 297 the Court of Appeal seemed to have adopted a wider interpretation of s6(1), holding that the accused – who moved a door from one flat to another flat owned by the same council – had an intention to permanently deprive the council of the door since he treated the door as his own regardless of the council's rights. If this interpretation is followed, Evan could be convicted of theft of the flowers, although it should be remembered that this interpretation may be in conflict with *Lloyd* and *Warner* (above).

The fact that Evan's mother pays Ian for the cigarettes which Evan takes from Ian will not in itself provide Evan with a defence since the issue is not whether the goods are paid for, but whether the accused was dishonest at the time he took them. Whether Evan was dishonest will be determined by the test laid down in *R v Ghosh* [1982] QB 1053. The primary test in *Ghosh* is objective, ie whether ordinary and decent people would regard what Evan has done as dishonest. It is submitted that most people would regard the taking of Ian's cigarettes as dishonest. However, there is also a subjective element to the *Ghosh* test.The accused must be aware that his conduct would be regarded as dishonest by the standards of the reasonable person. If Evan has been taking cigarettes from Ian for some time without Ian's objection, (because Evan's mother is secretly paying Ian for the cigarettes), Evan may believe that his conduct is acceptable and not know that his conduct is dishonest by the standards of ordinary people.

When Gareth demanded that Evan steal chocolate bars for him he incited Evan to commit theft contrary to the definition of incitement contained in *Race Relations Board v Applin* [1973] QB 815 which is to advise, encourage, persuade or threaten another to commit a crime. If Evan carries out the theft because of Gareth's threats, Gareth may also become an accessory to Evan's theft under s8 Accessories and Abettors Act 1861.

By threatening to expose Evan as a homosexual (which he knows to be untrue), Gareth has made an unwarranted demand with menaces and consequently may be charged with blackmail contrary to s21 TA 1968. However, it may be arguable whether, in the light of public acceptance of homosexuality, a threat to expose one as an (alleged) homosexual would be a threat which might cause a sober person of reasonable firmness to accede to the demand: see *Thorne v Motor Trade Association* [1937] AC 797. On the other hand, it should be remembered that characteristics of the victim which make him more susceptible to the threat may be taken into consideration (see *R v Clear* [1968] 1 QB 670), therefore the fact that Evan is only 13 years old will be taken into consideration.

It is unlikely that the threat to expose Evan's 'homosexuality' would entitle Evan to raise the defence of duress since this defence requires the accused to act because of a threat of 'death or serious personal injury' (*R v Graham* (1982) 74 Cr App R 235) and a threat to expose one's real or perceived 'immoral' behaviour is insufficient: *R v Valderrama-Vega* [1985] Crim LR 220.

Since Evan is over the age of ten there is no defence of infancy available to him: see s34 Crime and Disorder Act 1998.

## QUESTION FOUR

L went into M's supermarket to see if his favourite sweets, 'Grinders', were in stock. He thought that if he could take them without paying he would do so. When he arrived at the sweet counter there were no 'Grinders' left. Next, L went to the meat counter and was supplied with 250 grammes of cooked meat which, in error, the assistant underpriced. L decided to buy jam. He checked the prices marked on the various pots of jam and realised that one was marked with a very low price. L assuming that this pot was 'old stock' removed it together with a pot at the full price.

He put the cooked meat and two pots of jam in front of the cashier at the checkout. He then saw that the meat had been underpriced. The cashier rang up the indicated price and, in addition, rang up the price of the two pots of jam at the lower price. L said nothing though he saw what had happened. By mistake the cashier gave L £5.00 too much change which L put in his pocket. He was apprehended by a detective outside the store.

Advise L of his criminal liability.

University of London LLB Examination
(for External Students) Criminal Law June 1996 Q4

### General Comment

A question which would immediately have attracted those candidates who had revised theft and deception well, although the nature of the deception is a somewhat tricky issue.

### Skeleton Solution

Attempted theft of sweets (impossibility; burglary; obtaining property by deception) – theft of the meat and pots of jam – theft of £5.00 excess change.

### Suggested Solution

When L went into the supermarket intending to take 'Grinders' sweets without paying for them he may have committed attempted theft contrary to s1 Criminal Attempts Act (CAA) 1981. This act must be 'more than merely preparatory' towards the commission of the offence, which means that he must have gone beyond the preparatory stages and 'embarked on the crime proper': *R v Gullefer* [1987] Crim LR 195. By entering the shop and approaching the counter L has, arguably, done an act which is more than merely preparatory. He has the mens rea for the offence in that he clearly intends to steal the sweets. The fact that there are no 'Grinders' sweets in the shop will not be a defence since the defence of impossibility was removed by s1(2) CAA 1981, as confirmed by *R v Shivpuri* [1987] AC 1.

Since L entered a building intending to steal he could in theory be charged with burglary contrary to s9(1)(a) Theft Act (TA) 1968. The problem is that it would appear he is not a trespasser since the public has implied permission to enter a shop. However, in *R v Jones; R v Smith* [1976] 3 All ER 54 it was held that a person who enters a building intending to steal exceeds the scope of their permission to enter for lawful purposes and will therefore be a trespasser.

An interesting question is whether L could be convicted of obtaining property by deception by failing to tell the cashier that the latter rung up the wrong price. It would appear not to be a deception merely to take advantage of another's mistake (*Smith v Hughes* (1871) LR 6 QB 597) providing one does nothing to encourage the mistake or conceal the truth. Although the cashier may have been confused by the fact that L put two pots of jam down – one priced at the correct amount and one incorrectly priced – it is clear that L did so because he thought one pot was 'old stock' and did not do so with an intention of concealing the shop's mistake. Following a similar argument it is difficult to see how L could be said to have 'deceived' the shop into selling the meat at a lower price; although he was aware of their mistake he did nothing to encourage it or conceal the truth.

An alternative charge in relation to the meat and pots of jam would be theft contrary to s1 TA 1968 which does not require a deception. Although L took the meat and jam with the supermarket's consent, it is now established law that theft can be committed by dishonestly appropriating property with or without the owner's consent: see *R v Gomez* [1992] 3 WLR 1067. This of course begs the question as to whether it is dishonest to take advantage of a shop's mistake. L may be able to take advantage of s2(1)(a) TA 1968 which provides that a person cannot be dishonest if he believed he had the right to deprive the other of the property. If L believed he had the right to buy the goods at the lower price he cannot be convicted of theft even if his belief is wrong or unreasonable: *R v Bernard* [1938] 2 KB 264. Even if he did not have this belief, the prosecution can only secure a conviction if it could prove that he was dishonest under the test laid down in *R v Ghosh* [1982] QB 1053, which requires that reasonable people would regard the accused's act as dishonest and that the accused knew it would be so regarded. It is debatable whether reasonable people would regard taking advantage of a shop's mistake as dishonest and, even if they would, whether L knew that reasonable people would so regard his act.

Could L be convicted of the theft of the £5.00 excess charge? The essential problem here is that ownership passes to the person who receives property even if that property is given by mistake (*Moynes v Cooper* [1956] 1 QB 439), so that when L formed the (arguably) dishonest intent to keep the money after he had been given it, the property already belonged to him. A person cannot be convicted of dishonestly appropriating his own property! However, s5(4) TA 1968 provides that where a person receives property by another's mistake and is under an obligation to return it, for the purposes of a charge of theft it will be regarded as belonging to the person who gave it by mistake. Following the *Attorney-General's Reference (No 1 of 1983)* [1985] QB 182 it is likely that L is under an obligation to return the excess change in civil law and therefore that under s5(4) ownership of the money remains with the supermarket. The next issue is whether L is dishonest in keeping the excess change. It is unclear whether L is aware that he has been given excess change – if he is unaware than he clearly cannot be dishonest. If he is so aware, he may still be able to raise the (defence) under s2(1)(a) TA 1968 that he believed he had the right to keep the money. Alternatively, whether he is dishonest will be determined according to the *Ghosh* test outlined above. This would depend on whether reasonable people would regard failing to return excess change as dishonest.

QUESTION FIVE

C was in D's self service store.

a) She decided to help herself to a tin of salmon which she put in her coat pocket, but whilst in the check-out queue she decided to pay for the salmon and placed it in her basket before doing so.

b) C received excess change from the checkout girl. She put it in her pocket without examining it. She discovered the excess only when she was at home.

c) C decided to take out life assurance on her son and in two proposal forms she described her son as a non-smoker. This C knew to be incorrect. From company X, C obtained additional cover and from company Y a reduced premium because her son was thought to be a non-smoker.

Advise C about her criminal liability.

University of London LLB Examination
(for External Students) Criminal Law June 1986 Q2

*General Comment*

A question with three distinct and separate parts but all concerned with particular aspects of property offences. Parts (a) and (b) were straightforward. Part (a) in particular could have been anticipated in view of recent case law. Part (c) was not without its difficulties and a careful approach was required in order to deal with the two policies in their different ways.

*Skeleton Solution*

a) Section 1 Theft Act 1968 – s3 Theft Act 1968 – *R v Morris*: appropriation – *R v Ghosh*.

b) Section 1 Theft Act 1968: later appropriation – ss5(1) and 5(4) Theft Act 1968.

c) Sections 16(1) and 16(2) Theft Act 1968 – s15(4) Theft Act 1968 – operative deception.

*Suggested Solution*

a) Section 1 Theft Act 1968 provides that 'a person is guilty of theft if he dishonestly appropriates property belonging to another with the intention of permanently depriving the other of it'.

The question to be decided on the facts as given is whether the offence of theft is satisfied or whether there is merely an attempted theft.

The main issue here is whether, by putting the tin of salmon in her coat pocket, C has appropriated the tin as defined in s3 of the 1968 Act. If she has appropriated the tin she may be guilty of theft if all the other ingredients of the offence are established. If there has been no appropriation she may only be guilty of attempted theft. Section 3 defines an appropriation as 'any assumption by a person of the rights of an owner'. In *Lawrence* v *Metropolitan Police Commissioner* [1972] AC 626 the House of Lords held that an appropriation can occur even if the property has been taken with the owner's consent. However, the House of Lords in *R* v *Morris* [1984] AC 320 had thrown the issue into some doubt by stating, obiter, that an appropriation can only take place if the property has been taken without the owner's consent. The issue has now been settled by the House of Lords in *R* v *Gomez* [1992] 3 WLR 1067 where it was held that Lawrence was correct and the absence of consent is not a prerequisite for appropriation. The act of putting the tin of salmon in a coat pocket is of course without the shop's consent and consequently an appropriation would have taken place before or after *Gomez*.

It is submitted that an appropriation took place when C put the tin of salmon in her pocket and all the other ingredients of theft were also present at this time; she was dishonest according to the definition in *R* v *Ghosh* [1982] QB 1053 and intended to permanently deprive the shop of the item. The fact that she subsequently changed her mind is irrelevant as the offence is constituted once all the ingredients are present.

b)  When C receives excess change from the checkout girl no offence is shown when she put it in her pocket because at that stage she has no mens rea. Later when she discovers the excess she may be liable for the offence of theft as defined above.

Section 3 of the Theft Act 1968 which defines appropriation as any assumption of the rights of an owner further provides that there can be an appropriation where a person has come by the property (innocently or not) without stealing it, any later assumption of a right to it by keeping and dealing with it as owner can amount to an appropriation. On the facts in question C had appropriated by keeping the money.

The next point to consider is whether the money 'belongs to another' for the purposes of s1 Theft Act 1968.

Section 5(1) provides that property shall be regarded as belonging to any person having possession or control of it or having in it any proprietary right or interest (other than certain equitable interests).

Section 5(4) further provides that where a person gets property by another's mistake, and is under an obligation to make restoration (in whole or in part) then to the extent of that obligation the property shall be regarded as belonging to another, and an intention not to make restoration shall be regarded as an intention to deprive that person of the property.

If ownership of the money remains in someone other than C it is not necessary to rely on s4(4), s5(1) would be appropriate. However if ownership has passed to C then s5(4) will apply but only if the 'obligation to make restoration' is a legal obligation: *R v Gilks* [1972] 3 All ER 280.

The last point that requires brief consideration is that of dishonesty. Usually it is for the jury to decide whether a person is or is not dishonest (*R v Feely* [1973] 1 QB 530) applying where necessary the test as stated in *R v Ghosh*. However s2 Theft Act 1968 lists three instances where a jury must acquit. The only one that might be available on the facts in question would be if C believed she had the right in law to keep the property. If this were the case the jury must find that she was not dishonest however unreasonable the belief was.

c) Section 16(1) Theft Act 1968 provides that a person who by any deception dishonestly obtains for himself or another any pecuniary advantage shall commit an offence. Section 16(2) details the type of pecuniary advantages within s16(1) and provides (inter alia) that a pecuniary advantage within the meaning of the section shall be regarded as being obtained for a person where he is allowed to take out any policy of insurances or annuity contract or obtains an improvement of the terms on which he is allowed to do so. This particular aspect of s16(2) would appear to cover exactly the situation where C obtains insurance cover with a reduced premium from company Y but it is less clear whether the additional cover obtained from company X would be within s16(2) as the section appears to apply only where the cover is being taken out and not where it already exists.

In any event it must be remembered that it is still necessary to show that there was a deception which was the effective cause of the obtaining of the pecuniary advantage. Section 15(4) of the Theft Act 1968 defines a 'deception' as any deception (whether deliberate or reckless) by words or conduct as to fact or as to law, including a deception as to the present intentions of the person using the deception or any other person. The false statements in the proposal forms would come within s15(4) and certainly in the case of company Y the deception is the operative reason for the reduced premium being allowed.

There seems little doubt on the facts as given that C is dishonest although, as stated previously it is always for the jury to decide.

# Chapter 7

# Deception and Related Offences

7.1     **Introduction**

7.2     **Key points**

7.3     **Key cases and statutes**

7.4     **Questions and suggested solutions**

## 7.1 Introduction

Although theft and deception are closely related issues, and it is rare to get a question that concentrates solely on one area or the other, it is sensible to consider a range of questions which perhaps lean more heavily towards the deception range of offences. The interrelationship between the s15 and s16 deception offences, and those under s2 of the Theft Act 1978, is particularly to be noted here.

## 7.2 Key points

### Obtaining property by deception

a) Deception

Section 15(4) of the 1968 Act states that a deception may be as to fact, law or intention, by conduct or words and must be made deliberately or recklessly. On conduct and intention see: *DPP* v *Ray* [1974] AC 370.

b) Obtaining (s15(2) Theft Act 1968)

The deception must precede and cause the obtaining (*R* v *Collis-Smith* [1971] Crim LR 716) and influence the victim: *R* v *Hensler* (1870) 22 LT 691; *R* v *Rashid* [1977] 1 WLR 298.

The presentation of a cheque or credit card carries with it an implied representation that the user has authority to use the card or cheque and is therefore within their overdraft or credit limit: *Metropolitan Police Commissioner* v *Charles* [1977] Crim LR 615; *R* v *Lambie* [1981] 1 All ER 332.

c) Following *R* v *Gomez* (see Chapter 6) a charge under s15 may also give rise to a charge of theft under s1.

d) With respect to obtaining services by deception contrary to s1 of the Theft Act 1978 deception has the same meaning as described above.

e) The definition of dishonesty laid down in *R* v *Ghosh* (see Chapter 6) applies to all the deception offences but the s2(1) Theft Act 1968 excluded categories do not.

## Obtaining a pecuniary advantage by deception (s16 Theft Act 1968)

This offence can only be committed in one of five specified ways and a student should always point out which of these applies when answering a question. The five ways are where the accused obtains (or obtains better terms for) an overdraft insurance policy, annuity contract, employment or bet.

Note that the use of a cheque where there is insufficient funds in the account to meet the cheque may cause the account to go into overdraft and therefore constitute this offence (*R* v *Waites* [1982] Crim LR 369), although this is of course subject to a dishonest intention not to repay the overdraft.

### Obtaining a service by deception

This offence is created by s1(1) of the Theft Act 1978 which provides: 'A person who by any deception dishonestly obtains services from another shall be guilty of an offence.' A service is a benefit provided on the understanding that the benefit has been or will be paid for – hence gratuitous services are not protected by the Act: see *R* v *Atwal* [1989] Crim LR 293 and *R* v *Shortland* [1995] Crim LR 893

### Evasion of liability by deception

There are three separate offences under s2(1) of the Theft Act 1978:

a) Section 2(1)(a)

Securing the remission of a debt by deception (ie where a debtor deceives a creditor into letting the latter off the debt). Note that in *R* v *Jackson* [1983] Crim LR 617 it was held that the use of a stolen credit card would constitute this offence since the creditor (eg a shop) would look to the credit card company for payment rather than the user of the card.

b) Section 2(1)(b)

By deception, persuading a creditor to wait for payment – however it is important to note that the accused will not be guilty despite a deception unless he intends to permanently avoid payment. Note that inducing someone to accept a cheque may also create this offence: s2(3) Theft Act 1978; *R* v *Andrews and Hedges* [1981] Crim LR 106.

c) Section 2(1)(c)

The dishonest obtaining of an exemption from liability: see *R* v *Sibartie* [1983] Crim LR 470. Note that this can cover future liabilities.

## 7.3 Key cases and statutes

- *Davies* v *Flackett* (1972) 116 SJ 526
  Human mind must be deceived

- *DPP* v *Ray* [1974] AC 370
  Omission as deception

- *Metropolitan Police Commissioner* v *Charles* [1976] 1 All ER 659
  Overdraft by deception

- *R* v *Atwal* [1989] Crim LR 293
  Gratuitous services not covered

- *R* v *Barnard* (1837) 7 C & P 784
  Conduct as deception

- *R* v *Callender* [1992] 3 All ER 51
  Work obtained by deception

- *R* v *Doukas* [1978] 1 WLR 372
  Proving an operative deception

- *R* v *Ghosh* [1982] QB 1053
  Dishonesty in deception offences

- *R* v *Holt and Lee* [1981] 2 All ER 854
  Inducing a creditor to forgo payment

- *R* v *Jackson* [1983] Crim LR 617
  Securing remission of a liability by deception

- *R* v *Rai* [2000] 1 Cr App R 242
  Silence as deception

- *R* v *Sibartie* [1983] Crim LR 470
  Future liabilities covered by s2(1)(c) Theft Act 1978 offence

- *R* v *Silverman* [1987] Crim LR 574
  Opinion as deception

- Theft Act 1968, s15 – obtaining property by deception

- Theft Act 1968, s16(1) – obtaining a pecuniary advantage by deception

- Theft Act 1978, s1(1) – obtaining services by deception

- Theft Act 1978, s2(1) – evasion of a liability by deception

## 7.4 Questions and suggested solutions

### QUESTION ONE

Paul, aged 17 years, had run away from home where for years he had been subjected to mental cruelty by his stepmother. During an exceptionally cold winter he sneaked on to a train without paying and arrived in London hoping to find fame and fortune. He went to the social security office, which in compliance with the benefit regulations, refused to give him any money and advised him to return home. Next he went to a night shelter but there were no beds. Paul slept for three nights on the streets begging for money to eat. Quin, a fellow street dweller, introduced Paul to alcohol and Paul would often be drunk for days at a time, spending on drink all the money he had obtained as a result of begging. Finally, in desperation Paul went to the local police station to ask for help or a night in the cells so that he could sleep in the warm because he was freezing. This was refused. Paul spent another two days on the freezing street before going to the police station again and punching the desk sergeant in the face. He was arrested but the detention officer had decided to grant him bail when Paul refused to leave. Paul said, 'I will punch a policeman till I am kept in here out of this freezing weather.' The next day, Paul made similar threats to the magistrates but they refused to remand him in custody. Outside the magistrates' court, Paul punched the chairman of the bench and was arrested. On his arrest Paul was found to be severely malnourished.

Advise the parties about their criminal liability, if any.

University of London LLB Examination
(for External Students) Criminal Law June 1997 Q6

### General Comment

A difficult question in that it involves a wide range of offences ranging from non-fatal offences against the person, public order offences and even contempt of court. Candidates may find it difficult in some parts of the question to identify the point of some of the facts given.

### Skeleton Solution

Paul: obtaining services by deception – obtaining property by deception – necessity – making threats – contempt of court – non-fatal offences against the person.

### Suggested Solution

By travelling on the train to London without paying the fare, Paul has obtained a service by deception contrary to s1 Theft Act (TA) 1978. Travel by train would clearly fall within the definition of a service contained in s1(2) TA 1978 as the conferment of a benefit. Although Paul has not overtly lied to anyone, the definition of a deception contained in s15(4) TA 1968 includes a deception as to fact or one's present intentions. In boarding the train Paul will impliedly have represented that he has or is going to pay for the journey: *DPP* v *Ray* [1974] AC 370. The prosecution would have to prove that Paul was dishonest within the definition laid down in *R* v *Ghosh* [1982] QB 1053. The first limb of the *Ghosh* test is clearly met in that it is likely that ordinary and honest people would regard travelling on a train without paying the fare as dishonest. However, under the second limb of the *Ghosh* test Paul may argue that he believed that ordinary people would not regard his actions as being dishonest in the circumstances because he acted to avoid emotional abuse from his stepmother.

When Paul begged for 'money to eat', which he actually spent on purchasing alcohol, he has committed obtaining property by deception contrary to s15 TA 1968. Since s15(4) TA 1968 expressly states that a false representation as to one's intention may amount to a deception, Paul's representation that he wants the money to eat may constitute an actionable deception. However, the deception must cause the obtaining: see *R* v *Rashid* [1977] 1 WLR 298 and *R* v *Doukas* [1978] 1 WLR 372. It could be argued that people often give money to vagrants in the knowledge that it will or may be spent on alcohol and that Paul's deception as to what he was going to spend the money on had no effect on their decision to give money to him.

By punching the desk sergeant in the face, Paul has clearly committed an assault (defined as where the accused intentionally or recklessly causes the victim to apprehend immediate personal violence: *Fagan* v *Metropolitan Police Commissioner* [1969] 1 QB 439 and a battery (defined in Fagan as the intentional application of force to the body of another without the other's consent). If the punch has caused an injury which is 'more than trivial' (see *R* v *Chan Fook* [1994] 1 WLR 689) Paul may be guilty of an assault occasioning actual bodily harm contrary to s47 Offences Against the Person Act 1861.

Since the sergeant appears to have been acting in the course of his duty, Paul may be charged with assaulting a police officer in the execution of his duty contrary to s51 Police Act 1964.

By threatening to punch the magistrates, Paul will have committed an offence under s4 Public Order Act 1986 of threatening behaviour towards another person intending that other person to believe that immediate unlawful violence will be used against him. Any assaults on or threats to court staff in court will also constitute a contempt in the face of the court: see *Balogh* v *St Albans Crown Court* [1975] QB 73.

Punching the chairman of the magistrates outside the magistrates' court will constitute an assault and battery as defined above and actual bodily harm, if any injury was caused.

Paul may attempt to raise necessity as a defence to these charges. In *R* v *Pommell* [1995] 2 Cr App R 607 the courts recognised necessity as a complete defence to any charge except murder or attempted murder. The defence is available if the accused acted in order to prevent death or serious personal harm to himself or another, providing his response was reasonable and proportionate with the harm he was trying to avoid. In *R* v *Baker and Wilkins* [1997] Crim LR 497 it was held that the defence could only be used where the accused acted in order to prevent death or serious physical, not emotional or psychological, harm to himself or another. Consequently, Paul could not argue that he acted out of necessity to avoid the mental cruelty of his stepmother. Although he could in theory raise the defence on the basis that he acted to avoid freezing to death and starvation, it would be difficult to show that it was reasonable and proportionate to punch a policeman and a magistrate. It would also be difficult for Paul to raise the defence of necessity to the charge of obtaining money by deception because of his begging, since the product of his begging was spent on alcohol rather than food.

## QUESTION TWO

Stephen was an antique dealer who used to earn a living by calling at people's doors and buying antiques which Stephen later sold. Stephen called at Una's house and bought a rare jug for £80 though it was, as Stephen knew, worth £800. Inside Una's house there were many valuable things but Una refused to sell Stephen anything else. Stephen told Tom, a friend, about the contents of the house and Tom told Vic. Unknown to Stephen and Tom, Vic had convictions for burglary. Vic broke into Una's house and was in the process of looking round when he was disturbed by Una's son, WIlliam, who was a professional boxer. William struck Vic breaking Vic's jaw.

Stephen persuaded Xeries to let him have possession of an oil painting which Stephen was to take to have professionally valued. In fact, Stephen did not take it to be valued but, instead, merely told Xeries that it had been valued at £300. As a result Xeries agreed to sell it to Stephen for £480. In fact, it was worth only £200.

Advise the parties of their criminal liability.

University of London LLB Examination<br>(for External Students) Criminal Law June 1997 Q7

### General Comment

A question involving some straightforward points on offences against the person, burglary and self-defence but some rather difficult issues involving deception.

### Skeleton Solution

Obtaining property by deception – burglary – attempted theft – accessorial liability – non-fatal offences against the person – self defence.

### Suggested Solution

By purchasing the jug for £80 knowing that it is worth £800 it is debatable whether Stephen is guilty of obtaining property by deception contrary to s15 Theft Act 1968. The first problem the prosecution will encounter is to prove that Stephen deceived Una. In *R v King* [1979] Crim LR 122 it was established that a false representation as to one's belief may constitute a deception. If Stephen expressly told Una that the jug is worth approximately £80 knowing this to be false, he will have committed an actionable deception. A more problematic situation would arise, however, if Stephen purchased the jug from Una merely knowing that Una mistakenly believed that £80 was the approximate value of the jug and did nothing to correct her misapprehension. It is established law that in commercial transactions a party is under no obligation to correct another party misapprehensions: in *Smith* v *Hughes* (1871) LR 6 QB 597 it was said that 'the passive acquiescence of the seller in the self deception of the buyer does not entitle the buyer to avoid the contract'. If no such duty exists in civil law, it is unlikely that such silence would constitute a deception in criminal law. However, it is possible that Stephen's purchase of the jug may fall under the principle in *R* v *Silverman* [1987] Crim LR 574. In *Silverman* it was held that a price quote may contain an implied representation that it fair and reasonable if there is a relationship of mutual trust between the parties, if one party relied on the other's fair and reasonable conduct and the price quoted was dishonestly excessive. It is doubtful whether there is a relationship of mutual trust between a seller and someone who has called at their house to buy goods (although such a relationship may exist if there has a previous course of dealings between Una and Stephen, which is not clear from the facts). In the unlikely event that a relationship of trust is held to exist between Una and Stephen it is likely that a mark up of 800 per cent would be excessive. However, it would also have to be established that Stephen has acted dishonestly within the definition laid down in *R* v *Ghosh* [1982] QB 1053. This would depend on whether reasonable and honest people would regard overcharging by this amount as dishonest. It could be argued this was a commercial transaction which should be governed by the principle of laissez faire.

When Vic broke into Una's house he will have committed a burglary contrary to s9(1)(a) Theft Act 1968. It is irrelevant that nothing has actually been stolen since this offence is committed when the accused enters premises as a trespasser intending to steal – which Vic clearly has.

It is unlikely that Stephen and Tom could be convicted as accessories (contrary to s8 Accessories and Abettors Act 1861) to the burglary committed by Vic. Although Stephen and Tom have assisted Vic by providing him with information, they would appear to lack the mens rea for this offence. In *R* v *Bainbridge* [1959] 3 WLR 356 it was established that a person accused of being an accessory must know that the principle offender may act on his advice and commit an offence. This does not appear to be the case here.

By breaking Vic's jaw, William has prima facie committed an assault and battery. He has clearly caused Vic to apprehend immediate personal violence and has intentionally applied unlawful force to Vic's body without Vic's consent: *Fagan* v *Metropolitan Police Commissioner* [1969] 1 QB 439.

A fractured jaw would almost certainly constitute an injury which is 'more than trivial' (see *R* v *Chan Fook* [1994] 1 WLR 689) and William has also therefore committed the actus reus of an assault occasioning actual bodily harm contrary to s47 Offences Against the Person Act (OAPA) 1861. Since no mens rea is required as to the harm caused (*R v Savage*; *R v Parmenter* [1991] 3 WLR 914) William will have the mens rea of this offence even if he did not intend to break Vic's jaw.

William may also committed the actus reus of the offences under ss18 and 20 OAPA 1861. However, the actus reus of these offences requires the prosecution to prove that the injury sustained by the victim constitutes 'grievous bodily harm'. This was given a rather vague definition in *DPP v Smith* [1961] AC 290 as 'a really serious injury', but is essentially a jury question. If a fractured jaw does fall within this definition, whether William has committed the offence under s18 (where the maximum punishment is life imprisonment) or s20 (maximum five years' imprisonment) will depend on his mens rea. A conviction under s20 can be secured by proving that William intended or merely foresaw that his actions would cause Vic some harm: see *R v Savage*; *R v Parmenter*. A conviction under s18 could only be achieved upon proof that William intended to cause Vic serious harm.

To these charges William may raise the defence contained in s3 Criminal Law Act 1967. This allows the use of reasonable force in the prevention of crime (Vic of course was in the process of burgling the house). However the force used must be objectively reasonable: *R v Owino* [1996] 2 Cr App R 128. There is no evidence that Vic attacked William before William punched him, and although the fact that the accused may have acted in the heat of the moment will be taken into account (*Palmer v R* [1971] AC 814) the fact that William is a professional boxer may hinder any argument he puts forward that he may have panicked.

By pretending to Xeries that he had had the oil painting valued at £300 and subsequently purchasing it from her for £480, Stephen may have obtained property by deception contrary to s15 Theft Act 1968. He has clearly deceived Xeries into believing that the painting has been valued. We are told that Xeries sold the painting to Stephen as a result of the deception. Consequently, the essential element of causation is established: see *R v Rashid* [1977] 1 WLR 298 and *R v Doukas* [1978] 1 WLR 372. It is submitted that the fact that the painting is only worth £200 and that Stephen has made a loss is irrelevant. The question is whether he was dishonest within the meaning ascribed in *Ghosh* (above) at the time he purchased the painting.

QUESTION THREE

X put the appropriate coins in a car park barrier machine but it did not rise. X hit the machine with his fist. It disgorged a large quantity of coins from the change slot and did not work at all for the rest of the evening because of the blow. X put the coins in his pocket and removed his car from the car park. Later he used some of the coins in a vending machine to buy drinks. X then went to Y's shop where he used a stolen building society cheque to pay for a £50 coat which he had agreed to buy. X sold the coat to a market trader for £25. He returned to his car and noticed some groceries on the back seat of a neighbouring car. He forced open the car door, put the items in the boot of his car and was arrested by a policeman who had been keeping watch.

Advise X of his criminal liability.

University of London LLB Examination
(for External Students) Criminal Law June 1993 Q6

### General Comment

The only question which concentrates on offences against property on a paper which otherwise concentrates heavily on offences against the person. The question does not raise any awkward academic points although it does require a discussion of a wide variety of offences involving dishonesty as well as criminal damage.

### Skeleton Solution

Criminal damage to the machine – theft of the coins – making off without payment – possession of stolen property – obtaining property by deception – criminal damage to the car and theft of the items inside.

### Suggested Solution

*Criminal damage to the machine*

By striking the barrier machine and causing it not to work for the rest of the day X may be guilty of criminal damage contrary to s1 of the Criminal Damage Act 1971. Although X may not have damaged any individual parts of the machine it has been held in *Morphitis* v *Salmon* [1990] Crim LR 48 that damage includes not only physical harm but also the permanent or temporary impairment of value or usefulness. As the machine did not work for the rest of the evening its usefulness has been temporarily impaired. Although X may not have intended to damage the machine it is sufficient that he created an obvious risk that such damage might occur and it is irrelevant whether he was aware of the risk but went ahead regardless or he never thought about the risk: *Commissioner of the Police of the Metropolis* v *Caldwell* [1982] AC 341. Whether or not banging on the machine would create an obvious risk of damaging it would depend on how hard he hit it, where he hit it and how sturdy the machine appeared to be.

*Theft*

X may be guilty of theft of the coins from the machine contrary to s1 of the Theft Act 1968. It must be established that the coins belonged to another and although some of the coins may have been the ones X originally put in the machine, by analogy with the case of *Edwards* v *Ddin* [1976] 1 WLR 942 which held that property in petrol passes the moment it flows from the petrol pump into the petrol tank, it is submitted that ownership of the coins passed to the garage the moment they were put into the machine and accordingly, X would be appropriating coins belonging to another.

The prosecution must also establish that X has acted dishonestly with reference to s2(1) of the Theft Act 1968 and according to the standards of ordinary and reasonable people: *R v Ghosh* [1982] QB 1053. As X has already spent some of the money on a drink and does not intend to return it he has probably acted dishonestly with this money. With respect to the remaining unspent money, whether X is dishonest may well depend on what he intends to do with it – spend it, or perhaps he was merely safeguarding it until he could return it to the garage, although this would seem unlikely.

*Making off without payment*

As X appears to have removed his car from the car park without paying the parking fee he may be guilty of making off without payment contrary to s3 of the Theft Act 1978. To be convicted of this offence the accused must know that payment on the spot is expected of him and make off without making such payment – both requirements would appear to be met in this case. The accused must also have acted dishonestly within the meaning of *Ghosh* mentioned above and it is submitted that unless X intended to return to the garage at a later date and pay for the parking he would have acted dishonestly. The case of *R v Allen* [1985] AC 1029 requires the prosecution to prove an intention to permanently avoid payment and X will be entitled to an acquittal in the unlikely event that he had such an intention to return and pay at a later date.

*Possession of stolen property and obtaining property by deception*

As X is in possession of a stolen building society cheque he may have committed the offence of possessing stolen goods contrary to s22 of the Theft Act 1968 which would require that X knew or believed the cheque to be stolen. Since he bought the coat for £50 using the stolen cheque and later sold it for only half this amount it is likely that he knew that the cheque was stolen.

In purchasing the coat by using the stolen cheque X may also be guilty of obtaining property by deception contrary to s15 of the 1968 Act. In *Metropolitan Police Commissioner* v *Charles* [1977] AC 177 it was held that the presentation of a cheque carries an implied representation that the shop will be paid. If the cheque is stolen the shop will not be paid and this false representation if coupled with the appropriate mens rea will constitute a deception. However if X used a cheque guarantee card the building society would honour the cheque and this representation would no longer be false in which case the prosecution must look elsewhere to locate a deception. Charles appears to have solved this problem by holding that when a cheque is presented for payment not only is the presenter representing that the shop will be paid but also that he has authority to use the cheque. If the cheque is stolen this authority is lacking and once again if the accused has knowledge of this, a deception has occurred. It has been held that the deception must cause the obtaining (*R v Clucas* [1949] 2 KB 226) in consequence of which one may argue that if X used a cheque guarantee card the shop's only concern would have been that they would get paid and therefore the fact that X did not have authority to use the cheque would not have been a factor in the minds of the shop staff which induced them to accept the cheque and consequently did not cause the obtaining as required by s15. However, the House of Lords in *R* v *Lambie* [1981] 1 All ER 332 did not regard a similar argument as a bar to the conviction of the accused who had used her credit card in excess of the stipulated credit limit and therefore without authority.

*The groceries*

If, in forcing open the car door X caused any damage to the car, he may be guilty of criminal damage contrary to s1 of the Criminal Damage Act 1971. By removing the groceries and placing them in the boot of his car X has committed theft contrary to s1 of the 1968 Act.

## QUESTION FOUR

Peter was a house painter. He was contracted to paint a house for a particular fee and was given £50 with which to buy materials. Believing he had £50 at his home, Peter spent the £50 he was given on a suit. However, he discovered that his wife had spent the £50 at his home. Furious, he took his wife's favourite ring and threw it into a nearby river.

Peter visited his bank manager and told him that his wife was expecting their first baby, and he requested an overdraft facility of £50 to purchase some garments for the baby. The story was entirely untrue. His bank manager, however, readily agreed to the overdraft and added that there was no need for any explanation as to why it was required when the amount was so small. Peter cashed a cheque for £50 and bought the materials.

Peter met a friend, Brian, and told Brian that he was painting a house for charity and wondered whether Brian would like to assist him although, being a charitable work, there was no payment. Brian agreed to help and did do half the painting. Unknown to Peter, when the work was finished, Brian saw Peter being paid by the householder.

Brian kept silent but went around to Peter's house that evening, intent upon taking goods to the value of half what Peter had been paid. Peter's wife, Anne, let Brian in. Peter was out. Anne poured Brian a brandy and left the drawing room to make some sandwiches for Brian. Whilst she was out of the room Brian finished off the bottle of brandy.

Discuss the criminal liability of Peter and Brian.

Adapted from University of London LLB Examination
(for External Students) Criminal Law June 1981 Q7

*General Comment*

A straightforward examination of knowledge of the various elements of theft and burglary, and also deception.

## Skeleton Solution

Theft, 'appropriates', 'belonging to another', 'dishonestly': ss1–7 Theft Act 1968 – burglary, enters as trespasser: s9 Theft Act 1968 – deception, obtaining property/services: s15 Theft Act 1968; s1 Theft Act 1978 – obtaining pecuniary advantage: s16 Theft Act 1968.

## Suggested Solution

Peter may have committed offences contrary to the Theft Act 1968 and the Theft Act 1978.

When Peter used the £50 given to him to buy materials in purchasing a suit he may have committed an offence contrary to s1 of the Theft Act 1968 which states that it will be an offence to dishonestly appropriate property belonging to another with the intention of permanently depriving the other of it. However, on the facts of the question, there may be difficulty in showing first of all that Peter was dishonest and secondly, that the property did belong to another. Section 5(3) states that where a person receives property from or on account of another and is under an obligation to the other to retain and deal with that property in a particular way, the property shall be regarded as belonging to the other. Therefore, s5(3) will be useful in showing that prima facie, there is the actus reus of theft. To come within the section it would have to be shown that there was an obligation to deal with that particular property in a certain way. If Peter received the payment as a straightforward advance of remuneration, it would be unlikely that he would come within the scope of the section. However, the money has been received to buy materials and it is therefore submitted that this will bring his act within the scope of the actus reus of theft. However, it should be noted that in *R v Hall* [1973] 1 QB 126 it was stated that the obligation had to be a legal obligation, although this appears to be satisfied on the facts in question. The requirement for a legal obligation was reiterated in *DPP v Huskinson* [1988] Crim LR 620.

As to the question of dishonesty, it would be open to Peter to claim the benefit of s2 of the Theft Act 1968 on the basis that he believed that he would have had the owner's consent if the owner knew of the appropriation and the circumstances of it. However, it has to be shown subjectively that Peter did have such a belief. If this cannot be shown then the usual rule will apply. In *R v Feely* [1973] 1 QB 530, it was stated that the question of dishonesty was one always to be left to the jury and the jury would apply the standard of the ordinary decent person. However, if Peter raises his own subjective belief in the honesty of what he was doing the *R v Ghosh* [1982] QB 1053 direction must be given (*R v Price* [1990] Crim LR 200), ie did Peter regard himself as dishonest by his own standards and are those standards shared by the community, or has he been dishonest by the standards of the ordinary man and is he aware of that standard?

At the time when he spent the £50 on the new suit, he may have committed a further offence contrary to s15 of the Theft Act 1968 in that he dishonestly obtained the property (the suit) by deception with intention to permanently deprive the other of it. The same test for dishonesty would apply as for s1 of the Theft Act except that in relation to an offence other than theft, he would not be able to claim the benefit of s2. To come within s15, it would have to be shown that he intentionally or recklessly deceived the vendor of the suit. The deception may be by words or conduct as to fact or as to law including his deception as to the present intention of the person using the deception or any other person s15(4). Furthermore, it is not just enough to show that there was a deception as to the ownership of the money, it has to be shown that the deception was the operative factor in him obtaining the goods: *R v Kovacs* [1974] 1 All ER 1236. The question of whether it was the operative cause is one of fact to be left to the jury: *R v King and Stockwell* [1987] Crim LR 398. Therefore, on the facts of the question, it would have to be shown that Peter intentionally or recklessly deceived by implying that the money was his and that the deception enabled him to obtain the suit ie, that the vendor would not have sold the suit to him if he had known that the money was not Peter's to use in this particular way.

Peter may have committed a further offence of theft when he threw his wife's favourite ring into a river. By virtue of s30(1) of the Theft Act 1968 husband and wife can steal or, indeed, do any other offence within the Theft Acts 1968 and 1978 in relation to the property of the other. If the CPS does not wish to prosecute Peter for theft his wife would be able to bring a private prosecution (see Theft Act 1968, s30(2)), but any such prosecution would require the consent of the DPP: s30(4). The elements necessary to show theft of the ring appear to be satisfied. There is an appropriation when he takes the ring and throws it into the river in that he will have assumed the right of an owner at that stage. The property belongs to another and therefore the actus reus is complete. Once again, the question of dishonesty is to be left to the jury: *R v Feely*. Furthermore, his conduct evidences an intention to permanently deprive in that he treats the ring as his own to dispose of regardless of the other's rights: s6(1).

Peter may commit an offence contrary to s16 of the Theft Act 1968 when he asks his bank manager for an overdraft facility. Section 16(1) provides that a person who by any deception dishonestly obtains for himself or another any pecuniary advantage shall commit an offence. A pecuniary advantage obtained by Peter is that within s16(2)(b) in that he was allowed to borrow by way of overdraft. However, once again there may be problems in showing that there was a complete offence. Certainly there is a deception within s15(4) made intentionally by Peter. Furthermore, he does obtain a pecuniary advantage within s16. However, there may be problems in showing that Peter does indeed obtain an overdraft by deception. It has to be shown that there is a causal link between the deception and the obtaining of the overdraft: *R v Kovacs* and *R v Collis-Smith* [1971] Crim LR 716. If he would have obtained the overdraft without the deception, then there cannot be an offence within s16 although there may be an attempt under the Criminal Attempts Act 1981, s1(3).

When Peter persuades Brian to assist in the painting of the house for charity, there is prima facie an offence within s1 of the Theft Act 1978 which states that a person who by any deception dishonestly obtains services from another, shall be guilty of an offence. However, there would be problems within s1(2) because it provides that there will only be an obtaining of services within s1(1), where the other is induced to confer a benefit by doing some act or causing or submitting some act to be done on the understanding that the benefit has been or will be paid. Because Brian has agreed to receive no renumeration, there will be no offence within the section.

Brian may be liable for attempted theft when he enters Peter's house intending to take property to the value of half what Peter had been paid. However, once again, there would be a number of problems in showing such an offence. First of all, it would have to be shown that Brian had mens rea within s1 of the Theft Act 1968, which defines theft as dishonestly appropriating property belonging to another with intention of permanently depriving that other. There is certainly an intention to permanently deprive but it would not be so easy to show that Brian was dishonest.

It may be that he could claim the benefit of s2 of the Theft Act 1968 in that he believed that he had the right in law to the property. If he cannot claim the benefit of s2, then the question of dishonesty is one to be left to the jury: *R v Feely* and the *R v Ghosh* [1982] 1 QB 1053 direction given. In *R v Woolven* [1983] Crim LR 632 it was held that such a direction should cover all occasions where a claim of a right in law was made although in *R v Wootton and Peake* [1990] Crim LR 201 the sufficiency of a *Ghosh* direction in such cases was questioned. It is the honesty of Brian's belief in such a case by which his 'dishonesty' will be determined and not the reasonableness of such a belief: *R v Holden* [1991] Crim LR 478.

As to the actus reus of theft, it would have to be shown that Brian had done an act which was more than simply an act of preparation and was so proximate to the commission of the offence that it would amount to an attempt. The question of whether an act is or is not proximate, is one always to be left to the jury: *DPP v Stonehouse* [1978] AC 55. However, as Brian has not got in mind to steal particular items, but simply stating that Brian attempted to steal from the contents of the house, the charge should be successful: *R v Easom* [1971] 2 QB 315; *Attorney-General's References (Nos 1 and 2 of 1979)* [1979] 3 WLR 577.

It is necessary to consider whether s9 of the Theft Act 1968, is applicable. Section 9 of the Theft Act 1968, provides that a person is guilty of burglary, if:

a) he enters the building or part of the building as a trespasser with intent to steal, causing grievous bodily harm, rape or do criminal damage; or

b) having entered any building or part of a building as a trespasser, he steals or attempts to steal anything in the building or inflict or attempt to inflict on any person therein any grievous bodily harm.

The most obvious problem here would be whether Brian had entered as a trespasser or as an invitee. It could be argued that because Brian had the intention of taking property when he came into the building, he did indeed enter as a trespasser. If this view is correct, then providing what he intended to do would have amounted to theft, then he would commit an offence within s9(1)(a) in that he entered, as a trespasser, with intent to steal: *R v Jones and Smith* [1976] 3 All ER 54.

If the entry were established as trespassary then, having so entered, Brian may commit a further offence of theft by drinking the contents of the bottle of brandy while Anne was out of the room. Certainly, he has appropriated property belonging to another with intention to permanently deprive. However, once again, it would have to be shown that there was dishonesty and Brian may be able to invoke s2 again, based on the fact that Anne has already given him some of the brandy.

### QUESTION FIVE

Russell went to his local self-service garage and filled his car with ten gallons of petrol. On the pump was a notice that property in the petrol was not to pass till the petrol was paid for. Russell who had only limited cash with him, saw that the forecourt attendant's attention was elsewhere, so he started to drive off to avoid payment. Before leaving the forecourt he changed his mind, stopped the car and went to the attendant. He explained the position and the attendant reluctantly agreed to accept a cheque without a banker's card in full settlement. The cheque was dishonoured because of insufficiency of funds due to the fact that Russell's wife had drawn out a lot of money from their joint account without telling Russell.

Russell decided to purchase some oil and offered the attendant a £1 note. The attendant gave Russell change for a £5 note. Russell realised this but because of the assistant's unhelpful attitude he decided to say nothing. He resolved not to spend the excess change and left in his car. Had he been asked for it, he would have given it up.

Advise Russell about his criminal liability.

University of London LLB Examination<br>
(for External Students) Criminal Law June 1983 Q9

### General Comment

A detailed but straightforward question on the Theft Acts in which a well-prepared student could obtain very good marks.

### Skeleton Solution

Making off without payment: s3 Theft Act 1978 – obtaining property by deception: s15 Theft Act 1968 – deception, evasion of liability: s2 Theft Act 1978 – theft: ss1–7 Theft Act 1968.

### Suggested Solution

Russell should be advised that by starting to drive off from the garage without having paid for the petrol he may have committed an offence contrary to s3 of the Theft Act 1978. Under s3 a person who knowing that payment on the spot for any goods supplied or service done is required or expected from him dishonestly makes off without having paid as required or expected and with intent to avoid payment of the amount due shall be guilty of an offence.

Under s3 there is no requirement that any party be deceived in order to enable an accused to make off, but it must be shown that the accused acted dishonestly and intended to avoid payment, not simply to delay it: *R v Allen* [1985] AC 1029.

The question of dishonesty is always for the jury to decide: *R v Feely* [1973] 1 QB 530. In *R v Ghosh* [1982] QB 1053 the Court of Appeal considered the various cases concerning dishonesty and concluded that the test to be applied in all cases was subjective. However, it was not subjective in the sense that if an accused felt he was not dishonest he would not be liable. The test was whether firstly the jury was satisfied that according to the standards of the ordinary man, what was done was dishonest. If it was not dishonest by those standards that was the end of the matter and the prosecution failed. If, however, it was dishonest by those standards then the jury had to consider whether the person charged must himself have realised that what he was doing by those standards was dishonest. Furthermore, it is dishonest for a person to act in a way which he knows ordinary people consider to be dishonest, even if he genuinely believes that he is morally justified in acting as he does.

Applying those cases to the facts in question it would seem that the mens rea required under s3 may well be satisfied. However, the actus reus of the offence may not be made out because it could be argued that Russell had not 'made off' but merely attempted to make off. In *R v McDavitt* [1981] Crim LR 843 it was held that as the accused had not actually left the spot he had not 'made off' although the jury could return a verdict of attempt.

The need to show a 'making off' was reiterated in *R v Allen* (above). In *R v Brooks and Brooks* [1983] Crim LR 188 the Court of Appeal considered that the words 'dishonesty makes off' were easily understandable by any jury and therefore in the majority of cases required no elaboration in summing up. However, in a case where an accused was stopped before passing the spot where payment was required a jury should be directed that that might constitute an attempt.

On the facts in question, although Russell was not stopped but rather had a change of heart, it could be argued that until he had left the premises he had not 'made off' but had merely attempted the offence. Under s1 of the Criminal Attempts Act 1981 there will be an attempt to commit an offence provided an accused has done an act 'more than merely preparatory' to the full offence accompanied by the necessary full mens rea for the offence. It is for the jury to decide whether the accused's conduct has satisfied the test contained in s1: *R v Gullefer* [1987] Crim LR 195. Furthermore, the fact that Russell has a change of heart will in no way negative his liability providing the attempt elements were satisfied.

Although s3 of the Theft Act 1978 is the most likely offence to be shown on the facts in question Russell may commit other offences under the Theft Acts. If he intended not to pay before he went into the garage he may have committed an offence contrary to s15 of the Theft Act 1968. Under s15 it is an offence dishonestly by any deception to obtain property belonging to another intending to permanently deprive. The deception may be intentional or reckless by words or by conduct, express or implied, s15(4). However, it must be shown that the deception was the operative factor (in obtaining the property here) and that the deception operated on a human mind. Therefore unless the attendant saw Russell coming into the self-service garage to take petrol and therefore assumed that he was going to pay, there would be no operative deception. See further *R* v *Coady* [1996] Crim LR 518.

The fact that on the pump there was a notice saying that property was not to pass until the petrol was paid for means that Russell should be advised that he may face a charge of theft contrary to s1 of the Theft Act 1968. The general rule in relation to self-service garages is that property in the petrol passes to the customer on delivery: *Edwards* v *Ddin* [1976] 1 WLR 942.

If Russell had the necessary dishonest intention permanently to deprive the garage at that stage, the offence of theft may be complete. The fact that Russell was doing something he was authorised by the garage to do would not relieve him of liability for theft: see *R* v *Gomez* [1992] 3 WLR 1067. However, it would have to be shown that he had the necessary mens rea at the time of putting the petrol in the car. If he formed the mens rea after the petrol was put into the car and if the notice were effective, then it could be argued that at the time he drove off there was an appropriation of property belonging to another with a dishonest intention permanently to deprive. Under s3(1) of the Theft Act 1968 there is an appropriation where there is any assumption by the person of the rights of an owner and this includes a later assumption where that person had originally come by the property (innocently or not) without stealing it. In *R* v *Morris* [1983] 3 All ER 288 the court considered that it was unnecessary for the prosecution to prove that the defendant had assumed all the rights of the owner.

When Russell gives a cheque to the attendant which later is dishonoured it seems probable that he commits no offence under s15. At the time when he gives the cheque he is impliedly warranting that the cheque will be met on presentation: *Metropolitan Police Commissioner* v *Charles* [1977] AC 177. However, on the facts in question it seems that Russell believes that it would be met. Under s2(1)(b) of the Theft Act 1978 it is an offence dishonestly by deception to induce a creditor to wait for payment or forego payment of an existing liability with intent to make permanent default. On the facts this offence is not shown as there is no intention to default. Under s15(4) Theft Act 1968 'deception' means any deception (whether deliberate or reckless) by words or conduct as to fact or as to law including the deception as to the present intentions of the person using the deception.

It is arguable that Russell does not obtain the petrol by his presentation of the cheque and that any deception in relation thereto would more appropriately fall under s2 of the 1978 Theft Act as the deception comes after the liability to pay has been incurred.

Certainly it appears that Russell is not intentional in his deception. However, it could be argued that perhaps he was reckless as to whether or not the cheque would be met. Recklessness would be shown if he was aware of the risk. However, even if this element to the offence were found to be satisfied, it seems very unlikely on the facts in question that he would have satisfied the necessary 'dishonest' state of mind.

When Russell keeps the excess change given to him by the garage assistant he may commit a further offence of theft contrary to s1 of the Theft Act 1968. As already stated the actus reus of the theft is an 'appropriation of the property belonging to another'. The problem here is whether the property belongs to another or whether ownership has passed to Russell. If the mistake were 'fundamental' then it could be argued that there had been no intention to pass ownership to Russell. However, it would appear more likely that the attendant had intended to give that amount of money to Russell acting on a mistake of fact. If this is the case then ownership will have passed to Russell.

A charge of theft may still be satisfied if it is possible to apply s5(4) of the Theft Act 1968. This subsection provides 'where a person gets property by another's mistake and is under an obligation to make restoration (in whole or in part) of the property then to the extent of that obligation the property or proceeds shall be regarded (as against him) as belonging to the person entitled to restoration, and the intention not to make restoration shall be regarded accordingly as an intention to permanently deprive that person of the property or proceeds'.

A most difficult point to decide is when there is 'an obligation to make restoration of the property'. This is decided according to principles of civil law, although an important aspect of quasi-contractual liability is that of repaying money where it is received as a result of the payer's mistake of facts and therefore it could be argued that there is an obligation to make restoration on the facts in question. It would seem that in order to amount to an obligation under s5(4) it must be a legal obligation to make restoration not simply a moral obligation: *R v Gilks* [1972] 3 All ER 280.

It seems therefore that Russell, simply by keeping the excess change given to him, which indeed may belong to him in law, may commit the actus reus of theft by appropriation of property which because of the application of s5(4) belongs to another. It must now be considered whether he has the necessary mens rea to satisfy s1. The test for dishonesty has already been outlined: see *R v Feely* and *R v Ghosh*. However, it should be remembered that in certain circumstances where there is a charge of theft, the jury must find that an accused is not dishonest. These circumstances are outlined in s2 of the Theft Act 1968 and include a situation where an accused believes he has the right in law to deprive the other of the property. If Russell believed he had a right to keep the property then he will not be dishonest and must be acquitted of any charge of theft. Such a belief must be honestly held and the reasonableness or otherwise of that belief is irrelevant to the issue of 'dishonesty': *R v Holden* [1991] Crim LR 478. However, if that belief is not present it is for the jury to decide in accordance with the case law already outlined and the jury must be directed on the specific provisions of s2: *R v Wootton and Peake* [1990] Crim LR 201.

There is no definition of 'an intention permanently to deprive' under the Theft Act. Under s6 of the Theft Act 1968 there are two examples of circumstances which would amount to an intention permanently to deprive. However, it would seem likely that on the facts in question even though Russell had no intention to spend the excess change and indeed would have given it up had he been asked for it, simply by keeping it when he could have returned it he is in effect treating it as his own and so long as he intends to keep it over a period then he may well have satisfied this element of theft. Ultimately, however, it would be for a jury to decide on this point.

# Chapter 8

# Robbery, Burglary, Blackmail and Related Offences

8.1    **Introduction**

8.2    **Key points**

8.3    **Key cases and statutes**

8.4    **Questions and suggested solutions**

## 8.1 Introduction

Although the two main areas of the Thefts Acts of interest to students are theft and deception, examination questions frequently involve consideration of what might be called ancillary offences, such as robbery, burglary and blackmail. Whilst robbery and burglary both involve theft in some or all instances, blackmail is a somewhat distinct offence in that no property needs to be taken and it does not require proof of dishonesty. As will be noted from the questions selected for consideration these topics rarely occupy a whole question in themselves, and points covered in the two preceding chapters may need to be considered here as well.

## 8.2 Key points

### Robbery – s8 Theft Act 1968

The accused must commit theft fulfilling all the requirements under s1 of the Theft Act 1968. For example, if the accused believed he had the right to take the property he cannot be convicted of robbery (although he may of course be convicted of offences against the person): *R v Robinson* [1977] Crim LR 173. Note that the force must be used before or at the time of the theft and in order to steal: *Corcoran v Anderton* [1980] Crim LR 385. Thus force used after the theft has taken place (eg in order to escape) would not sustain a charge of robbery. However, the doctrine of 'continuing appropriation' should be noted in this respect: see *R v Hale* (1978) 68 Cr App R 415. What amounts to force is a question of fact for the jury: *R v Dawson* (1976) 64 Cr App R 170.

### Burglary

Note that there are two distinct types of burglary and a good student should always specify which is being referred to: s9(1)(a) Theft Act 1968 – where the accused has entered with the intention of stealing, raping or committing criminal damage; and s9(1)(b) Theft Act 1968 – where the accused has entered without any of these intents, but once inside commits theft or grievous bodily harm or attempts to do either.

The accused must be a trespasser at the time the burglary takes place. This would apparently prevent anyone who is in a building lawfully but commits one of the above-mentioned prohibited acts from being convicted for burglary. However, note that a dishonest intent may exceed the scope of the accused's permission to enter the premises and therefore make him a trespasser: *R v Jones and Smith* [1976] 3 All ER 54. Also, a person may have permission to enter part of a building but become a trespasser when he enters another part: *R v Walkington* [1979] 2 All ER 716.

Note that the entry must be 'effective' (*R v Brown* [1985] Crim LR 212) but need not be substantial and effective (*R v Collins* [1972] 2 All ER 1105). Consequently, an accused who puts his arm through a window in order to steal may be guilty of burglary.

Note that for a charge of aggravated burglary under s10 the accused must have the weapon of offence with him at the time of the burglary. Thus a person who arms himself after entering a building cannot be said to have committed an aggravated s9(1)(a) burglary. However, an aggravated burglary may still occur if such a person subsequently commits a s9(1)(b) burglary while having the weapon with him: *R v O'Leary* (1986) 82 Cr App R 341.

Note also that any item may be converted to a weapon of offence if it is adapted or the moment it is intended to be used as a weapon: *R v Kelly* [1993] Crim LR 763.

### Blackmail – s21 Theft Act 1968

Note the different ways in which 'demands' may be made (*Treacey v DPP* [1971] AC 537) and what will constitute a 'menace': *R v Harry* [1974] Crim LR 32; *R v Garwood* [1987] Crim LR 476.

Note also the occasions where an accused's belief that he was entitled to get his property back from another by these methods may provide a defence: *R v Harvey* (1980) 72 Cr App R 139.

### Taking a conveyance – s12 Theft Act 1968

Again the definition must be known and the component parts understood.

'Taking' – *R v Bogacki* [1973] QB 832; *R v Bow* (1977) 64 Cr App R 54; *R v Marchant* (1985) 80 Cr App R 361; 'owner's consent' or 'lawful authority' – *R v Phipps and McGill* [1970] RTR 209; *Whittaker v Campbell* [1984] QB 318; *R v Peart* [1970] 2 QB 672.

'Conveyance' – *Neal v Gribble* (1977) 64 Cr App R 54. Note also that it is an offence to allow oneself to be carried in or on a conveyance knowing it has been so taken, and the offence of unauthorised taking of a pedal cycle.

## Removal of articles

Students should be aware of the specific offence under s11 of the 1968 Act dealing with removal of articles displayed to the public and how it differs from theft and burglary. Most importantly, the lack of a requirement for intention permanently to deprive must be appreciated (as with taking a conveyance).

## Going equipped

The offence of 'going equipped', ie having with one any article for use in connection with any burglary, theft or cheat – s25 Theft Act 1968 – is one which is often overlooked in answering questions: *R v Rashid* [1977] 2 All ER 237; *R v Bundy* [1977] 2 All ER 382; *R v Minor* (1987) 52 JP 30.

## Handling

a)  This is an important and relatively complex offence and its elements ought to be known in some depth.

   The concept of 'handling stolen goods' must be appreciated – the feeling among legislators is that, without 'fences' – ie receivers and handlers – there would be little theft. Therefore handling is viewed more seriously, and punished more harshly than theft. It follows that the thief cannot be the handler.

b)  The offence can be committed in many different ways (18 to be precise).

   The handler must be dishonest. He must also 'know or believe' the goods to be stolen and these words are to be given their ordinary meaning: *R v Harris* (1987) 84 Cr App R 75. In *R v Hall* (1985) 81 Cr App R 260 the Court of Appeal laid down guidelines for directing juries on this matter and it was held that where the accused 'cannot say for certain that goods are stolen but there can be no other reasonable conclusion in the light of all the circumstances', such knowledge would suffice. Mere suspicion is not enough.

c)  The various ways in which the offence may be committed must be known:

   i)   receiving (or arranging to do so). The meaning of 'receive' should be clearly understood: see *R v Cavendish* [1961] 1 WLR 1083; *R v Kanwar* [1982] 1 WLR 845; *R v Smith* (1850) 1 Den 510;

   ii)  undertaking the retention, removal, realisation or disposal by or for the benefit of another (or arranging to do so). On the meaning of 'assisting' (which like 'receiving' often occurs in examinations) see *R v Brown* [1969] 3 WLR 370; *R v Pitchley* [1972] Crim LR 705; *R v Kanwar* [1982] 1 WLR 845;

   iii) assisting in the retention, removal, realisation or disposal by or for the benefit of another (or arranging to do so).

d)  'Stolen goods' must be understood – ie goods obtained by theft, blackmail, deception, or similar offences abroad which would have constituted theft, blackmail or deception had they been committed in England.

Note should be taken of when goods cease to be 'stolen' and the arguments arising in *Haughton* v *Smith* [1975] AC 476 and *R* v *King* [1938] 2 All ER 662.

e) Note that an accused may only be convicted of handling by any method other than receiving if the handling is done for the benefit of someone other than the accused himself: see *R* v *Bloxham* [1983] 1 AC 109.

f) Note that 'stolen goods' are not confined to the goods which were originally stolen but also include anything exchanged for those goods and which then 'represent stolen goods': see s24(2) Theft Act 1968.

g) Note the circumstances in which money drawn from a bank account may be stolen goods: see *Attorney-General's Reference (No 1 of 1974)* [1974] 2 WLR 891.

### Forgery and counterfeiting

Very briefly, it is useful to remember that there exist separate offences of forgery and counterfeiting. Forgery is basically making or using a document, stamp, tape etc which 'tells a lie about itself'. Counterfeiting involves making or using counterfeit currency or coins.

## 8.3 Key cases and statutes

*Robbery*

- *R* v *Dawson* [1976] Crim LR 692
  Use of force

- *R* v *Hale* (1978) 68 Cr App R 415
  When theft occurs

- Theft Act 1968, s8(1) – defines offence

*Blackmail*

- *R* v *Clear* [1968] 1 QB 670
  Whether demand menacing

- *R* v *Collister and Warhurst* (1955) 39 Cr App R 100
  Whether demand made

- *R* v *Garwood* [1987] 1 WLR 319
  Test for menaces

- *R* v *Harvey* (1980) 72 Cr App R 139
  Whether demand unwarranted

- Theft Act 1968, s21(1) – defines offence

- Theft Act 1968, s34(2) – 'gain' and 'loss' in s21

### Burglary

- *Norfolk Constabulary* v *Seekings and Gould* [1986] Crim LR 167
  Nature of building

- *R* v *Collins* [1973] QB 100
  Nature of trespass and entry

- *R* v *Jones and Smith* [1976] 3 All ER 54
  Trespass in excess of permission

- Theft Act 1968, s9(1) – defines offence

### Taking a conveyance

- *R* v *Bogacki* [1973] QB 832
  Defines 'taking'

- *R* v *Bow* (1977) 64 Cr App R 54
  Defines 'taking'

- *R* v *Marchant* (1985) 80 Cr App R 361
  Defines 'taking'

- *R* v *Peart* [1970] 2 QB 672
  Whether owner consented

- *R* v *Phipps and McGill* [1970] RTR 209
  Whether owner consented

- *Whittaker* v *Campbell* [1984] QB 318
  Whether owner consented

- Theft Act 1968, s12 – defines offence

### Going equipped

- *R* v *Rashid* [1977] 2 All ER 237
  Whether equipped for a cheat

- Theft Act 1968, s25 – defines offence

### Handling

- *R* v *Bloxham* [1983] 1 AC 109
  Whether acting for another's benefit

- *R v Hall* (1985) 81 Cr App R 260
  Mens rea for handling

- *R v Kanwar* [1982] 1 WLR 845
  Modes of receiving

- *R v Pitchley* [1972] Crim LR 705
  Whether assisting

- Theft Act 1968, s22 – defines offence

## 8.4 Questions and suggested solutions

QUESTION ONE

Q was a well-known shoplifter. She went into a Merks and Spanner store and was seen putting two packets of tights into her shopping bag. She tasted a grape to see if they were sweet though she had no intention of buying any grapes. She went through a staff entrance where she was met by R, a member of staff. Q had previously threatened R that, unless he assisted her, she would tell the store about their previous sexual relationship. R had gone along with Q's proposal but he did not, in fact, intend to allow her to leave the store with any stolen goods. With R's assistance, Q put three dresses (for which she did not intend to pay) into a store bag. On the way out, Q replaced the tights on the shelf. At the door a security officer stopped Q and R and arrested them. Q tried to run away by pushing over the security officer but she was detained.

Advise the parties of their criminal liability.

University of London LLB Examination
(for External Students) Criminal Law June 1999 Q4

*General Comment*

Quite a complicated question with several linked burglary issues based on possible thefts in the store and thefts in the 'staff only' area. Care needs to be taken to identify where various events occur. Note that the facts state that Q is a well-known shoplifter – this is relevant to mens rea. Many other subsidiary items arise that need to be dealt with concisely if the question is to be answered in the time allotted in an examination, including conspiracy (with mens rea problems), non-availability of duress and participation.

*Skeleton Solution*

Q commits burglary on entering the store: consider mens rea – theft of the tights: does she intend to keep them? – theft of the grapes: is she dishonest? – entering a restricted area: mens rea on entry – theft of the dresses; also burglary – does Q blackmail R? – Q running away could be making off; robbery attempt – is R guilty of a conspiracy; does not intend to commit crime – R as an accomplice – no defence of duress.

### Suggested Solution

By placing the tights in her own shopping bag Q has committed the actus reus of theft as defined in s1(1) of the Theft Act 1968. The tights are property (s4) and belong to another as against Q: s5. Appropriation is defined in s3 as any assumption by a person of the rights of an owner. In *R v Morris* [1983] 3 All ER 288 Lord Roskill explain that this encompassed any assumption of any right of the owner. The store would not consent to Q's actions, but even if it were argued that it did, this would not prevent her actions amounting to an appropriation: see *R v Gomez* [1993] 1 All ER 1. Q's appropriation of the goods must be dishonest. Resort will be had first to s2(1) of the Theft Act 1968. It provides that Q's appropriation of property belonging to another is not to be regarded as dishonest if she appropriates the property in the belief that she has in law the right to deprive the store of it (s2(1)(a)), or she appropriates the property in the belief that she would have the store's consent if store knew of the appropriation and the circumstances of it: s2(1)(b). There is no evidence to suggest that she could escape liability under either sub-section. Failing this the trial judge could direct the jury in terms laid down in *R v Ghosh* [1982] QB 1053. The jury should first consider whether the prosecution has proved that Q was acting dishonestly according to the ordinary standards of reasonable and honest people. If so, did Q realise that what she was doing was by those standards dishonest? Given that she is a regular shoplifter there would seem to be little doubt that Q was dishonest.

What of the fact that Q eventually returns the tights on her way out? The prosecution must establish that she had intention to permanently deprive the owner of the tights and Q will argue that her returning of the tights is evidence that she had no such intent. The key is to look at Q's intention at the time of the appropriation. If at that time she intended to permanently deprive then theft will be made out. The fact that she subsequently changed her mind will only go to mitigation. Once all five elements of theft come together the offence is committed. The problem for the prosecution is an evidential one in establishing that she had intention to permanently deprive at the time of the taking.

The grape eaten by Q is property belonging to another. By eating the grape Q appropriates it as explained above. Again Q might argue that she was not dishonest. She has no intention of making a purchase but is simply curious to know if they are sweet. She might argue that she honestly believed she had the legal right to eat the grape under s2(1)(a) – she does not have to have any such legal right – she merely has to believe that she does. Alternatively she might rely on s2(1)(b) and contend that she honestly believed the store would not mind – this is perhaps a better argument. Failing this it would seem that no jury would regard her eating of the grape as dishonest – see the *R v Ghosh* (above) direction. Her intention to permanently deprive the store of the grape is evident.

The facts also throw up the possibility of burglary contrary to s9 of the 1968 Act. If Q entered the store intending to steal she would have done so as a trespasser as she would have been entering the store for a purpose in excess of her implied permission to do so: see *R v Jones and Smith* [1976] 3 All ER 54. If she had the intention to steal liability under s9(1)(a) of the 1968 Act could be made out. Indeed, if she entered as a trespasser and then stole the tights there could also be liability under s9(1)(b). No liability for burglary can arise if she entered as an honest shopper and then decided to steal the tights – she would not have entered the store as a trespasser. Given that the facts state she is a regular shoplifter it can probably be established that she entered as a trespasser.

By entering a staff-only area Q is almost certainly entering a part of a building as a trespasser simply because she does not have permission to be there. The facts do not state what her intention is at the time. If she has an intention to steal she can be guilty of a further burglary contrary to s9(1)(a) of the 1968 Act as indicated above.

The threat made to R could amount to blackmail contrary to s21(1) of the Theft Act 1968. She issues a demand to R – that he must assist her. The threat to reveal their previous relationship to his employers could be the menaces. Perhaps he would lose his job if this were made known? According to *R v Clear* [1968] 1 QB 670 words or conduct which would not intimidate or influence anyone to respond to the demand cannot be menaces, but threats and conduct of such a nature and extent that the mind of an ordinary person of normal stability and courage might be influenced or made apprehensive so as accede unwillingly to the demand can be put to the jury for their decision. Note in particular that, following *R v Garwood* [1987] 1 WLR 319, where the threats in fact affected the mind of the victim, although they would not have affected the mind of a person of normal stability, the existence of menaces is proved providing that Q was aware of the likely effect of her actions upon R.

Q does make the demand with a view to gain for herself – getting the goods. The demand would presumably be unwarranted. There is no evidence that Q makes the demand in the belief that she has reasonable grounds for making the demand, and that the use of the menaces is a proper means of reinforcing the demand.

Putting the dresses in the bag could be a theft committed by Q as explained above – she appropriates property belonging to another. The mens rea is evident. If she entered the restricted area as a trespasser, this theft could also give rise to liability under s9(1)(b) of the 1968 Act.

Pushing the security guard would amount to the use of force for the purposes of a charge of robbery contrary to s8(1) Theft Act 1968. Q uses the force at the time of stealing as she is still appropriating the dresses, and she uses the force in order to steal; see *R v Hale* (1978) 68 Cr App R 415. The act of appropriation does not suddenly cease. It is a continuous act and it is a matter for the jury to decide whether or not the act of appropriation has finished.

A charge under s3 of the Theft Act 1978 – making off without payment – might also be considered. The allegation would be that Q, knowing that payment on the spot for the dresses was required or expected from her, dishonestly made off without having paid as required or expected and with intent to avoid payment of the amount due. Given that she never actually made it out of the store a charge of attempting to commit the offence may be more appropriate: see *R* v *McDavitt* [1981] Crim LR 843.

Turning to R's liability, he could be charged with conspiracy to steal – in that he agreed with Q's plan. He will contend that he did not want the plan to work but this may not be enough to protect him. In *R* v *Anderson* [1985] 2 All ER 961 Lord Bridge held that, beyond the mere fact of agreement, the mens rea of conspiracy was established if the accused, when he entered into the agreement, intended to play some part in the agreed course of conduct in furtherance of the criminal purpose. In *R* v *Siracusa* (1990) 90 Cr App R 340, the mens rea element was marginalised even further so that it became enough that the defendant knew what was going on, and his intention to participate in the furtherance of the criminal purpose could be established by his failure to stop the unlawful activity. R is, therefore, at risk of conviction for conspiracy even if he intended to report Q. Much will depend on how the discretion to prosecute is exercised. Alternatively R could be charged as an accomplice to Q's theft/burglary as regards the dresses. He clearly gives her some assistance and contemplates the offence that she is going to commit. The fact that he did not intend her to be able to leave the store with the goods can be taken as evidence negativing his mens rea. Much depends on whether he is to be believed or not. In relation to these charges R might to raise the defence of duress per minas, based on the assertion that he was forced to become involved. Unfortunately for R, the defence will not be available as it must be based on threats to kill or do grievous bodily harm. The threat of losing his job will not suffice.

## QUESTION TWO

H, who had been drinking, had forgotten his front door key. He climbed into the back bedroom of what he took to be his house. In fact, it was an identical house belonging to a neighbour, I. He climbed into what he thought was his bed and failed to recognise that the occupant was not his girlfriend but I's wife, J, who had taken a sleeping pill. I returned to find the two asleep in bed and was so angry that he threw the two of them out of the bedroom window. J was killed by the fall.

Advise the parties of their criminal liability.

University of London LLB Examination
(for External Students) Criminal Law June 1992 Q3

*General Comment*

This question involves some speculation about the possible commission of a number of crimes. From the information provided the only crimes that have clearly been committed stem from the assault on H and the death of J. Possible crimes arise from H's intoxication, his entry into a house belonging to another and his climbing into bed with J.

## Skeleton Solution

Drunk and disorderly: s91 Criminal Justice Act 1967; public order offences, no evidence – criminal damage: honest belief his own property (*R v Smith*); relevance of intoxication (*Jaggard v Dickinson*) – burglary: Theft Act 1968 s9; trespass alone not enough (*R v Collins*) – indecent assault: ingredients (*R v Court*); right minded people (*R v Culyer*); intoxication unambiguous assault; unaware of external facts; J unaware of indecency (*R v Johnson*) – harm to H: battery; provocation only a defence to murder – death of J: intent to cause grievous bodily harm/death; provocation; mistake as to facts (*R v Brown*).

## Suggested Solution

### Drunk and disorderly

From the evidence provided it is not possible to tell if H has committed any offence as a consequence of his drinking before he arrives at what turns out to be the wrong house. H may have been drunk and disorderly contrary to s91 of the Criminal Justice Act 1967 if he was intoxicated and acting in a disorderly manner in a public place. Other bad behaviour by H while on the public highway may have amounted to one or other of the public order offences in the Public Order Act 1986. However, from the information provided no offence by H is disclosed.

### Criminal damage

If H, when climbing into the wrong house, caused any damage he will not have committed the offence of criminal damage under s1(1) of the Criminal Damage Act 1971. Although it is not clear whether or not H causes damage to the property on entering, his criminal liability should be considered. No offence is committed under this section if a person destroys or causes damage to property belonging to another if he does it in the mistaken belief that the property is his own. Provided that the belief is honestly held it is irrelevant to consider whether or not it is a justifiable belief: see *R v Smith* [1974] QB 354. As long as the mistake negatives the mens rea, however egregious the error may have been, no offence is committed: see also *R v Langford* (1842) Car & M 642. H will be able to rely on his level of intoxication as evidence, simply that it made his honest mistake more credible. A denial which might be incredible in the case of a sober man may be readily accepted where there is evidence that H was drunk and the fact that the belief was only honestly held because of intoxication is not relevant: see *Jaggard v Dickinson* [1981] QB 527. The situation will of course be different where H is merely the tenant of his own house and he is aware that he is damaging the property of his landlord, who would not consent to damage being caused, rather than damaging his own property.

### Burglary

When H enters the property he has potentially committed a burglary contrary to s9 of the Theft Act 1968, as he has entered another's property as a trespasser. However, H does not have the necessary intent for the offence to have been committed and trespass alone is not sufficient to amount to a criminal offence: per Edmund Davies LJ in *R v Collins* [1973] QB 100. For H to have committed a burglary he must have entered the property as a trespasser with intent to rape, cause grievous bodily harm, to steal anything in the property, or cause unlawful damage to the building or anything therein. According to the evidence provided H has no such intent before entering the building. Having entered the building as a trespasser H will only be guilty of burglary if he steals or attempts to steal anything, or inflicts or attempts to inflict on any person therein grievous bodily harm (under s9(1)(b) of the Theft Act 1968). He has therefore not committed the offence of burglary.

*Indecent assault*

When H climbs into bed with J, I's wife, he has potentially committed an indecent assault on her contrary to s14 of the Sexual Offences Act 1956 (as amended by the Sexual Offences Act 1985). 'The offence of indecent assault includes both a battery or touching and psychic assault without touching. If there was no touching, then to constitute an indecent assault the victim must be shown to have been aware of the assault and of the circumstances of indecency': see *R v Court* [1987] 1 All ER 120. J has taken a sleeping pill and is asleep, therefore she cannot be subjected to a psychic assault. According to the information H clearly has not done any more than touch J; there is no question of intercourse taking place. If H touches J in a manner that right-minded people would consider to be indecent and he knows or is reckless as to whether she consents, he is guilty – as in *R v Culyer* (1992) The Times 17 April where indecent assault was found to be a crime of basic intent where the assault was unambiguously indecent. H's climbing into bed with J who is presumably dressed only in night attire would, it is submitted, amount to an unambiguous indecent assault, whether H has an indecent purpose or not, provided only that he is aware of the external circumstances. In the present case H is not aware that the woman in the bed is not his girlfriend, which is part of the external circumstances of the alleged offence. In any event H will not have committed an indecent assault on J if he did not handle her indecently, even if his behaviour was indecent (for example if he were naked) as J did not see and was unaware of H's indecency: see *R v Johnson* [1968] SASR 132.

*Harm to H*

H presumably sustains some harm as a result of being defenestrated but the question does not specify what that harm, if any, might be. Suffice to say that I must have committed at least a battery in picking H up and causing him to collide with the ground outside the bedroom window. The appropriate charge will depend upon the harm done. It should be noted that provocation will not avail him as it is only a defence to murder.

*Death of J*

I causes the death of his wife J. If I intended to cause her grievous bodily harm or intended her death he can be charged with murder. A jury will be entitled to infer this intent if there is evidence that he foresaw death or grievous bodily harm as being a virtually certain consequence of his actions – much would depend, for example, on how far above the ground the bedroom window was. If charged with murder I could raise the defence of provocation. It is a long accepted principle that if I has acted in a sudden and temporary loss of self-control against what he perceives to be his adulterous wife and her lover he will be guilty of voluntary manslaughter and not murder. A jury will have to be satisfied that a reasonable man with the defendant's characteristics would have been provoked by the events, as he perceived them. The fact that I is provoked by a mistake of fact makes no difference; he is entitled to be treated as if the facts were as he mistakenly supposed them to be: see *R* v *Brown* (1776) Leach 148.

## QUESTION THREE

B decided to steal a diamond from a local jewellery exhibition. In order to 'case' the exhibition B bought an entry ticket. After inspection B decided it would be too difficult to steal the jewel. On the way out from the exhibition he took a coat from a staff cloakroom. B was challenged by a commissionaire whom B pushed aside before running away.

Advise B of his criminal liability.

Adapted from University of London LLB Examination
(for External Students) Criminal Law June 1985 Q1

### General Comment

A straightforward question testing the broad elements of theft and burglary with particular regard to trespassary entry.

It must be borne in mind that, although the jewel is at an exhibition, any theft of it (ie taking with an intention of permanently depriving the owner) will still be theft and not an offence under s11 of the Theft Act 1968 – removal of articles on display to the public. It is all too easy to assume that the question concerns s11 at first glance.

### Skeleton Solution

Attempted theft – burglary under s9(1)(a) Theft Act 1968 – burglary under s9(1)(b) Theft Act 1968 – theft – robbery – assault and battery.

### Suggested Solution

When B buys the ticket in order to 'case' the exhibition he may commit an offence contrary to s9(1)(a) of the Theft Act 1968. Under s9(1)(a) the offence of burglary is committed where there is entry by an accused into a building as a trespasser with intent to steal. The entry must be 'effective and substantial' and the accused must have intention or at least recklessness as to the facts which make him a trespasser: *R* v *Collins* [1973] QB 100. Considering the facts in question there are two main difficulties.

First, B has bought himself a ticket and therefore it could be argued that he has not entered the building as a trespasser. However, B's permission to enter was not given to help plan a theft. B has entered the building for a purpose other than the purpose for which he was given permission and therefore he may have entered 'as a trespasser': *R v Jones and Smith* [1976] 3 All ER 54.

Second, it seems doubtful that B entered with intent to steal. B's entry was done with the purposes of assisting him in planning the burglary and therefore the requirement of an intention to steal would not appear to be satisfied unless B had a more general intention to steal anything that took his fancy while in the building: *Attorney-General's References (Nos 1 and 2 of 1979)* [1979] 3 WLR 577.

B could not be liable for an attempt to steal the diamond because he must have done an act which is more than merely preparatory to the full offence with full mens rea, s1(1) Criminal Attempts Act 1981. His acts seem to be just that – ie acts which are preparatory to the theft – and so this would seem unlikely on the facts here, although it is for the jury to decide. If there was an attempt to steal the diamond there may be a further offence under s9(1)(b).

When B removes a coat from the cloakroom he commits the offence of theft contrary to s1 Theft Act 1968. Under s1 a person is guilty of theft if he dishonestly appropriates property belonging to another with the intention of permanently depriving the other of it.

Section 3 provides that an assumption by a person of the rights of an owner will amount to an appropriation. In *R v Morris* [1983] 3 WLR 697 the House of Lords held that it was not necessary for the prosecution to prove that an accused assumed all the rights. It is sufficient to prove that he assumed any of the rights.

Furthermore, the concept of appropriation involved an act by way of 'adverse interference with or usurpation of those rights'. The question of dishonesty must be left to the jury who should apply the test as stated in *R v Ghosh* [1982] QB 1053.

Additionally, we are told that it is a staff cloakroom and therefore, even if B's ticket were sufficient authority to negative an original trespass, the room is beyond that permission to enter and therefore he would be guilty of entering a part of a building either intending to steal (s9(1)(a)) or having so entered, stealing property: s9(1)(b).

When B pushes the commissionaire aside he may be liable for assault and battery. Assault is shown where a victim is put in immediate fear of force. A battery is a direct infliction of force. They may be performed either intentionally or recklessly: *R v Venna* [1975] 3 All ER 788. There is nothing to indicate that the victim is injured so the more serious assaults under the Offences Against the Person Act 1861 will not be considered. The offence of robbery is committed under s8 of the Theft Act 1968 where a person steals and immediately before or at the time of the theft he uses force on any person in order to steal.

There are two possible problems arising from the definition of robbery. First, it is not entirely clear whether the force was used immediately before or at the time of the theft. While an appropriation of the property may continue for a period of time while the process of stealing is taking place (*R v Hale* (1978) 68 Cr App R 415), on the facts in question it would seem that the theft is over.

Second, the force must be 'in order to steal'. It is not sufficient that force is used in order to escape, which seems to be what happened in the facts.

We are not told of any injuries to the commissionaire and, unless he suffers grievous bodily harm, the assault upon him will not suffice to support a charge of burglary (s9(1)(b)) under this head.

### QUESTION FOUR

C entered the local antique shop to make enquiries about a clock he had seen in the shop window. Inside the shop he decided to look round to see if there was anything worth stealing. He saw a Swansea teapot and decided to try to steal it. While the shopkeeper was serving another customer, C put the teapot in his bag. He felt guilty and replaced it before the shopkeeper returned. C left the shop having purchased the clock. C had paid the price requested by the shopkeeper which was less than on the price label because, as C knew, the shopkeeper by mistake had misread the price label.

Advise the parties. What difference, if any, would it make to your advice if the teapot had been kept behind the shop counter?

*University of London LLB Examination*
*(for External Students) Criminal Law June 1990 Q2*

### General Comment

The question clearly requires a sound grasp of the law of theft, not least the current debate as to the nature of appropriation, and the complexities of s5(4) of the 1968 Act.

It is necessary to consider burglary, if only to explain why such a charge could not be sustained. Given the difficulties in establishing liability for theft of the clock, it is suggested that alternatives such as deception ought to be considered.

### Skeleton Solution

Attempted theft of items unknown – theft of the teapot: consider intent to deprive – burglary, no liability – theft of the clock on alternative assumptions – consider s5(4) – consider appropriation debate – consider problems with dishonesty – consider alternative charges.

### Suggested Solution

When C enters the shop to see if there is anything worth stealing the prosecution could charge him with attempted theft of property unknown. The indictment does not have to specify the property C was attempting to steal: see *Scudder* v *Barrett* [1979] 3 WLR 591. Neither will it avail C to argue that there was nothing in the shop worth stealing. Impossibility is not a defence to a charge of attempted theft: see the Criminal Attempts Act 1981, as interpreted by the House of Lords in *R* v *Shivpuri* [1987] AC 1. The major problem in actually securing such a conviction would be proof that he had taken steps more than merely preparatory to stealing, simply by looking around the shop: see *R* v *Gullefer* [1990] 3 All ER 882. An alternative charge would be under s9(1)(a) of the Theft Act 1968, ie that C entered the shop as a trespasser with intent to steal: see *Attorney-General's References (Nos 1 and 2 of 1979)* [1979] 3 WLR 577.

C is more likely to be convicted of theft following his act of placing the teapot in his own bag. The teapot is property belonging to another as against C: see ss4(1) and 5(1) of the Theft Act 1968. In placing the teapot in his bag, C is assuming one of the rights of the owner; see the definition of appropriation provided by s3(1) of the 1968 Act. In *R* v *Morris* [1984] AC 320 the House of Lords held that an appropriation occurred when any of the owner's rights were usurped; it was not necessary that all of the rights were usurped or infringed. By putting the teapot in his bag he has assumed the owner's right of possession even though he is still inside the shop. If any difficulty arises in relation to this theft charge it must be as regards the defendant's mens rea. Firstly he must be dishonest. C does not appear to come within any of the negative concepts of dishonesty as determined by s2 of the 1968 Act. It is submitted that, applying the common law definition of dishonesty provided by the Court of Appeal in *R* v *Ghosh* [1982] 1 QB 1053, ordinary decent people would regard such behaviour as dishonest, and that C must surely have realised this. The remaining issue is that of C's intention to permanently deprive. C will undoubtedly contend that the fact that he replaced the teapot is evidence that he did not intend to keep it. Whilst his actions might be evidence of his remorse, and thus might be of relevance in considering the appropriate sentence, they are of little relevance to the substantive offence. The crucial issue is whether or not C intended to permanently deprive the owner of the teapot at the moment when he appropriated it by placing it in his bag. If he did, the theft is complete at that moment. Once the theft is complete it cannot be undone. It is submitted, however, that his action of replacing the teapot will create some evidential difficulties for the prosecution.

If C entered the shop intending to steal he will have entered for a purpose in excess of his implied permission to do so, and thus as a trespasser: see *R* v *Jones and Smith* [1976] 3 All ER 54. Hence, if C then steals the teapot whilst inside the shop he may have also committed burglary contrary to s9(1)(b) of the 1968 Act. If C did not form an intention to steal until he had entered the shop this would be fatal to any burglary charge as he will not have entered as a trespasser, and there is no evidence to suggest that he enters any other part of the building occupied by the shop with an intent to steal.

On the alternative facts given, ie that the teapot was behind the counter, C could be guilty of burglary even if he did not enter the shop as a trespasser. The area behind the counter could be regarded as a separate part of the building that, as a customer, he did not have permission to enter: see *R* v *Walkington* [1979] 2 All ER 716. If he formed the intention to steal the teapot prior to going behind the counter he could have committed an offence under s9(1)(a) – enters as a trespasser with intent to steal. Alternatively, he could be guilty under 9(1)(b) when he actually steal the teapot, given that he would have entered that part of the shop as a trespasser and stolen therein.

C's liability for theft of the clock may depend upon whether he took it to the counter himself or not. If he selected the clock and took it to the counter, his touching the clock could be the appropriation of property belonging to another. On the basis of *R* v *Gomez* [1992] 3 WLR 1067 C can appropriate the clock simply by assuming any right of the owner, and can appropriate even if the owner consents to his actions. Liability would thus turn on C's mens rea. It is submitted that it would be very difficult for the prosecution to establish dishonesty. C could argue that he is not dishonest because he believes he has the right in law to try to buy the property at whatever price: see s2(1)(a) Theft Act 1968. In contract law he would simply be making an offer to buy the clock. The shop would not have to accept his offer.

If the shopkeeper fetches the clock for C and does not hand it over until C has paid the lower (incorrect) price, the prosecution will still face formidable difficulties in establishing theft. C will argue that, following the contract of sale, property has passed to him, and thus he has not appropriated property belonging to another by removing the clock from the shop. Against this the prosecution can cite *R* v *Hinks* [2000] 4 All ER 833, which holds that a defendant can steal property even though the owner validly transferred title in the property to him. If this is the case, the focus of the argument will shift to whether or not the defendant was dishonest in taking the clock that had been sold to him.

In the present case the mistake as to price arguably renders the contract voidable, but the principle in *Hinks* would still hold true.

An alternative route for the prosecution might be to rely on s5(4) of the 1968 Act. This provision states that where a defendant gets property by another's mistake, and is under an obligation to make restoration of that property or its proceeds, then to the extent of that obligation the property or its proceeds shall be regarded (as against him) as belonging to the person entitled to restoration. Prima facie this section would seem to apply to C, thus effectively preventing property in the clock from passing to him, for the purposes of theft, because of the shopkeeper's mistake. The difficulty for the prosecution, however, is that s5(4) does not of itself create an obligation to restore goods obtained by another's mistake. Such an obligation must already exist in law. It is beyond doubt that such an obligation does exist where one obtains money as a result of another's mistake, but it is far less clear that any such obligation arises where the property so obtained takes some other form. It is instructive to note that s5(4) was specifically drafted to deal with the problem that arose from the decision in *Moynes* v *Coopper* [1956] 1 QB 439, ie a defendant receiving too much cash in his wage packet. It has been applied to similar situations since its enactment, eg *Attorney-General's Reference (No 1 of 1983)* [1984] 3 All ER 369, but has not been applied to a situation where a defendant has received goods by mistake.

Unless the prosecution can argue that the shopkeeper retains some equitable interest in the clock (see s5(1)), notwithstanding the voidable contract of sale, a charge of theft can only be made out by recourse to the reasoning (or lack of it!) in *R v Hinks*. As indicated above, there will, in any event, be difficulties in establishing dishonesty. It is submitted that C might raise two arguments by way of defence on this point. Firstly, that he honestly believed he had a right in law to take the item: see s2(1)(a) of the Theft Act 1968. In contract law terms C will contend that he had at least voidable title to the clock. Secondly, C could argue that, following *R v Ghosh*, ordinary decent people would not regard his actions as dishonest, or at least that he did not realise that they would regard them as dishonest. Whether or not this latter argument succeeds would depend largely upon the amount by which the price of the clock was mis-stated by the shopkeeper. C's intention to permanently deprive the owner of the clock is evident.

There is the possibility that C could be guilty of obtaining the clock by deception, contrary to s15 of the 1968 Act, but the difficulty would lie in establishing a deception on his part. The prosecution may cite *DPP v Ray* [1974] AC 370, and contend that by remaining silent C was representing that he honestly believed the price requested by the shopkeeper to be correct when this was not the case. The chief difficulty here is, of course, the fact that the price of the clock was determined by the shopkeeper, not C! Proving dishonesty would also be problematic, for reasons already given.

## QUESTION FIVE

a) N and O, aged 17 years and 13 years, decided to borrow their father's car without asking. They suspected, though they did not know, that he would have refused. N drove them to a nearby cafe.

   Advise N and O.

   *Adapted from University of London LLB Examination*
   *(for External Students) Criminal Law June 1984 Q5*

b) G and I were students at the same college. G wrote to H, I's millionaire father, demanding payment to rag funds in return for I's release. I agreed to write to H saying that he had been held against his will. This was not true.

   H was alarmed by the contents of the letters and paid the money to the rag fund. Earlier, G and friends had blocked the roads near the college demanding payment before permitting vehicles to pass.

   Advise G and I on their criminal liability.

   *Adapted from University of London LLB Examination*
   *(for External Students) Criminal Law June 1985 Q3*

## General Comment

a) A fairly simple examination of s12 with particular regard to 'consent' and the aggravating factor of the age of the accused.

b) A fairly straightforward examination of making 'demands with menaces' and the possible overlap with deception.

## Skeleton Solution

a) Conspiracy: CLA 1977 – no age based defence – taking a conveyance and being carried thereon: s12 TA 1968.

b) Blackmail: s21 TA 1968 – attempted deception: s15 TA 1968 – deception: s15 TA 1968 – robbery: s8 TA 1968.

## Suggested Solution

a) When N and O decide to borrow their father's car without his approval, they may commit a conspiracy contrary to s1 of the Criminal Law Act 1977 in that they have agreed on a course of conduct which if carried out in accordance with their intention will necessarily amount to the offence contained in s12 of the Theft Act 1968. N is 17 years old and therefore for the purpose of criminal law is treated as an adult. Following the enactment of s34 of the Crime and Disorder Act 1998 the fact that O is 13 will not afford him any defece based on infancy. For the purposes of establishing mens rea he will be treated as any other adult offender. The fact that N and O suspected, although they did not know, their father would have refused would not give them a defence to any change contrary to s12. Under s12(6) a person would not commit the offence of taking a conveyance if:

i) he believed he had lawful authority to take the conveyance; or

ii) he believed that he would have the owner's consent if the owner knew of the circumstances.

Neither of those requirements are satisfied on the facts in question.

When N drives the car and O is carried in the car they commit offences under s12 of the Theft Act 1968. N would be liable for taking and driving a conveyance without the consent of the owner and O would be liable, presuming that he has mischievous discretion, for allowing himself to be driven in a conveyance, knowing that it has been taken without the consent of the owner. The 'taking' of the conveyance occurs at the moment of some movement: *R v Bogacki* [1973] QB 832. Furthermore, the taking and driving was in this case for use as a conveyance in that both N and O were transported in the vehicle: *R v Bow* [1977] Crim LR 176 and *R v Stokes* [1982] Crim LR 695.

b) When G writes to I's father demanding payment to rag funds in return for I's release he may commit the offence of blackmail contrary to s21 Theft Act 1968. A person is guilty of blackmail if he makes an unwarranted demand with menaces with a view to gain for himself or another or to cause loss to another in money or other property.

A 'demand' can be made in any number of ways and on the facts in question it would be complete when the letter is posted. It is immaterial whether or not it is received by the victim: *Treacy* v *DPP* [1971] AC 537. The term 'menaces' is not defined in the Act. In *R* v *Clear* [1968] 1 QB 670 it was held that the demand was only menacing if it was accompanied by threats of such nature and extent that an ordinary person of normal stability would be influenced so as to accede to the demand. In *R* v *Harry* [1974] Crim LR 32 the organisers of a student rag wrote letters to local shopkeepers offering them immunity from rag activities if they contributed to rag funds. While some shopkeepers complained this was held not to be menacing because an average person would not have been affected.

A demand with menaces is unwarranted unless:

i)   the accused believes that he has reasonable grounds for making the demand; and

ii)  the accused believes that the use of menaces is a proper means of reinforcing the demand.

When I writes to his father saying falsely that he is being held against his will he may be liable for an attempt to obtain money by deception contrary to s15 Theft Act 1968. Section 15 of the Theft Act 1968 provides that a person who by any deception dishonestly obtains property belonging to another with intention to permanently deprive shall commit an offence. The deception must satisfy s15(4) and therefore must be either intentional or reckless and can be by words or conduct, as to fact or as to law, including a deception as to the present intentions of the person using the deception, or any other person.

The deception must be shown to be the operative reason for the obtaining of the property (in this case the money).

Undoubtedly, there is an intention to permanently deprive although it may not be so easy to satisfy the requirement for dishonesty. The question of dishonesty must be left to the jury to decide. In *R* v *Ghosh* [1982] QB 1053 the Court of Appeal adopted an essentially subjective approach. When deciding whether or not a person was acting dishonestly the jury had to decide whether according to the ordinary standard of reasonable and honest people the accused's conduct was dishonest. If it was not then the accused should be acquitted. If it was the jury should then consider when the accused viewed his conduct as dishonest by ordinary standards. If he realised that his conduct was dishonest by these standards he would still be dishonest even if he believed that he was morally justified in acting in the way he did act.

When H pays the money to the rag fund a full offence contrary to s15 of the Theft Act 1968 may have been committed. The defendants will have obtained property by deception, or at least enabled the rag fund to do so. The issue of dishonesty will have to be considered again, *R* v *Ghosh* being the guiding authority. As the money was intended for the rag fund the defendants might contend that they were not dishonest, if there was no intention to gain any personal benefit. They may also believe it to be acceptable to trick a very wealthy person into making a large contribution. Technically there is also an offence of theft when the funds are obtained by deception: see *R* v *Gomez* [1992] 3 WLR 1067.

When G and friends blocked the road demanding payment before allowing vehicles to pass, a further offence under s21 may be shown although it seems much less likely that their demands would be found to be menacing. As we are not told of any force or threatened force used towards the drivers it is unlikely that a charge of robbery under s8 of the Theft Act 1968 would be made out.

# Chapter 9

## Criminal Damage

9.1    Introduction

9.2    Key points

9.3    Key cases and statutes

9.4    Questions and suggested solutions

## 9.1  Introduction

Criminal damage is an area of criminal law that is relatively straightforward and which usually forms the basis of at least one examination question. As with the Theft Acts offences, definitions should be learnt together with statutory defences.

## 9.2  Key points

a) The elements of the basic offence of criminal damage under the Criminal Damage Act 1971 are:

i)   Property – note the definition in s10(1).

ii)  The property must belong to another – see s10(2) and note especially that a person may be guilty of damaging his own property if it is co-owned, if another has lawful custody and control of it or has a charge on it: *R v Denton* [1982] 1 All ER 65.

iii) The property must be destroyed or damaged (defined in *Morphitis* v *Salmon* [1990] Crim LR 48 as including 'not only permanent or temporary harm but also permanent or temporary impairment of value or usefulness').

iv)  'Without lawful excuse' – under s5(2)(a) the accused will have a lawful excuse if he believed that the person entitled to give consent would have consented had he known of the circumstances. Note that the accused need only have a genuine belief, the belief need not be reasonable: s5(3) and *Jaggard* v *Dickinson* [1980] Crim LR 717.

Under s5(2)(b) the accused will have a lawful excuse if he believed the property was in need of immediate protection and if he believed that the measures he took were reasonable. Note again that the accused need only have the requisite belief, whether it is reasonable or not is irrelevant. The accused must believe that the property is in immediate need of protection: *R v Hunt* [1977] Crim LR 740; *Johnson v DPP* [1994] Crim LR 673. See also: *R v Ashford and Smith* [1988] Crim LR 682; *Lloyd v DPP* [1991] Crim LR 904.

v) Note that there are two alternative mens rea to the offence and a candidate should endeavour to specify which he thinks is appropriate when answering a question, ie the accused intended to damage property or was reckless as to whether property was damaged in the *Caldwell* sense (*Commissioner of Police of the Metropolis v Caldwell* [1981] 2 WLR 509). The ingredients of *Caldwell* recklessness (see Chapter 2) must be analysed if the candidate believes the accused has recklessly as opposed to intentionally damaged property.

b) Note that criminal damage by fire is charged as arson (s1(3)).

c) Under s1(2) a person may be guilty of the more serious offence of aggravated criminal damage if he commits criminal damage and intended or was reckless (in the Caldwell sense) as to whether life would be endangered. Note that it is not necessary that life is actually endangered, it being sufficient that the accused had the requisite mens rea with respect to the endangerment: *R v Dudley* [1989] Crim LR 57. Care should be taken to note that the prosecution will have to prove that D intended that the criminal damage itself (as opposed to the act causing the criminal damage) should endanger life, or that he was reckless as to whether or not it would do so: see *R v Steer* [1987] 2 All ER 833.

d) Note the offences of making threats to damage property (s27) and possession of articles intended for use to damage property (s3).

## 9.3 Key cases and statutes

* *Commissioner of Police of the Metropolis v Caldwell* [1982] AC 341
  Recklessness in criminal damage

* *Hardman v Chief Constable of Avon and Somerset Constabulary* [1986] Crim LR 330
  Nature of damage

* *Jaggard v Dickinson* [1981] QB 527
  Intoxication and lawful excuse

* *Morphitis v Salmon* [1990] Crim LR 48
  Nature of damage

* *R v Denton* [1982] 1 All ER 65
  Whether D has lawful excuse

* *R v Hunt* (1977) 66 Cr App R 105
  D's belief in lawful excuse

* *R v Smith* [1974] QB 354
  Belief in ownership of property

- *R* v *Steer* [1987] 2 All ER 833
  Whether criminal damage intended to endanger life

- Criminal Damage act 1971, s1(1) – creates basic offence

- Criminal Damage act 1971, s1(2) – creates aggravated offence

## 9.4  Questions and suggested solutions

QUESTION ONE

M, a cleaning lady, mistook N for a friend of O, the owner of the house which she cleaned. She admitted N to the house. From there he removed a portable computer belonging to O. N found a list of O's sexual partners in the machine. N wrote to P, Q and R, who were listed in the machine, threatening to disclose their relationship with O unless they paid him £ 50 a month. P sent N £ 50. Q was so frightened that she committed suicide. R told her husband, S, about the contents of the letter. S was angry and drove for two hours to where N lived. There he hit N over the head with the portable computer. N was severely injured and the computer damaged.

Advise the parties of their criminal liability. What difference, if any, would it make to your advice if N had died two years later from the blow?

University of London LLB Examination
(for External Students) Criminal Law June 1999 Q3

*General Comment*

This question involves a curious mixture of Theft Act offences and offences against the person. Particular points to note include the issue of whether a blackmailer who receives money from his victim also commits theft. Where a blackmailer's victim commits suicide difficult issues of liability for manslaughter arises because of causation and the fact that the unlawful act must be dangerous. Note the aggravated criminal damage point arising out of *R* v *Steer*. The time limit issue is now very simple following the enactment of the Law Reform (Year and a day Rule) Act 1996.

*Skeleton Solution*

N may commit burglary; did he have permission; theft of machine – blackmail of those listed on machine – theft in receipt of money paid – blackmail as a cause of death; whether any homicide charge possible – R commits criminal damage; aggravated offence and assaults – S causes death; murder; provocation; unlawful act manslaughter; time limits removed – elements of unlawful act manslaughter.

*Suggested Solution*

In entering O's house and removing a computer N may have committed the offence of burglary. Under s9(1) Theft Act 1968 the prosecution must prove that he enters the building or part of it as a trespasser and with intent to steal. When N enters the house he clearly enters a building. Does he do so as a trespasser? M can clearly give certain persons permission to enter, but may not have had authority to give complete strangers with no legitimate business to be there permission to enter. This alone would be enough to render N a trespasser. If it could be proved that N has the intention to steal something when he first entered the house the prosecution's task becomes simpler. Entering with such an intent would render N a trespasser on the basis of the ruling in *R v Jones and Smith* [1976] 3 All ER 54. A person is a trespasser under s9 if he enters premises of another knowing that he is entering in excess of the permission that has been given to him, or being reckless as to whether he is entering in excess of the permission. Provided the facts are known to N that enable him to realise that he was acting in excess of the permission given by M, or that he was acting recklessly as to whether he exceeded that permission, the jury can conclude that he was in fact a trespasser.

Removal of the computer would constitute theft. The computer is property belonging to another as against N: see ss4(1), 5(1) and 3(1) of the Theft Act 1968. N's actions appear to be dishonest. The only uncertain issue is whether or not N had intention to permanently deprive. This would have to be inferred from the facts. If N entered O's house as a trespasser and stole the computer he could also be charged under s9(1)(b) of the 1968 Act. There are various complications surrounding these burglary charges. If N entered the house with some innocent purpose it will be difficult to establish entry as a trespasser. If he moves from the hallway to another room where the computer is located the prosecution would have to consider hi intent when he entered the room – he could become a burglar by entering part of the house as a trespasser with intent to steal. The facts are not sufficiently clear to enable specific advice to be given on this point.

Given that M is mistaken as to N's identity there is insufficient evidence to consider charging her as an accomplice to N. In terms of actus reus it could be said that she aids and abets the commission of the theft and burglary, but there is no evidence that she contemplates the commission of these offences by N: see *R v Bainbridge* [1959] 3 WLR 356.

N writes to P, Q, and R demanding money under threat of revealing embarrassing information. In doing so he may have incurred liability for the offence of blackmail contrary to s21(1) of the Theft Act 1968. The offence is made out if it can be proved that N, with a view to gain, made an unwarranted demand with menaces. For these purposes a demand with menaces is unwarranted unless N makes it in the belief that he has reasonable grounds for making the demand; and that the use of the menaces is a proper means of reinforcing the demand.

The letter is clearly a demand. Words or conduct which would not intimidate or influence anyone to respond to the demand would not be menaces, but threats and conduct of such a nature and extent that the mind of an ordinary person of normal stability and courage might be influenced or made apprehensive so as accede unwillingly to the demand would be sufficient to put before a jury. Basically, the demand would be regarded as having been made with menaces if the average person would be been menaced by it. P and Q appear to have been menaced. There is no evidence as to whether or not R was menaced. Even if she was not, the test would still be satisfied if it could be shown that an average person would have been: see *R v Clear* [1968] 1 QB 670.

N clearly makes the demand with a view to gain for himself. The test for whether or not it is warranted is subjective. The evidence does not indicate why he made the demand. If he was simply exploiting an opportunity to embarrass others into giving him money it is unlikely that he will be able to persuade a court that the demands were warranted. There is, therefore, strong evidence that the offence of blackmail has been committed.

When P receives £50 from P he could be guilty of theft. The fact that P 'consents' to N receiving the money is no bar to liability. *R v Gomez* [1993] AC 442 makes it clear that there can be an appropriation of property belonging to another even though the owner consents to the defendant taking it. If N is found to have been dishonest in keeping the money and he intended to deprive P of it the elements of theft will be made out.

Will N incur any liability for the death of Q? N has caused her death in fact – applying the 'but for' test – but for the blackmail Q would not have died: see *R v White* [1910] 2 KB 124. The issue of causation in law is more complicated. N will argue that Q's suicide constitutes a novus actus interveniens that breaks the chain of causation. The prosecution will rely on the ruling in *R v Blaue* (1975) 61 Cr App R 271, to the effect that N must take his victim as he finds her. N should try to distinguish his case from Blaue on the basis that his was not an offence of violence, and on the basis that Blaue involved a refusal of help, not a deliberate act by the victim causing her death. In the absence of any clear authority it is impossible to advise as to how the courts will resolve this matter. Public policy perhaps dictates that blackmailers who drive their victims to suicide should be at risk of conviction for some form of homicide.

Assuming N is found to have caused Q's death in fact and in law, it will be necessary to consider what form of homicide he should be charged with. For murder he will have to be shown to have intended to kill or do grievous bodily harm: see *R v Woollin* [1998] 4 All ER 103. This seems most unlikely on the facts unless it can be shown N was aware of Q's especial vulnerability. The alternative is a manslaughter charge, in the form of unlawful act manslaughter. The unlawful act would be the blackmail, detailed above. The difficulty for the prosecution would lie in establishing that the unlawful act satisfied the common law test for 'dangerousness'.

On the basis of *R v Church* [1965] 2 All ER 72, the unlawful act must be one that all sober and reasonable people would inevitably recognise must subject the other person to, at least, the risk of some harm resulting therefrom, albeit not serious harm. *R v Dawson* (1985) 81 Cr App R 150 develops this further by determining that the foreseeable harm must be physical harm. The test for foreseeability is based on the knowledge gained by a sober and reasonable man as though he were present at the scene of and watched the unlawful act being performed. In other words, he has the same knowledge as N.

The reasonable person may foresee that Q would be frightened by the blackmail but it would be extreme to argue that a reasonable person would have foreseen any risk of physical harm.

It is submitted that a prosecution for unlawful act manslaughter would fail on this ground. Killing by gross negligence would not be appropriate on the facts.

When R hits N over the head with the computer he commits a number of offences. The computer is obviously property belonging to another. R damages it. Hence he commits the actus reus of 'simple' criminal damage contrary to s1(1) of the Criminal Damage Act 1971. He must be shown to have intended the damage or to have been reckless as to whether such damage would occur. The recklessness here would be as defined by the House of Lords in *Commissioner of Police of the Metropolis v Caldwell* [1982] AC 341. It would suffice that R created an obvious risk that property would be damaged, and that he gave no thought to that risk. This would appear to be made out on the facts. R could only escape liability by contending that he thought about the risk of damaging the computer and decided there was no risk: see *R v Reid* [1992] 1 WLR 793. R could also be charged with 'aggravated' criminal damage contrary to s1(2) of the 1971 Act on the basis that he damaged property intending to endanger life or being reckless as to whether life would be endangered. The key point to stress here is that, following *R v Steer* [1987] 3 WLR 205, the prosecution must prove that R was at least reckless, as defined above, as to whether the criminal damage to the computer would endanger life. It is not enough under s1(2) that he was aware of the risk that hitting another with the computer would endanger life.

The severe injuries suffered by N would undoubtedly suffice for the purposes of grievous bodily harm as defined in *R v Saunders* [1985] Crim LR 230. R could be charged with causing grievous bodily harm with intent contrary to s18 of the Offences Against the Person Act 1861. The actus reus is evident. The intent would be as defined in *R v Woollin* (above). Much depends on what harm R foresaw. Unless the jury can conclude that he foresaw at least grievous bodily harm as virtually certain they cannot infer that he intended it. The lesser charge would be inflicting grievous bodily harm maliciously contrary to s20 of the 1861 Act. Again the actus reus would be evident. On the basis of *R v Mowatt* [1967] 3 All ER 47, R will have acted maliciously if he foresaw some physical harm to N, albeit of a minor character, might result. It is difficult to conceive of how he could not have foreseen this given his actions.

If R entered N's house intending to do some grievous bodily harm he would have also committed the offence of burglary contrary to s9(1)(a) of the Theft Act 1968. The offence is made out if he enters a building as a trespasser with intent to do some grievous bodily harm. There can be no doubt that he would have been a trespasser if he entered with such intent: see *R v Jones and Smith* (above).

If N had died from his injuries 2 years later R could be charged with some form of homicide. The fact that there is a gap in time between the attack and the death is no longer a bar to liability, following the enactment of the Law Reform (Year and a day) Act 1996.

Causation is evident. R can be charged with murder if he intended to kill or do grievous bodily harm. As to the meaning of intent see *R v Woollin* (above). R may seek to raise the defence of provocation if charged with murder. *R v Duffy* [1949] 1 All ER 932 provides that provocation is some act or series of acts done by the dead man to the accused which would cause in any reasonable person and actually causes in the accused, a sudden and temporary loss of self-control, rendering the accused so subject to passion as to make him for the moment not master of his mind. This has to be read in the light of s3 of the Homicide Act 1957, which adds that the question whether the provocation was enough to make a reasonable man do as the defendant did shall be left to be determined by the jury; and in determining that question the jury shall take into account everything both done and said according to the effect which, in their opinion, it would have on a reasonable man. Hence anything can be provocation. R was clearly provoked. The crucial issue will be the objective test – how would a reasonable man have reacted? There do not appear to be any particular circumstances or characteristics that need to be taken into account when applying this test in R's case: see *DPP v Camplin* [1978] 2 All ER 168. If the defence succeeds R's liability will be reduced to manslaughter. If the mens rea for murder is not present R will be guilty of unlawful act manslaughter based on the attack on N. The dangerousness of the unlawful act is evident, see above, and R appears to have had the mens rea for the unlawful act.

### QUESTION TWO

G, aged 13 years, and F, aged 21 years, had taken their father's car without his permission. This had been reported to the police and eventually a police car was in pursuit. G threw an empty bottle of beer out of the window at the windscreen of the police car intending thereby to slow it down. However, he missed. Next, F drove the car at high speed off the road through a gap in a fence. The police car tried to follow but it crashed into the hedge and a passenger in the police car was killed. K, who had been walking on the pavement near to the crash, witnessed these events and suffered a nervous breakdown as a result and was in hospital for six months.

Advise F, G and the police driver of their criminal liability. (Offences under the Road Traffic Acts can be ignored.)

University of London LLB Examination
(for External Students) Criminal Law June 1996 Q3

### General Comment

A question which may seem difficult at first because the relevant issues and offences are not immediately apparent. However, once the relevant the issues and offences have been identified the question is relatively straightforward, although some candidates may not have revised the offence of aggravated vehicle taking.

*Skeleton Solution*

F: taking a vehicle without the owner's consent; aggravated vehicle taking – G: attempted criminal damage; attempted grievous bodily harm – mens rea of attempt – defence of infancy: G accessory to the offences committed by F – police officer: manslaughter by gross negligence; actual/grievous bodily harm to K.

*Suggested Solution*

When F took and drove away his father's car he has probably committed the offence of taking a vehicle without the owners consent contrary to s12 Theft Act (TA) 1968. It is unlikely that F could argue that he believed his father would have consented since, if he had this belief, there is no reason why he should have attempted to escape from the police.

In addition, F is likely to be convicted of the more serious offence of aggravated vehicle taking contrary to s12A TA 1968. This offence is committed when an accused takes a vehicle without the owner's consent contrary to s12 and drives it in a dangerous manner. Fleeing from the police and driving through a hedge is likely to constitute dangerous driving and therefore F will be convicted of the offence under s12A which carries a maximum sentence of two years' imprisonment.

When G threw the empty bottle at the windscreen he may have committed the offence of attempted criminal damage contrary to s1 Criminal Attempts Act (CAA) 1981. The difficulty concerns the mens rea of the offence which requires that the accused intends to bring about the prohibited consequence (in this case criminal damage). G could use a similar argument to that which was successfully raised in *R v Mohan* [1976] QB 1, that he intended to stop the car and not specifically to damage the windscreen. However, in *R v Walker and Hayles* (1990) 90 Cr App R 226 it was held that an accused 'intended' a consequence for the purpose of s1 CAA 1981 if it was his 'purpose' to cause the consequence or if he foresaw it as ' virtually certain' to result. Therefore, even if G did not intend to smash the windscreen, he will be convicted of attempting to do so if he foresaw this as a 'virtual certainty'. It is less likely that he would have foreseen injury to the police inside the vehicle as a virtual certainty and therefore, in the absence of any evidence that he specifically intended to injure any of the police officers, he could not be convicted of attempting to cause grievous bodily harm.

F could be charged as an accessory (contrary to s8 Accessories and Abettors Act 1861) to the attempted criminal damage committed by G but only if throwing bottles at the pursuing police car was part of their 'common design': *R v Bainbridge* [1960] 1 QB 129. It should be noted that although G is only a passenger in the car being driven by F, he will be charged with the full offence of taking a vehicle without the owner's consent rather than being an accessory to the taking committed by F. This is because s12 of the TA 1968 states that any person who takes a vehicle knowing that the owner has not consented or who allows himself to be carried in or on it will be guilty of the full offence.

G will not be able to raise any defence based on his age as such. A child under the age of ten cannot incur criminal liability but, further to the enactment of s34 of the Crime and Disorder Act 1998, the rebuttable presumption of criminal law that a child aged between ten and 14 was incapable of committing an offence has been abolished. G's age may, however, be a factor in establishing the extent to which he foresaw the consequences of his actions, and therefore had the required mens rea. On the assumption that attempted criminal damage requires proof of an intention to cause harm to property, G may contend that he did not foresee this harm occurring. This is a matter of fact for the jury to determine.

The police driver may be charged with the manslaughter by gross negligence of the passenger in the police car. The prosecution would have to establish that the manner in which the police officer drove went beyond more 'civil negligence' and amounted to negligence which the jury thought deserving of criminal punishment: *R v Adomako* [1994] 3 WLR 288. Although the police may take greater risks than usual when pursuing a fleeing suspect car they will still be expected to give public safety a high priority. Whether the police officer's driving is 'grossly negligent' is a question of fact for the jury and more information about the incident would be required before expressing an opinion. However, we do not know who the passenger in the police car is, and it may be grossly negligent in continuing a high speed chase with a passenger in the car if, for example, that passenger was a civilian.

By causing K a nervous breakdown the police driver will have inflicted grievous bodily harm contrary to s20 of the 1861 Act, or will have occasioned actual bodily harm contrary to s47 Offences Against the Person Act (OAPA) 1861. *R v Ireland; R v Burstow* [1998] AC 147 establishes that psychiatric injury can constitute actual bodily harm, or even grievous bodily harm, providing it amounts to a specific psychiatric condition. Section 20 requires proof of an infliction of harm, but *R v Ireland; R v Burstow* also confirms that this does not require proof of a direct assault. However, following *R v Savage; DPP v Parmenter* [1992] 1 AC 699 the prosecution would have to prove that at the time of the chase the police driver intended or foresaw that he would cause some harm to the public. A charge under s47 could be problematic in that the offence does expressly require either an assault or battery by the defendant. It is difficult to see how the police driver has committed an assault or battery on these facts.

Finally, it is also possible that, by inducing the police into a dangerous pursuit, F may be said to be an 'operating and substantial cause' of the passenger's death and could in theory be charged with the passenger's homicide, although a conviction for manslaughter by gross negligence seems unlikely.


QUESTION THREE

T decided that he needed to pull down three out-buildings to make room for a new house which he intended to build. The out-buildings were made of wood and were near to sheds on U's adjacent land. T told U that he intended to burn down the outbuildings because he could not afford the considerable expense of demolishing them professionally. He placed buckets of water near the buildings to be set alight. He checked from the local weather station about the state of the wind. Finally, T set alight to his buildings despite U's protests. The fire spread from T's buildings to U's sheds. Unknown to T and U, a tramp, V was asleep in one of U's sheds. U's buildings were severely burned and V asphyxiated from the smoke.

Advise T. What difference, if any, would it make if T had considered that there was no possibility of the fire spreading to U's sheds?

University of London LLB Examination
(for External Students) Criminal Law June 1995 Q4

## General Comment

A relatively straightforward question involving a discussion of offences under the Criminal Damage Act 1971, offences against the person and homicide.

## Skeleton Solution

Criminal damage – arson – aggravated criminal damage – offences against the person.

## Suggested Solution

Criminal damage is defined by s1 of the Criminal Damage Act 1971 as when the accused unlawfully, intentionally or recklessly damages property belonging to another. It is quite clear that T has damaged both his own and U's property. Under s1(3) of the 1971 Act criminal damage by fire must be charged as arson. The significance of this is that the maximum sentence for arson is life imprisonment, as opposed ten years for the offence of criminal damage simpliciter. However, a person cannot be charged with criminal damage or arson to his own property, but only to property belonging to another. Thus, subject to the discussion of the mens rea below, T may be guilty of arson to U's sheds but not his own property.

In order to convict T of arson to U's sheds the prosecution will need to show that T intended or was reckless as to whether he would damage U's property. It is clear from the facts that T had no such intention and thus a charge would have to be based on recklessness.

It was held in *Commissioner of Police of the Metropolis* v *Caldwell* [1981] 2 WLR 509 that a person is reckless for the purposes of a charge under s1 of the 1971 Act if he takes an obvious risk that property would be damaged and either was aware of that risk or had never thought about the possibility of there being a risk.

Thus, the first issue to discuss is whether, by setting fire to his property, T created an obvious risk that the fire might spread to U's property. This would be a question for the jury and insufficient information is given in the question to conclusively determine this issue. On the one hand the buildings are made out of wood and are said to be 'near' to each other, but on the other hand we are told that T has checked the weather report for the state of the wind and that he has buckets of water ready. It should be noted that whether the risk was obvious means whether the risk would be obvious to a reasonable man, and it is irrelevant that it was not obvious to the particular accused: see *Elliott v C (A Minor)* [1983] 2 All ER 1005.

The next issue is whether T was aware of the risk of the fire spreading, or had not given the matter any thought either case would justify a conviction. It cannot be said that he had not given the matter any thought because he had clearly taken precautions to avoid the fire spreading, and therefore must have thought about the risk. T may argue that he positively believed that there was no risk because of the precautions he took, and that consequently it cannot be said that he was aware of the risk at the time he started the fire, or that he had not given the matter any thought. In this case he falls under what has come to be termed the 'lacuna' in *Caldwell* recklessness someone who falls between the two limbs stated by Lord Diplock in that case. It should be noted, however, that if T was aware, that despite his precautions, there was still some risk of the fire spreading, however small, he would not fall under the lacuna but rather the first limb of *Caldwell* recklessness and thus may be convicted: see *Chief Constable of Avon and Somerset v Shimmen* (1986) 84 Cr App R 7.

T may also be guilty of the offence under s1(2) of the 1971 Act of criminal damage intending or reckless as to whether the life of another is endangered. The maximum sentence for this offence is life imprisonment. However, for this offence it is insufficient (and indeed unnecessary) to show that life was actually endangered (which it clearly was in this case). It must be established that T either intended to endanger life (which does not appear to be the case here), or that he was reckless as to whether life would be endangered. *Caldwell* recklessness applies to this offence and consequently it must be shown that T took an obvious risk that life would be endangered. One may argue that since there was no reason to believe that one of U's sheds would be occupied by a tramp there was no such obvious risk.

We are informed that V was asphyxiated by the smoke, but not whether V consequently died. If V died from the asphyxiation, T could be charged with the homicide of V, but if V survived T would have to be charged with one of the non-fatal offences against the person.

If V died, it is unlikely that T would be convicted of murder because the mens rea of murder was established in *R v Woolllin* [1998] 4 All ER 103 as an intention to kill or cause grievous bodily harm. It is clear from the facts given that T's intention was to burn down the outbuildings and there is no evidence of an intention to kill.

T could be charged with manslaughter by gross negligence as defined in *R v Adomako* [1994] 3 WLR 288, where the accused owes the victim a duty and breaches that duty causing death, and the jury are satisfied that the conduct of the defendant was so negligent as to amount in their judgment to a criminal act or omission. The first problem the prosecution will encounter is to prove that T owed V a duty of care. In

*Adomako* the House of Lords did not define precisely when one person owes a duty of care to another. However, the court did indicate that such a duty may be imposed where it is reasonably foreseeable that one's actions may cause harm to another person (similar to the duty of care test applicable in the case of negligence). Although the point is arguable, it is submitted that T did not owe V a duty of care since he had told the owner of the shed (U) that he intended to set fire to the buildings and could not reasonably have foreseen that a tramp would be trespassing on U's property. Even if such a duty was owed, it is arguable in the light of the precautions T took to prevent the fire from spreading whether T in fact was in breach of this duty. Under the final test laid down in *Adomako* the jury must be satisfied that T's breach of duty goes beyond mere negligence and amounts to a criminal breach of duty. It should be noted that this is purely an objective test and T's lack of awareness of the danger of the fire spreading, or of someone being killed or injured, is irrelevant.

If V died, T may be charged with a variety of offences against the person. If the consequences of being asphyxiated were serious T may be charged with maliciously inflicting grievous bodily harm contrary to s20 of the Offences Against the Person Act 1861. For the purpose of this offence 'grievous bodily harm' was defined in *DPP v Smith* [1960] 3 All ER 161 as 'really serious harm'. A charge of intentionally causing grievous bodily harm contrary to s18 of the 1861 Act is unlikely since there is no evidence that T intended to cause harm, let alone serious harm, to anyone.

Asphyxiation is likely to amount to actual bodily harm for the purposes of a charge of an assault occasioning actual bodily harm contrary to s47 of the 1861 Act. Actual bodily harm was defined in *R v Chan Fook* [1994] Crim LR 432 as 'any injury which is more than trivial'. However, the problem here is that to be guilty of this offence the accused must have assaulted the victim, causing actual bodily harm. An assault did not take place on these facts.

T could be charged with maliciously administering a poison or noxious substance so as to cause grievous bodily harm, or endangering life contrary to s23 of the 1861 Act. One could argue that smoke is a noxious substance. However, the main problem with this charge is the need for the prosecution to prove that the smoke was administered maliciously, ie intentionally or recklessly. In *R v Cunningham* [1957] 2 QB 396 is was held that reckless in the context of s23 required the prosecution to prove that the accused was aware of the danger of administering the poison or noxious substance to another. There is no evidence that T was so aware and it is therefore submitted that T would be acquitted of such a charge.

If T believed that he had eliminated all risk of the fire spreading, then, as discussed above, he will fall outside the two limbs of *Caldwell* recklessness. It is not settled law whether a person who falls within this 'lacuna' would be entitled to an acquittal. In *Shimmen* (above) it was stated, obiter (since it was held in *Shimmen* that the accused was aware of the risk and therefore did not fall under the lacuna) that such a person should be acquitted. This interpretation has been confirmed by the House of Lords in *R v Reid* [1992] Crim LR 814, although again, this statement was obiter.

## QUESTION FOUR

A disliked B, a well known local councillor. A believed that B was a rogue who had made secret profits from his office. A threw paint at B's car intending to frighten B as B was being driven past. A shouted, 'It is necessary to teach you a severe lesson and draw your behaviour to public notice.' The paint damaged the car and obscured B's driver's view and as a result the car crashed into a bus queue injuring a mother and her three children. B was slightly injured in the collision and B's driver suffered severe nervous shock.

Advise A of his criminal liability.

Adapted from University of London LLB Examination
(for External Students) Criminal Law June 1990 Q1

### General Comment

A complicated and lengthy question combining non-fatal assaults, criminal damage, and homicide. Note that both types of criminal damage require consideration. The nature of the injuries suffered by the children is not specified. It is suggested that they are merely discussed in general terms.

### Skeleton Solution

Common law assault – words as an assault – simple and aggravated criminal damage – homicide, causation, disregard murder – unlawful act manslaughter, whether unlawful act is dangerous – non-fatal assaults.

### Suggested Solution

A may have committed common law assault in throwing the paint at the car. The actus reus of the offence requires proof that the victim apprehended immediate physical violence: see *Logdon* v *DPP* [1976] Crim LR 121. The determining factor will be the perception of the victim. The reasonable bystander would realise that the paint would not make physical contact with the victim, and that there was in fact no threat of direct physical violence. The victim, however, might have momentarily thought that the paint was going to hit him.

The mens rea for common assault is intention or recklessness: see *R* v *Venna* [1976] QB 421. In Venna the court took recklessness to mean subjective recklessness, basing this decision on the earlier case of *R* v *Cunningham* [1957] 2 QB 396. Subjective recklessness requires proof that the defendant was aware of the risk that the victim would apprehend immediate physical violence. It would appear that the application of this form of recklessness to assault remains unaffected by developments in cases such as *Commissioner of Police of the Metropolis* v *Caldwell* [1982] AC 341. *R* v *Spratt* [1991] 2 All ER 210 and *R* v *Parmenter* (1991) 92 Cr App R 68 both of which confirm that, as far as assault occasioning actual bodily harm contrary to s47 of the Offences Against the Person Act 1861 is concerned, *Cunningham*-type recklessness applies. It is submitted that the same reasoning should apply to the offence of assault at common law. On the facts it may be that A will say that, as he was throwing the paint at the windscreen of the car, he could not have foreseen any risk that the victim would apprehend physical contact, but it is submitted that he may have some difficulty in persuading any court to believe this.

A's act of shouting at B can of itself constitute the offence of common law assault. Words alone can constitute an assault: see *R* v *Ireland* [1997] 3 WLR 534.

It would appear that A has committed the offence of 'simple' criminal damage contrary to s1(1) of the Criminal Damage Act 1971. The car is clearly property belonging to another as against A. The paint has caused damage to the bodywork of the car. Damage can occur even where the effects can be rectified relatively easily: see *Hardman* v *Chief Constable of Avon and Somerset Constabulary* [1986] Crim LR 330. A appears to have had the necessary mens rea for the offence, either intention or recklessness.

A more difficult question is that of whether or not A could be convicted of the more serious offence of 'aggravated' criminal damage contrary to s1(2) of the 1971 Act. The aggravating factor lies in the mens rea. A must be proved to have had either an intention to endanger life, or at least to have been reckless as to whether life would be endangered. Following the House of Lords' decision in *R* v *Steer* [1988] AC 111, the prosecution must establish that the defendant intended the criminal damage itself to endanger life, or that he was reckless as to whether it would endanger life. It is not sufficient, for example, merely to show that he was reckless as to whether the act causing the criminal damage might endanger life. On the facts of the problem, the minimum that the prosecution would have to establish in relation to the mens rea for the aggravated offence would be that A gave no thought to an obvious risk that obscuring the driver's view, by covering the car windscreen with paint would endanger the lives of others. The test for recklessness here is that laid down by the House of Lords in *Caldwell* (above). It is submitted that on the facts, the prosecution might be able to establish the necessary mens rea.

A has caused injuries to the woman's children. If causation is established in relation to the homicide it is submitted that it will be established in relation to these unspecified non-fatal offences. The precise charge brought against A will depend to a large extent on the nature of the harm done to the children. In any event it is unlikely that A will be convicted of anything more serious than malicious wounding, or maliciously inflicting grievous bodily harm contrary to s20 of the Offences Against the Persons Act 1861, since he appears not to have intended to cause any such harm.

The injuries to B and his driver are likely to constitute actual bodily harm contrary to s47 of the 1861 Act, in that they are injuries which interfere with the health and comfort of the victim: see *R* v *Miller* [1954] 2 QB 282. The mens rea for this offence is intention or recklessness as described above. The prosecution would have to prove that A was at least aware of a risk of the victims being frightened by his actions, which on the facts, seems likely.

QUESTION FIVE

P, an anti-bloodsports demonstrator, spread chemicals on fields to make the hounds sneeze and to impair their sense of smell.

Advise P of his criminal liability if any.

Adapted from University of London LLB Examination
(for External Students) Criminal Law June 1985 Q6

### General Comment

A straightforward examination of simple damage and its component parts.

### Skeleton Solution

Criminal damage under s1(1) Criminal Damage Act 1971 to land – attempted criminal damage to hounds – s1(2) of the Criminal Damage Act 1971 – possessing articles – s3 CDA 1971.

### Suggested Solution

When P spreads chemicals on the land in order to divert the hounds from their trail he may commit an offence contrary to s1(1) of the Criminal Damage Act 1971

Section 1(1) provides that a person who without lawful excuse destroys or damages any property belonging to another intending to destroy or damage any such property or being reckless as to whether any such property would be destroyed or damaged shall commit an offence.

The expression 'destroy or damage' speaks for itself to a great extent although it should be noted that an article or object may be damaged even though it is not actually broken in any way and can serve to carry out its normal purpose: *Hardman* v *Chief Constable of Avon and Somerset Constabulary* [1986] Crim LR 330.

Section 10(1) of the Criminal Damage Act contains the definition of property for the purposes of criminal damage. 'Property' means property of a tangible nature whether real property or personal property.

Applying these principles to the facts in question when P spread chemicals onto the land he was damaging property belonging to another in that the chemicals were to a degree spoiling the property. Undoubtedly P would wish to claim that he was acting with lawful excuse and therefore not liable for any offence.

A partial definition of 'lawful excuse' may be found in s5 of the Act. P's conduct would not fall within any of the specific situations mentioned in s5 ie belief that the owner would consent or defence of property. It would therefore be up to the jury to decide whether they thought he had a lawful excuse for his conduct. The mens rea of s1(1) is satisfied where in addition to acting without lawful excuse the destruction or damage of the property is shown to be either intentional or reckless in the *Commissioner of Police of the Metropolis* v *Caldwell* [1982] AC 341 sense.

While D may not intentionally damage the land he would be 'reckless' within the *Caldwell* definition in that he created an obvious risk that the property would be damaged and either he had given no thought to the possibility of the risk or he had seen the risk but had nevertheless gone on to take it.

P may commit a further offence under the Criminal Damage Act by attempting to damage property belonging to another. When he spreads the chemicals he does so in order to make the hounds sneeze and impair their sense of smell. The hounds would be 'property belonging to another' and what he intended would be sufficient to amount to 'damage'. In order to establish an attempt it must be shown that his act is more than merely preparatory: s1 Criminal Attempts Act 1981. This is for the jury to decide. Furthermore the mens rea for any attempt is generally the same as for the full offence except that as this is a result crime it must be shown that P intended the damage. Recklessness is not sufficient.

Additionally, by having the chemicals in his custody or under his control intending, without lawful excuse to use it to destroy or damage property belonging to some other person, P commits an offence under s3 of the Act.

# Chapter 10

## Inchoate Offences and Accessorial Liability

**10.1 Introduction**

**10.2 Key points**

**10.3 Key cases and statutes**

**10.4 Questions and suggested solutions**

## 10.1 Introduction

Although accessorial liability and inchoate offences (incitement, conspiracy and attempt) are separate issues they are brought together in this chapter because of the interrelationship between them, and because of the extent to which examination questions tend to raise the issues together. Bear in mind that both accessorial and inchoate liability are part of the general principles of criminal law and can come up in relation to any substantive offence on the syllabus. Be aware also that the law relating to the mens rea of accomplices, particularly in those cases where the principal carries out acts that were not agreed between the parties, is in a somewhat complex and unsatisfactory state.

## 10.2 Key points

### Incitement

It was held in *Race Relations Board* v *Applin* [1973] QB 815 that an incitement was not confined to urging another to commit an offence but also included threats, pressure and persuasion. The incitement must reach the mind of the incitee. The incitee must know of the facts that render the conduct incited an offence: see *R* v *Curr* [1968] 2 QB 944. The accused must intend that the incitee should commit the offence (although it is not necessary that the incitee actually commits the offence): *Invicta Plastics* v *Clare* [1976] RTR 251.

Impossibility – *R* v *Fitzmaurice* [1983] 1 All ER 189 held that impossibility because of the ineptitude of the methods of committing the crime suggested was no defence. Impossibility would be a defence where it was 'total' in the sense that no one could commit the offence. On this basis it would appear that legal impossibility would still be a defence at common law.

## Statutory conspiracy

a) A conspiracy is defined in s1 of the Criminal Law Act 1977 as where two or more people agree on a course of conduct which, if carried out, would lead to the commission of an offence. Note that the actus reus is agreement and no steps need actually be taken towards the commission of the offence.

b) With respect to the mens rea, note the conflict between *R* v *Anderson* [1986] AC 27 and *Yip Chiu-Cheung* v *R* [1994] Crim LR 824 on whether the prosecution must prove that the accused actually intended that the agreement be carried out. The answer lies in the Court of Appeal decision in *R* v *Siracusa* (1990) 90 Cr App R 340 – D can be guilty of conspiracy simply by agreeing with others that a criminal course of conduct is pursued. He does not have to intend to play any active part.

c) Impossibility – under s1(1)b of the 1977 Act impossibility is no defence on a charge of statutory conspiracy.

## Common law conspiracy

The offence of conspiracy contrary to common law still exists in two forms: conspiracy to defraud and conspiracy to corrupt public morals. In *R* v *Scott* [1975] AC 819, Viscount Dilhorne defined the offence as involving an agreement to deprive a person dishonestly of something which is his or of something to which he is or would or might but for the perpetration of the fraud be entitled: see further *Wai Yu-Tsang* v *R* [1991] 3 WLR 1006.

Impossibility – on the basis of *DPP* v *Nock* [1978] AC 979, impossibility would be a defence where it was 'total' in the sense that no one could commit the offence. On this basis it would appear that legal impossibility would still be a defence at common law.

## Attempt

The offence exists now only under statute, namely the Criminal Attempts Act 1981. D must do an act that is more than merely preparatory towards the commission of the offence. This is a question of fact that should be debated by the candidate in the examination if necessary. In *R* v *Gullefer* [1990] 3 All ER 882 it was held that an accused does an act which is more than merely preparatory when he embarks on the crime proper or the actual commission of the offence. The mens rea is intent to cause the prohibited consequence as determined by the crime in question: see *R* v *Walker and Hayles* (1990) 90 Cr App R 226. It is sufficient that D is reckless as to any circumstances that have to be established: see *R* v *Khan* (1990) 91 Cr App R 29.

Impossibility – it should be noted that the previous complex rules on impossibility are redundant due to s1(2) and (3) of the 1981 Act which provides to the effect that impossibility is no longer a defence to a charge of attempt: see also *R* v *Shivpuri* [1986] 2 All ER 334.

## Participation: actus reus

Section 8 of the Accessories and Abettors Act 1861 (as amended by the Criminal Law Act 1977) provides:

'Whosoever shall aid, abet, counsel, or procure the commission of any indictable offence whether the same be an offence at common law or by virtue of any Act passed or to be passed, shall be liable to be tried, indicted, and punished as a principal offender.'

Aiding involves helping, usually at the scene of the crime. Abetting involves encouraging the commission of the offence, again normally at the scene of the crime. To counsel the commission of an offence involves an accomplice in advising, encouraging, persuading, instructing, pressurising, or even threatening the principal into committing the offence. Procuring involves D in setting out to see that the offence is committed and taking the appropriate steps to produce that happening: see *Attorney-General's Reference (No 1 of 1975)* (1975) 61 Cr App R 118. Procuring is the only mode of participation that actually requires proof of causation between the act of the accomplice and the commission of the offence. In all other cases there must simply be some connection. Mere presence at the scene of a crime will, coupled with a failure to prevent its commission, not of itself be enough to justify a conviction: see *R v Coney* (1882) 8 QBD 534 and *R v Clarkson* [1971] 1 WLR 1402.

## Participation: mens rea

An accomplice must have mens rea, even if the principal is charged with a strict liability offence: *Johnson v Youden* [1950] 1 KB 544. In most cases of aiding and abetting it is sufficient that D contemplated the type of crime committed by the principal offender: see *R v Bainbridge* [1959] 3 WLR 356. As regards procuring, *Attorney-General's Reference (No 1 of 1975)* (above) appears to support a narrower approach, Lord Widgery commenting that to procure meant setting out to see that the desired consequence happens and taking the appropriate steps to produce that happening. His words are suggestive of more than mere contemplation of a consequence on the part of the procurer, perhaps requiring proof of something closer to intention.

## Participation: liability for unintended consequences

An accomplice will be a party to any unintended and accidental consequences of the common design, ie resulting from the principal offender acting as agreed: see *R v Baldessare* (1930) 22 Cr App R 70 and *R v Betts and Ridley* (1930) 22 Cr App R 148.

## Participation: joint enterprise

Where the principal and accomplice are acting in concert at the scene of the crime there may be what the courts call a 'joint enterprise'. In such cases, where for example the principal offender is convicted of murder, the accomplice will also be convicted of murder if the principal commits acts that were contemplated and the accomplice contemplated death or grievous bodily harm as a possible consequence of those acts being performed: see *R v Powell and Daniels*; *R v English* [1997] 3 WLR 959. It will not avail an accomplice that he thought either result might occur but hoped that it would not. Only if he considers the possibility of death or grievous bodily harm occurring and dismisses it as genuinely negligible will he escape liability.

Where the principal offender deliberately departs from the agreed or contemplated course of conduct and kills, an accomplice can escape liability even though he did contemplate death or grievous bodily harm as a consequence of the common design being carried out. Consider the following:

a)  Suppose A and P agree to attack V using fists and A agrees to hold V down with P to do the punching. Suppose also that A contemplates that this might result in grievous bodily harm to V. During the attack P produces a knife which he uses to stab V to death. Assume that A was unaware that P had the knife. The use of the knife would be a deliberate departure from the common design by P. Even though A contemplated grievous bodily harm he will not be an accomplice to murder because the death results from a deliberate act by P that was not agreed or contemplated: see again *R v Powell and Daniel*; *R v English* [1997] 3 WLR 959. The same applies where A contemplates P attacking V with a piece of wood and P of his own accord pulls out a gun to shoot V dead. Where, however, A contemplates the use of a knife by P and P uses a gun to kill V the courts are likely to hold that A will be an accomplice to murder on the basis that the weapon used was 'as deadly' as the weapon contemplated. There is authority to suggest that if A contemplates the use of a gun by P to cause grievous bodily harm to V, and P uses a knife to kill V, A might yet escape liability because the weapon was used in a 'more deadly' way: see *R v Gamble* [1989] NI 268 (approved by Lord Hutton in *R v Powell and Daniels*; *R v English*, above).

b)  Suppose A and P agree to attack V, the agreement being to hurt V but not seriously. A does not, therefore, contemplate V being killed or suffering grievous bodily harm – although he does contemplate V suffering some harm. Suppose that during the attack P hits V as agreed, but with more force than A contemplated, and with intent to kill or do grievous bodily harm – with the result that V dies. P will be guilty of murder. A cannot be an accomplice to murder as he lacks the mens rea. On the basis of *R v Stewart and Scholfield* [1995] 1 Cr App R 441, however, A could be an accomplice to manslaughter – the key question will be whether A contemplated the actions of P that caused V's death. The fact that A does not contemplate the mens rea with which P acts is irrelevant.

### Participation: transferred malice and accomplices

If the accomplice agrees to assist in the killing of X, and the principal offender deliberately chooses a different victim, Y, the accomplice will not be a party to the killing of Y: see *R v Saunders and Archer* (1573) 2 Plowd 473.

## Participation: withdrawal

*R* v *Becerra and Cooper* (1975) 62 Cr App R 212 provides that for withdrawal to be effective there must be timely communication of the intention to abandon the common purpose from those who wish to dissociate themselves from the contemplated crime to those who desire to continue in it. In *R* v *Whitefield* (1983) 79 Cr App R 36 the court expressed the view that if D's participation is confined to advice or encouragement, he must at least communicate his change of mind to the other, and the communication must be such as will serve unequivocal notice upon the other party to the common unlawful cause that if he proceeds upon it he does so without the aid and assistance of those who withdraw. The emphasis is, therefore, on communication of withdrawal to the others parties: *R* v *Rook* [1993] 1 WLR 1005.

## 10.3 Key cases and statutes

### Incitement

*   *Invicta Plastics* v *Clare* [1976] RTR 251
    Mens rea needed

*   *R* v *Curr* [1968] 2 QB 944
    Knowledge needed by incitee

*   *R* v *Fitzmaurice* [1983] 1 All ER 189
    Where impossibility might still provide a defence at common law

*   *R* v *McDonough* (1962) 47 Cr App R 37
    Impossibility no defence – general incitement

*   *R* v *Most* (1881) 7 QBD 244
    Incitement can be unilateral

*   *Race Relations Board* v *Applin* [1973] QB 815
    Actus reus of incitement

### Conspiracy

*   *DPP* v *Nock* [1978] AC 979
    Impossibility may be a defence to specific common law conspiracies

*   *R* v *Anderson* [1985] 2 All ER 961
    Mens rea required for conspiracy

*   *R* v *Reed* [1982] Crim LR 819
    Nature of agreement

*   *R* v *Siracusa* (1990) 90 Cr App R 340
    Mens rea required for conspiracy

- Criminal Law Act 1977, s1(1) – statutory basis for conspiracy

## Attempt

- *R v Gullefer* (1990) 91 Cr App R 356
  Direction on actus reus

- *R v Khan* (1990) 91 Cr App R 29
  Mens rea for statutory attempt

- *R v Shivpuri* [1986] 2 All ER 334
  No defence of impossibility

- *R v Walker and Hayles* (1989) 90 Cr App R 226
  Mens rea for statutory attempt

- Criminal Attempts Act 1981, s1(1) – statutory basis for the offence

- Criminal Attempts Act 1981, s1(2) and (3) – no defence of impossibility

## Accessorial liability

- *Attorney-General s Reference (No 1 of 1975)* [1975] 3 WLR 11
  Defines procuring

- *Davies v DPP* [1954] AC 378
  Where principal deliberately exceeds scope of joint enterprise

- *DPP for Northern Ireland v Maxwell* [1978] 3 All ER 1140
  Where accomplice gives 'blank cheque'

- *Johnson v Youden* [1950] 1 KB 544
  Accomplice must have mens rea

- *R v Anderson and Morris* [1966] 2 QB 110
  Where principal deliberately exceeds scope of joint enterprise

- *R v Bamborough* [1996] Crim LR 744
  Accomplice liability for manslaughter where principal commits murder

- *R v Becarra and Cooper* (1975) 62 Cr App R 212
  What is needed to prove withdrawal

- *R v Betts and Ridley* (1930) 22 Cr App Rep 148
  Accomplice a party to accidental consequences

- *R v Clarkson* [1971] 1 WLR 1402
  Mere presence at the crime insufficient

- *R v Gilmour* (2000) The Times 21 June
  Accomplice liability for manslaughter where principal commits murder

- *R v Powell and Daniels; R v English* [1997] 4 All ER 545
  Joint enterprise rules

- *R v Rook* [1993] 2 All ER 955
  What is needed to prove withdrawal

- *R v Saunders and Archer* (1573) 2 Plowd 473
  Where principal chooses a different victim

- *Thornton v Mitchell* [1940] 1 All ER 339
  Liability where principal acquitted

- Accessories and Abettors Act 1861, s8 – sets out modes of participation

## 10.4 Questions and suggested solutions

QUESTION ONE

A left the following message on B's answer phone. 'Let's break into D's house and take his stamp collection.' B, who was a friend of D, decided not to reply to A's message or to tell the police about A's plan. Subsequently, A persuaded C to join him instead. Four days later C was driving A to D's house when C told A that he no longer wanted to go through with it and stopped the car. A threatened C that unless C drove him to D's house, A would 'disfigure' C's daughter. A had a reputation for being very violent. Reluctantly, C drove A to D's house but A failed to enter the house because there were too many burglar alarms and A was unable to bypass them.

Advise A, B and C of their criminal liability, if any.

University of London LLB Examination
(for External Students) Criminal Law June 1998 Q1

*General Comment*

A question providing an opportunity to explore the nature of the three inchoate offences and the relationship each has with the problem of impossibility. Accessorial liability arises in connection with the substantive offence. Note the problems surrounding the availability of duress. For the sake of clarity, the substantive offences committed by the principal offender A are considered first.

*Skeleton Solution*

Liability of A for attempted burglary; impossibility – C's liability as an accomplice; withdrawal from the scheme; availability of duress – conspiracy between A and C and incitement of C by A; impossibility regarding both – A's incitement of B and impossibility.

*Suggested Solution*

When A tried to enter the house he may have committed the offence of burglary contrary to s1 of the Criminal Attempts Act 1981 and s9(1)(a) of the Theft Act 1968 in as much as he took steps more than merely preparatory to the commission of the burglary. The burglary would have comprised of entering the property as a trespasser with intent to steal. There is no doubt that A had the intent to commit the offence, the only issue is whether or not his actions were more than merely preparatory. This is essentially a question of fact for the jury: see *R v Gullefer* (1990) 91 Cr App R 356 and *R v Geddes* (1996) The Times 16 July. The fact that it is impossible for A to carry out the burglary will be no bar to liability. Impossibility of means has never been recognised as a defence in English criminal law. In any event the matter is dealt with by the Criminal Attempts Act 1981. Section 1(2) provides that a person may be guilty of attempting to commit an offence even though the facts are such that the commission of the offence is impossible, and s1(3) adds that the defendant is to be judged on the facts as he believed them to be. Hence the question becomes – did A take steps that he believed to be more than merely preparatory to the commission of the offence? See further *R v Shivpuri* [1986] 2 All ER 334.

C could be charged as an accomplice to A. It is possible to be an accomplice to an attempt: see *R v Dunnington* [1984] QB 472. By driving A to the scene of the crime he could be regarded as having aided and/or abetted the commission of the offence by A. Mens rea would not be a problem as C clearly contemplated the type of crime committed by A: see *R v Bainbridge* [1959] 3 WLR 356. There are two issues that C could raise in response to a charge of aiding and abetting the attempted burglary. The first is that he had withdrawn from the common enterprise and hence was no longer acting as an accomplice at the time A committed the attempted burglary. The question is whether or not he did enough to effectively withdraw. On the basis of *R v Becarra and Cooper* (1975) 62 Cr App R 212 there must be something more than a mere mental change of intention and physical change of place by C. In so far as it is possible he must give A a timely communication of his intention to abandon the common purpose. He will need to provide evidence of some communication, verbal or otherwise, that served unequivocal notice on A that he was proceeding without the further aid and assistance of C. Again, whether or not C can establish evidence of this will be a matter of fact for the jury. Stopping the car may be significant in this respect.

The second issue to be raised by C is the defence of duress. He will argue that he was forced to continue with his participation in the scheme because of the threats made by A. On the basis of *R v Graham* [1982] 1 All ER 801, the jury will be directed to consider whether C was impelled to act as he did because, as a result of what A had said, he had good cause to fear that if he did not do what A asked, A would kill or cause serious physical injury. If so satisfied the jury will then have to determine whether or not a sober person of reasonable firmness, sharing the characteristics of C would have responded to the threats by taking part in the offence.

There is no doubt that A does specify a crime to be committee by C and does make a threat to cause serious harm. There may be a question as to whether or not the threat was sufficiently imminent – did C have an opportunity to stop the threat being carried out: see *R v Hudson and Taylor* [1971] 2 QB 202. In deciding whether such an opportunity was reasonably open to C the jury should have regard to his age and circumstances, and to any risks to him which may be involved in the course of action relied on.

C may have a problem in relying on the defence of duress if the prosecution argue that he voluntarily joined a criminal association and them found himself forced to commit an offence by another member of that association. In *R v Shepard* (1987) 86 Cr App R 47 it was held that the defence of duress will be denied in such situations if it is proved that in joining a criminal enterprise the defendant appreciated the nature of the enterprise itself and the attitudes of those in charge of it, so that when he was in fact subjected to compulsion he could fairly be said by a jury to have voluntarily exposed himself and submitted himself to such compulsion.

An alternative charge for the prosecution would be that A and C conspired to commit the burglary. The conspiracy would be charged contrary to s1(1) of the Criminal Law Act 1977 as amended. The prosecution would have to prove that A and C agreed on a course of conduct that (if the agreement had been carried out in accordance with their intentions) would have necessarily amounted to, or involved the commission of, any offence. There was clearly an agreement. A obviously had the intention to carry out the agreement. The fact that C would not have actually been carrying out the burglary as a principal offender would be no bar to a prosecution for conspiracy. On the basis of *R v Siracusa* (1990) 90 Cr App R 340 it would be sufficient that C knew what was going on and the intention to participate in the furtherance of the criminal purpose could be established by his failure to stop the unlawful activity. The fact that he subsequently changes his mind would have no bearing on the fact that a conspiracy would have been committed.

The fact that the burglary proved impossible to carry out would be no bar to a prosecution for statutory conspiracy. The Criminal Law Act 1977 (as amended by the Criminal Attempts Act 1981) provides that A and C can be convicted of conspiracy provided, at the time of the agreement, they believed the plan was capable of being executed. They will be judged on the facts as they believed them to be at the time.

If necessary the prosecution could charge A with inciting C to commit the offence of burglary with him. By communicating his idea to C A commits the actus reus of the offence. The incitement reaches the mind of the incitee: see *Race Relations Board v Applin* [1973] QB 815. There seems to be no doubt that C knows that what is being suggested would be a criminal offence: see *R v Curr* [1968] 2 QB 944 The mens rea requirement, as laid down in *Invicta Plastics v Clare* [1976] RTR 251 is that A should intend to communicate, and should have knowledge of the facts that constitute the offence. He should also have an intention that the offence should be committed. All of these elements seem to be evident on the facts. Again the issue of impossibility arises. As incitement is a common law offence it falls outside the scope of the Criminal Attempts

Act 1981. On the basis of *R v Fitzmaurice* [1983] 1 All ER 189 impossibility will not be a bar to conviction provided the offence was capable of being committed by someone (ie someone who knew how to circumvent the alarms). Impossibility would only provide a defence to common law incitement where it could be shown that the offence incited was totally impossible (eg suggesting that C kill Queen Victoria).

Finally A may be charged with inciting B to commit burglary. The actus reus and mens rea for the offence is as outlined above in relation to C. The fact that B was indifferent as to the plan does not prevent A being guilty of incitement. The suggestion reached the mind of the incitee. There does not have to be any evidence that he was persuaded by what he heard. B's failure to notify the police would probably not result in any liability. In theory he could be regarded as 'helping' the commission of the offence by not warning the victim, but evidentially it would be impossible to establish liability.

## QUESTION TWO

Andrew fell madly in love with Brenda who was married to Chas, a quick tempered man of small stature. Andrew was determined to win Brenda. He wrote anonymously to Chas saying that Brenda had been sleeping with their neighbour Donald. This was untrue. When Chas showed Brenda the letter they quarrelled. Eventually she called Chas a 'thick midget'. Chas hit Brenda under the chin with his umbrella and she fell backwards. In fact her skull was fractured by the fall. When Andrew heard what had happened he paid Donald, who was a prison officer, to attack Chas who was being held on remand in prison. Donald took the money though he had no intention to hurt Chas.

Advise the parties about their criminal liability, if any. What difference, if any, would it make to your advice if (a) Brenda had died or, alternatively, (b) Brenda had been wrongly treated by an overworked doctor in casualty who failed to treat her correctly?

University of London LLB Examination
(for External Students) Criminal Law June 1997 Q1

### General Comment

A reasonably straightforward question, although one involving a wide range of offences on the syllabus. The conspiracy issues need to be considered very carefully and a knowledge of *R v Anderson* and *R v Siracusa* is required.

### Skeleton Solution

Chas: liability for non-fatal offences against the person – Andrew: incitement – Andrew and Donald – conspiracy; if Brenda had died; murder, provocation and diminished responsibility; if the doctor failed to treat Brenda correctly; whether inappropriate medical treatment constitutes a novus actus interveniens.

## Suggested Solution

By punching Brenda on the chin, Chas has almost certainly committed an assault, which was defined in *Fagan* v *Metropolitan Police Commissioner* [1969] 1 QB 439 as where the accused intentionally or recklessly causes the victim to apprehend immediate personal violence. Brenda has certainly been put in fear of violence and Chas has done so intentionally. The punch would also fall within the definition of a battery, which was defined in *Fagan* as the 'intended use of unlawful force to another person without his consent'.

Chas may also be charged with an assault concerning actual bodily harm contrary to s47 Offences Against the Person Act (OAPA) 1861. This offence requires an assault (which is clearly present here) that causes actual bodily harm. Actual bodily harm was defined in *R* v *Chan Fook* [1994] 1 WLR 689 as 'any injury which is not so trivial as to be wholly significant'. A fractured skull would certainly constitute a more than insignificant injury. Does Chas have the mens rea for the s47 offence? The House of Lords established in *R* v *Savage*; *R* v *Parmenter* [1991] 3 WLR 914 that the only mens rea required for the offence is that required for the assault, and that the prosecution need not prove that the accused intended or foresaw that his act would cause any injury. Since Chas deliberately assaulted Brenda and this assault has caused actual bodily harm within the definition laid down in *Chan Fook*, it is submitted that Chas may be convicted of the s47 offence.

Chas may also be charged with grievous bodily harm to Brenda contrary to ss18 and 20 OAPA 1861. In *DPP* v *Smith* [1961] AC 290 the court refused to lay down a detailed definition of what may or may not amount to 'grievous bodily harm', holding merely that it meant a 'very serious injury', and that in effect this is essentially a question of fact for the jury. In my opinion a fractured skull is a serious and potentially life threatening injury and would fall within the definition of grievous bodily harm. However, Chas could only be charged under s18 OAPA 1861 (which carries a maximum sentence of life imprisonment) if the prosecution could prove that he specifically intended to cause Brenda serious harm. Chas may or may not have had this intention but it is submitted in the absence of any confession by Chas to this effect that it would be difficult for the prosecution to discharge its burden beyond any reasonable doubt that Chas intended a single punch to cause serious harm. The prosecution are more likely to succeed under s20 OAPA 1861 where, following *R* v *Savage*; *R* v *Parmenter* (above), they need only prove that Chas intended or foresaw that the punch would cause Brenda some harm.

If the prosecution could prove that Chas intended to kill Brenda, Chas may be convicted of attempting to murder Brenda contrary to s1 Criminal Attempts Act 1981. However, it is submitted that the prosecution would find it difficult to prove the mens rea of this offence since it was established in *R* v *Whybrow* (1951) 35 Cr App R 141 that the mens rea required for attempted murder was specifically an intention to kill – an intention to cause even serious harm would be insufficient, although such an intention was sufficient mens rea for the full offence of murder.

By paying Donald to attack Chas, Andrew may be convicted of an incitement to commit actual or grievous bodily harm. An incitement was defined in *Race Relations Board* v *Applin* [1973] QB 815 as where the accused urges, advises or encourages another to commit a crime. Andrew has clearly urged Donald to attack Chas by paying him to do so. The offence is complete so long as the accused has urged another to commit an offence intending that that other should carry out the offence; it is irrelevant whether the other actually acts on the advice: *R* v *Curr* [1968] 2 QB 944.

When Donald agreed to attack Chas both he and Andrew may have committed a conspiracy to commit actual or grievous bodily harm contrary to s1 Criminal Law Act 1977. Since Donald accepted the payment, an agreement has clearly been arrived at. The issue is whether a charge of conspiracy can succeed if one of the parties is merely pretending to participate in the agreement for some ulterior purpose but actually has no intention of carrying out the offence agreed upon. The House of Lords in *R* v *Anderson* [1986] AC 27 upheld the conviction of a person charged with conspiring to help a prisoner escape even though the accused had only agreed to assist in the escape in order to receive payment and never intended to carry out the plan. The court held that a charge of conspiracy did not require the prosecution to prove an intention to carry out the offence. In *R* v *Siracusa* (1990) 90 Cr App R 340 the Court of Appeal went further, holding that a defendant can be guilty of conspiracy simply by agreeing that an offence be committed without intending to take any active part at all in securing the commission of the offence. This has been confirmed by the Privy Council in *Yip Chiu-Cheung* v *R* [1994] 3 WLR 514. Hence Andrew's lack of intention to carry out the attack on Chas will not be a bar to his conviction for conspiracy.

If Brenda had died, Chas could be charged with murder. However, the prosecution would need to prove that Chas intended either to kill Brenda or cause her serious harm: *R* v *Woollin* [1998] 4 All ER 103. If the prosecution were able to establish this mens rea, Chas may be able to raise the partial defence of provocation. This defence would have the effect of reducing the conviction from murder to manslaughter, thereby attracting a discretionary sentence and avoiding a mandatory sentence of life imprisonment applicable for murder. Following *R* v *Duffy* [1949] 1 All ER 932 Chas could raise this defence if he suffered a 'sudden loss of control' as a result of what Brenda said to him. Although the defence of provocation as defined in *Duffy* was originally confined to provocative acts, the defence was extended to provocative acts or words by s3 Homicide Act 1957. Following the House of Lords' decision in *R* v *Smith (Morgan)* [2000] 4 All ER 289 the question for the jury (assuming there is evidence of provocation) will be whether or not Chas displayed what was, for him, reasonable self-control. For these purposes no distinction should be drawn between characteristics that explain the gravity of the provocation to Chas (ie he may well be an unintelligent person of short stature), and those characteristics that relate to self-control. The jury would still be directed, however, to ignore matters such as the defendant's bad temper, jealousy or possessiveness. Hence Chas' quick temper should be ignored for the purposes of asking whether he displayed reasonable self-control. If the prosecution were unable to prove that Chas intended to kill Brenda or cause her serious harm and therefore unable to succeed on a charge of murder, Chas may be charged with the unlawful act of manslaughter of Brenda. This offence was defined in *R v Church* [1966] 1 QB 59 as where the accused causes the death of the victim by an unlawful act which all sober and reasonable people would inevitably recognise would expose another person to the risk of some harm albeit not serious harm. The assault and battery perpetrated on Brenda by Chas would constitute the unlawful act and it is submitted that punching someone in the face is clearly dangerous in the sense mentioned in *Church*. The prosecution need only prove the mens rea for the unlawful act and that it is objectively dangerous. It is unnecessary to prove that the accused had any intention or foresight to kill or even harm the victim: *R v Ball* [1989] Crim LR 730.

It is submitted that the overworked doctor failing to treat Brenda correctly would be unlikely to break the chain of causation. It has been held (*R v Smith* [1959] 2 QB 35) and confirmed in *R v Cheshire* [1991] 1 WLR 844 that the accused's act remains a legal cause of death as long as it is an 'operating or substantial' or a 'significant' cause of death; the accused's act need not be the sole or even the main cause of death. In neither of the above cases did the failure of the medical profession to administer the appropriate medical treatment amount to a novus actus interveniens breaking the chain of causation. Incorrect medical treatment will only break the chain of causation if it amounts to an independent cause of death rendering Chas's act merely part of the history.

## QUESTION THREE

A wrote to B and asked B to help him steal from C's house where A believed there was a collection of valuable china. B replied that he was willing to help. In fact, B had decided to go along with A's suggestion because he wanted to report A to the police because B had a grudge against A. B went to the police and told them what he was doing. The police were interested in the arrangement because they wanted to see to whom the china would be disposed. They hoped to catch the 'handler' of such stolen goods. B drove with A to C's house at the arranged time. B opened a window catch with a piece of wire. A climbed in and found that the china collection was not there. A returned to the car where B was waiting. Both were seized by the police.

Advise the parties which offences they have committed.

University of London LLB Examination
(for External Students) Criminal Law June 1995 Q1

### General Comment

A fairly straightforward question involving a discussion of burglary, inchoate offences and accessorial liability, although a sound knowledge of the Privy Council ruling in *Yip Chiu-Cheung v R* is essential.

*Skeleton Solution*

A: incitement?; conspiracy?; burglary?; attempt?; impossibility – B: conspiracy?; accessorial liability.

*Suggested Solution*

When A wrote to B suggesting that they stole from C's house A may have committed the offence of incitement to commit theft. An incitement was defined in the case of *Race Relations Board* v *Applin* [1973] QB 815 as including 'to urge, spur on, persuade or encourage another to commit a crime', which A has evidently done. The problem here is that A incited B to steal a china collection which it transpires is not at C's house and therefore the issue of impossibility arises. It was held in *R* v *Fitzmaurice* [1983] 1 All ER 189 that the law on impossibility relating to incitement was that stated in *Haughton* v *Smith* [1975] AC 476, to the effect that factual impossibility is a defence to a charge of incitement. Consequently, it is likely that A will be acquitted of this offence (this is of course assuming that the china collection was not at C's house at the time A incited B, rather than being removed by the police after being informed by B).

When B replied that he was willing to help, both A and B may be guilty of a conspiracy to commit theft and burglary contrary to s1 Criminal Law Act 1977. The actus reus of this offence is an agreement to carry out a course of conduct that will lead to the commission of an offence. The problem area here is that it appears that B only agreed with A so that he could inform the police, and that he pretended to go along with A so as to entrap him. In *R* v *Anderson* [1986] AC 27 Lord Bridge held that it was necessary to prove that the accused intended that the course of conduct agreed on should necessarily be pursued even though he only intended to play some part. Subsequently in *R* v *Siracusa* (1990) 90 Cr App R 340, O'Connor LJ clarified this by explaining that D can be guilty of conspiracy simply by agreeing with others that a criminal course of conduct is pursued. He does not have to intend to play any active part. This interpretation does cause difficulties for undercover police officers who go along with criminals and their plans in order to help secure convictions. The Privy Council decision in *Yip Chiu-Cheung* v *R* [1994] 2 All ER 924 makes clear that there is no public policy exemption for undercover police officers, but the answer may lie in the authorities not exercising the discretion to prosecute in such cases. Accordingly B could be convicted of conspiracy even though he intended that A should be arrested before he succeeded in committing the offence.

When A climbed through the window into C's house he committed the offence of burglary contrary to s9(1)a of the Theft Act 1968. He has clearly entered the building as a trespasser with an intention to commit theft. It is irrelevant for a charge under s9(1)a that the accused in fact fails to commit theft; the intention to do so is sufficient.

When A entered the building to look for the china collection he has probably committed the offence of attempted theft contrary to s1 of the Criminal Attempts Act 1981. For a charge of attempt, the accused must do an act which is 'more than merely preparatory' towards the commission of the offence. Under s4(3) of the 1981 Act this is a mixed question of law and fact? the judge must decide whether the accused's act is capable of being more than merely preparatory, and the jury then decide whether it was in fact more than merely preparatory. The phrase has not been precisely defined but it was held in *R v Gullefer* [1990] 3 All ER 882 that the accused must have 'embarked on the crime proper'. By entering C's house to look for the china collection it is submitted that A has clearly done an act which is more than merely preparatory towards the theft of that collection. However, the problem of impossibility arises again, except this time with different results. Section 1(2) of the 1981 Act states to the effect that impossibility is no longer a defence to a charge of attempt (reversing the position in *Haughton v Smith* (above) which still applies to incitement). This has been confirmed by the House of Lords in *R v Shivpuri* [1987] AC 1, which overruled *Anderton v Ryan* [1985] 2 WLR 968.

When B drove A to C's house and opened the window for him, B may be guilty as an accessory under s8 of the Accessories and Abettors Act 1861 to the offences committed by A. By opening the window for A he has clearly assisted him to commit the offence, and burglary and attempted theft were within B's contemplation: see *R v Bainbridge* (1960) 43 Cr App R 194.

When B opened the window catch with a piece of wire, he may be guilty of criminal damage contrary to s1 of the Criminal Damage Act 1971 if he caused any damage to the window.

## QUESTION FOUR

F and his friend G agreed that they would beat up H, with whom they had quarrelled in a pub the previous Saturday. It was agreed between them that F would hold H and G would punch him. They waited inside a shop till H left his house and walked past the shop. F and G came out and seized him. They dragged H down an alleyway. There, as agreed, F held H while G punched him. G pulled out a knife and was about to stab H when F finally shouted, 'Don't do that!' It had been clearly understood between F and G that only fists would be used, though F was suspicious of G because he was known to be unreliable and given to uncontrolled bouts of violence. G thrust at H with the knife but missed and instead F was stabbed.

Advise the parties of their criminal liability.

University of London LLB Examination
(for External Students) Criminal Law June 1995 Q6

### General Comment

A fairly straightforward question on inchoate offences, offences against the person and accessorial liability. The most likely problem area for the reasonably well-prepared student was the issue of F's mens rea as an accessory.

### Skeleton Solution

F & G: conspiracy?; false imprisonment?; kidnapping – G: grievous bodily harm?; attempted murder – F: accessory to the offences committed by G – G: grievous bodily harm to F.

### Suggested Solution

When F and G agreed to beat up H they may have committed the offence of conspiring to assault, batter or occasion actual bodily harm contrary to s1 of the Criminal Law Act 1977. They have committed the actus rea of this offence by agreeing to beat up H.

When F and G seized H, they have committed the offence of false imprisonment, which was defined in *R v Rahman* (1986) 81 Cr App R 349 as 'the unlawful and intentional or reckless restraint on a person's freedom of movement from a particular place'. By seizing H, F and G have restricted H's freedom of movement and have done so intentionally.

When they dragged H down an alleyway, F and G have technically committed the offence of kidnapping, which was defined in *R v D* [1984] AC 778 as 'the taking or carrying away of a person by force or fraud without their consent and without lawful excuse'. F and G have clearly taken H by force, against his will.

When G punched H, G may have committed a variety of offences, depending on the severity of the injuries caused to H. Certainly G would have committed an assault and battery, and is likely to have committed an assault occasioning actual bodily harm contrary to s47 of the Offences Against the Person Act 1861. A punch is likely to have resulted in some harm to H and therefore the definition of actual bodily harm laid down in *R v Chan Fook* [1994] Crim LR 432 as 'any injury which is more than trivial' is likely to be satisfied.

F is almost certainly guilty of being an accessory (under s8 of the Accessories and Abettors Act 1861) to the assault, battery and possible actual bodily harm committed by G. F has clearly committed the actus of the offence by assisting G, and has the mens rea, in that assault, battery and actual bodily harm are offences which were within his contemplation when he agreed with G to beat up H: *R v Bainbridge* (1960) 43 Cr App R 194.

When G stabbed F with a knife it is likely that he committed wounding or grievous bodily harm contrary to s18 of the Offences Against the Person Act 1861. The stab wound may amount to either of the two alternative actus reus of this offence: 'wounding' which requires simply that both layers of the skin must be broken (*JJC (A Minor) v Eisenhower* [1984] QB 331), or 'grievous bodily harm', defined as 'really serious harm' in *DPP v Smith* [1960] 3 All ER 161.

The mens rea required for this offence is that the accused intended to cause the victim grievous bodily harm. Although G intended to cause H harm, this mens rea can be transferred to F under the doctrine of transferred malice: *R v Latimer* (1886) 17 QBD 359.

If G caused F grievous bodily harm, but the prosecution cannot prove that he intended to cause such serious harm, then he may be charged with maliciously wounding or inflicting grievous bodily harm contrary to s20 of the Offences Against the Person Act 1861. The actus reus of this offence is similar to the s18 offence, but with respect to the mens rea it is sufficient if the prosecution proves that G merely intended or was reckless as to whether he caused some harm. G could be convicted by transferring the intention to cause some harm from H to F under the doctrine of transferred malice (see above), or by arguing that although G was trying to stab H, he foresaw that he may injure G: *R v Savage, R v Parmenter* [1991] 3 WLR 914.

G may also be liable for the attempted murder of H contrary to s1 of the Criminal Attempts Act 1981. G has clearly done an act which is 'more than merely preparatory' but the prosecution would have to prove that G intended to kill H (*R v Whybrow* (1951) 35 Cr App R 141), or, that he foresaw death as virtually certain: see *R v Walker and Hayles* (1990) 90 Cr App R 226 and *R v Woollin* [1998] 4 All ER 103.

An interesting question is whether F can be convicted as an accessory to the offences committed by G involving the use of the knife. If the principal offender deliberately exceeds the scope of the agreed common design and uses a weapon, he will be regarded as acting on his own account. The accomplice ceases to be a party to such actions; see *R v Powell and Daniels*; *R v English* [1997] 4 All ER 545. Consequently, since F did not know that G was carrying a knife it follows that under *R v Powell and Daniels*; *R v English* should not be convicted for any offences associated with the use of that knife.

### QUESTION FIVE

L telephoned M suggesting that they should enter Z's house, 'to do it over'. Z was their teacher. M understood L to be suggesting that they should look over the house and hide one or two of Z's things and leave messages in shaving soap on Z's mirrors. L meant that they should take anything of value and damage the rest of Z' s property with paint. M said, 'Alright I'll see you at 8 pm tonight.'. In fact, M failed to turn up having thought the matter over. Later, L recruited O to his plan and together they went to Z's house. Unexpectedly, Z returned home and discovered L and O. L hit Z over the head with a poker.

Advise L, M and O as to their criminal liability.

Adapted from University of London LLB Examination
(for External Students) Criminal Law June 1991 Q4

*General Comment*

The question raises a wide range of issues. Particular trick points to watch for are the possibility of attempted incitement, and the possible absence of any agreement with regard to the conspiracy. The attack upon Z clearly requires reference to the Wilson and Jenkins point on burglary.

## Skeleton Solution

Incitement – *R* v *Curr* point – possible attempt – conspiracy – whether any agreement – conspiracy with O – burglary – s9(1)(a) – assault on Z – s9(1)(b) – *R* v *Wilson and Jenkins* – principal deliberately departs from the common design.

## Suggested Solution

### Incitement and conspiracy

L suggests the commission of a number of offences to M. He may incur liability for common law incitement. The actus reus of incitement is committed where a defendant suggests the commission of an offence to another person. It has to be shown that the suggestion from the incitor has reached the mind of the incitee, but there is no need to provide evidence that the incitee acted on the suggestion: see comments of Lord Denning MR in *Race Relations Board* v *Applin* 1973] QB 815. Generally, the incitee must know of the facts that make the conduct incited criminal. Hence, for example, an incitor can only be guilty of incitement to handle stolen goods if the incitee knew or believed the good in question to be stolen: see *R* v *Curr* [1968] 2 QB 944. In that case the defendant ran a loan business whereby he would lend money to women with children in return for their handing over their signed Family Allowance books. He would then use other women to cash the family allowance vouchers. He was convicted of inciting the commission of offences under s9(b) of the Family Allowance Act 1945, which made it an offence for any person to receive any sum by way of Family Allowance knowing it was not properly payable, but appealed successfully to the Court of Appeal, where it was held that the trial judge had erred in not directing the jury to consider whether those women, who were being incited to use the signed allowance books to collect money on behalf of the defendant, had actually known that what they were being asked to do was unlawful. In the present case L may contend that as he and M were at cross purposes, M may not have realised that what was being incited was unlawful. If this were the case, L might be charged with attempted incitement: see *R* v *Ransford* (1874) 13 Cox CC 9.

It would appear that L did have the mens rea for incitement. In *Invicta Plastics* v *Clare* [1976] RTR 251, the Divisional Court defined it as involving not only an intention to incite, but also an intention that the incitee should act upon the incitement.

L and M may be charged with statutory conspiracy given that they agree to enter Z's house for an unlawful purpose, but there are difficulties here. Section 1(1) of the Criminal Law Act 1977 (as amended) provides that if a person agrees with any other person that a course of conduct shall be pursued which, if the agreement is carried out in accordance with their intentions, either will necessarily amount to or involve the commission of any offence or offences by one or more of the parties to the agreement, he is guilty of conspiracy to commit the offence or offences in question. The problem is that there is no meeting of the minds. Arguably the parties have not even agreed that any offence will be committed. Note that L cannot be charged with attempted conspiracy as the offence was abolished by s5 of the 1977 Act.

From the evidence provided it appears that there is much clearer evidence of a conspiracy between L and O, and that both could be charged with conspiracy to commit burglary contrary to the 1977 Act.

*Burglary*

The evidence provided indicates that when L entered the property owned by Z he intended to steal and commit criminal damage. O appears to have been fully aware of this. Under s9(1)(a) of the Theft Act 1968, a person is guilty of burglary if he enters any building or part of a building as a trespasser and with intent, inter alia, to commit the theft of anything in the building, or with the intent of doing unlawful damage to the building or anything therein. L and O clearly enter a building and have no permission to be there.

*Assault on Z*

In striking Z on the head with the poker, L commits an assault, quite probably grievous bodily harm or wounding, depending upon the severity of the injuries. The harm appears to have been inflicted intentionally, thus L may incur liability under s18 or s20 of the Offences Against the Persons Act 1861. A further possibility is that L might be charged under s9(1)(b) of the 1968 Act which provides (inter alia) that a person is guilty of burglary if having entered any building as a trespasser and inflicts on any person therein any grievous bodily harm. Whether or not L entered as a trespasser has already been discussed. Note that, under s9(1)(b) of the Theft act 1968, L need not have had the intention to steal or inflict grievous bodily harm when he entered the building as a trespasser; such intent can be formed subsequent to entry. The infliction of grievous bodily harm under s9(1)(b) does not have to constitute an offence; it simply requires L to have inflicted grievous bodily harm upon Z. The Court of Appeal in *R v Wilson and Jenkins* [1983] 1 All ER 993 contemplated that a defendant would be guilty under s9(1)(b) where he entered a house as a trespasser and was observed by an occupant of whose presence he was unaware. Should the occupant suffer a stroke as a result of this shock, the defendant would have inflicted grievous bodily harm regardless of his lack of mens rea. The House of Lords, although allowing the defendant's appeal in *R v Wilson and Jenkins*, did not dissent from the above analysis of s9(1)(b).

O will contend that he is not guilty under s9(1)(b) since the attack upon Z was not part of the original agreement. The general rule is that an accomplice will be liable for all the accidental, or unforeseen consequences that flow from the common design being carried out, but where the principal deliberately departs from the common design, an accomplice ceases to be a party to his actions. Thus in *Davies v DPP* [1954] AC ˈ˙8, which concerned a gang fight in which the principal offender had killed an or with a knife, the defendant accomplice was acquitted of being an accompli˙ murder or manslaughter because the use of a knife during the attack w˙ scope of what had been contemplated by him: see further *R v Powe*ˡ *English* [1997] 3 WLR 959. Thus the attack upon Z is likely to be s˙ contemplated by O when he agreed to accompany L.

# Chapter 11

## General Defences – Insanity and Intoxication

11.1 **Introduction**

11.2 **Key points**

11.3 **Key cases and statute**

11.4 **Questions and suggested solutions**

## 11.1 Introduction

There are certain defences that are regarded as 'general' in the sense (in theory) they apply in respect of any criminal offence. Two such general defences – insanity and intoxication – are significant in that they relate to the defendant's state of mind. In a sense they can be seen as denials of fault, or as denying the capacity for fault. These topics typically arise as elements of problems questions or, occasionally, as topics for specific essay questions.

## 11.2 Key points

### Intoxication

Principally, intoxication is associated with alcohol, although the effects of drugs other than alcohol should also be considered.

Students should note that where drugs are known to produce aggressive or unpredictable behaviour, such drugs will be classed with alcohol for 'intoxication' purposes: *R* v *Hardie* [1985] 1 WLR 64.

a) Note that intoxication generally is not a defence. It may, however, negate the required mens rea.

Where a specific or ulterior intent is required, self-induced intoxication may preclude that intent: *R* v *Bailey* [1983] 2 All ER 503. Drunkenness may, for instance, prevent D from forming the intent required for murder – *R* v *O'Connor* [1991] Crim LR 135.

However note the decision in *Attorney-General for Northern Ireland* v *Gallagher* [1963] AC 349 in relation to drinking for 'dutch courage', having already formed the relevant intention.

b) Voluntary intoxication will not be a defence for crimes of basic intent: *DPP* v *Majewski* [1977] AC 443.

Such offences are capable of being committed recklessly, a criterion which is itself met by the accused's becoming voluntarily intoxicated.

Where D because of self-induced intoxication forms a mistaken belief that he is using force to defend himself that plea of self-defence will fail: *R* v *O'Grady* (1987) 85 Cr App R 315.

However, an accused may form an honest belief whilst so intoxicated and thereby find a statutory defence such as 'lawful excuse' to damage another's property: *Jaggard* v *Dickinson* [1981] QB 527.

c) Where intoxication is through a drug such as a sedative: *R* v *Hardie* – that intoxication may provide a defence even for crimes of basic intent if there is evidence that D was not reckless in consuming the substance

d) It is not clear whether involuntary intoxication may be a defence to a charge of basic intent. The House of Lords in *R* v *Kingston* [1994] Crim LR 846 held that involuntary intoxication may also be a defence to a charge of specific intent, but only where the intoxication deprived the accused of the requisite mens rea: it would not be an adequate defence for the accused to show that, although he still had the requisite mens rea, he would not have committed the offence were he sober. The better view regarding basic intent crimes is that if D does not form the requisite mens rea because of the effects of involuntary intoxication he should be acquitted, unless he can be shown to have been reckless in bring about the state of affairs.

### Insanity (insane automatism)

The three limbs of the definition of insanity provided in *McNaghten's Case* (1843) 10 Cl & F 200 must be understood:

a) The accused must be suffering from a 'defect of reason': *R* v *Clarke* [1972] 1 All ER 219.

b) Arising from 'a disease of the mind' (note that any condition which produces the required defect of reason may amount to a disease of the mind – the brain itself need not be affected): *R* v *Kemp* [1956] 3 All ER 249. Further, a disease of the mind giving rise to the defence of insanity must arise from an internal cause (such as disease or psychological illness) and not an external cause (such as injury or the consumption of drugs): *Bratty* v *Attorney-General for Northern Ireland* [1961] 3 All ER 523.

c) The 'disease of the mind' must produce either of two effects and the candidate in an examination should specify which he thinks is appropriate: either the accused did not know what he was doing or, if he did, that he did not know that it was wrong.

d) Automatism (ie non-insane automatism) was considered in Chapter 1. It should be noted that the relationship between insanity and automatism is a complex area which is often examined. A person who does not know what he is doing may claim the defence of insanity or automatism. The determinative criteria for distinguishing between the two defences appear to be whether the condition causing the accused to commit the offence is likely to recur (insanity) or not (automatism) and whether the cause of the condition is internal (insanity) or external (automatism): *R* v *Bratty* (above).

See especially: *R* v *Quick & Paddison* [1973] 3 All ER 347 and *R* v *Hennessy* (1989) 89 Cr App R 10 (diabetes); *Bratty* v *Attorney-General for Northern Ireland* [1961] 3 All ER 523 and *R* v *Sullivan* [1984] AC 156 (epilepsy); *R* v *Burgess* [1991] 2 All ER 769 (sleepwalking); *R* v *Rabey* (1977) 37 CCC (2d) 461 (Ont) and *R* v *T* [1990] Crim LR 256 (psychological trauma); *Attorney-General's Reference (No 2 of 1992)* [1993] 3 WLR 982 (driving without awareness).

## 11. 3 Key cases and statute

*Insanity*

- *Bratty* v *Attorney-General for Northern Ireland* [1963] AC 386
  Rationale for classification of conditions

- *McNaghten's Case* (1843) 10 Cl & F 200
  Definition of insanity

- *R* v *Burgess* [1991] 2 WLR 1206
  Violent sleepwalking can be a disease of the mind

- *R* v *Hennessy* [1989] 1 WLR 287
  Diabetes resulting in hyperglycaemia can be a disease of the mind

- *R* v *Kemp* [1957] 1 QB 399
  Arteriolosclerosis can be a disease of the mind

- *R* v *Sullivan* [1983] 1 All ER 577
  Epilepsy can be a disease of the mind

- *R* v *Windle* [1952] 2 QB 826
  D must know actions are illegal

- Criminal Procedure (Insanity) Act 1964, s1 – basis for special verdict

*Intoxication*

- *DPP* v *Beard* [1920] AC 479
  What is intoxication

- *DPP* v *Majewski* [1976] 2 All ER 142
  Basic/specific intent dichotomy

- *R v Hardie* [1984] 3 All ER 848
  Non-reckless self-intoxication

- *R v Kingston* [1994] 3 WLR 519
  No defence of disinhibition

- *R v Lipman* [1970] 1 QB 152
  Intoxication no defence to basic intent crimes

## 11.4 Questions and suggested solutions

QUESTION ONE

'The defence of "insanity" is now hopelessly out of date and should be replaced by some other concept.'

Discuss.

University of London LLB Examination
(for External Students) Criminal Law June 1998 Q7

*General Comment*

A very specific question that should clearly only be attempted by candidates with a good working knowledge of the issues. The greatest danger here is that candidates will simply write all they know about the defence of insanity. Whilst a good answer clearly involves a description of the defence, what is actually needed is an informed critique that brings out the inconsistencies in the law and accurately pinpoints the gaps.

*Skeleton Solution*

Set out the nature of the defence – explain the basis for raising insanity – what conditions can give rise to insanity – the link with automatism – the need to protect the public – the *Bratty* formulation – defendants who opt for insanity – the link with diminished responsibility – the need for a much broader defence – the views of the Butler Committee – the draft Criminal Code Bill.

*Suggested Solution*

The statement under consideration suggests that the defence of insanity is out of date and should be replaced by another concept. It is submitted that whilst the term insanity might be retained, the scope of the concept needs be radically altered if it is to offer a defence that is actually of any use.

The basis for the modern law is the definition laid down in the *'McNaghten Rules'* *McNaghten's Case* (1843) 10 Cl & F 200. This provides that the defence is made out where the jury is satisfied that, at the time of the committing of the act, the party accused was labouring under a defect of reason, from disease of the mind, as not to know the nature and quality of the act he was doing; or, if he did know it, that he did not know he was doing what was wrong.

The concept of disease of the mind is very widely drawn. It obviously covers the major mental diseases, which the doctors call psychoses, such as schizophrenia. It also covers diseases of the body that affect the working of the mind. Hence, in *R v Kemp* [1957] 1 QB 399 it was held that hardening of the arteries was a disease shown on the evidence to be capable of affecting the mind in such a way as to cause a defect, temporarily or permanently, of its reasoning, understanding and as such to amount to a disease of the mind within the meaning of the Rules. This reasoning has been extended to bring others suffering from relatively common conditions within the potential scope of the insanity defence. Hence in *R v Sullivan* [1983] 1 All ER 577 a sufferer from psychomotor epilepsy was held to be insane, because of the temporary and intermittent suspension of the mental faculties of reason, memory and understanding resulting from the occurrence of an epileptic fit. In *R v Hennessy* [1989] 1 WLR 287 diabetes was held to be a disease of the body giving rise to insanity in so much as hyperglycaemia, high blood sugar, caused by an inherent defect, and not corrected by insulin was a disease that caused a malfunction of the defendant's mind.

Many would find it abhorrent that sufferers from such common conditions are being labelled by the courts as criminally insane. The reason lies in the paucity of suitable defences in English criminal law.

First, it must be recognised that defendants in these cases are not raising the defence of insanity of their own volition. In *Sullivan* and in *Hennessy* the defendants sought to rely on the defence of automatism. The attractions of this are obvious. The defendant merely has to provide an evidential basis for the defence, albeit in the form of expert testimony; the defence does not raise issues of mental illness as such; most importantly of all the defence of automatism, if made out, results in a complete acquittal – the defendant walks free. This last point is the key. In many cases the courts are concerned at the prospect of a defendant being released with out the court having any jurisdiction over him or her. The court, rightly, sees itself as having a duty to protect the public from potentially dangerous defendants.

What happens, in cases such as *Sullivan* and others, is that the defendant pleads not guilty on the grounds of automatism. The trial judge expresses the view that he will not put the defence of automatism to the jury. The defendant thereupon changes his plea to guilty and appeals on the ground that the trial judge erred in not allowing the defence of automatism to be put to the jury. Why is the trial judge making such a ruling? Because he will have heard evidence as to the defendant's condition and will have concluded that, if the defendant were allowed the defence of automatism, he would be at large in society and would be a danger to the public. Hence the automatism route is blocked.

As Lord Denning explained in *Bratty v Attorney-General for Northern Ireland* [1963] AC 386 any mental disorder which has manifested itself in violence and is prone to recur is a disease of the mind. The court will not take the risk that the accused may offend again. The only 'excuse' open to the defendant is insanity. The key difference being, of course, that a successful plea or finding of insanity results in what is known as the 'special verdict'. Under s1 of the Criminal Procedure (Insanity) Act 1964 the finding is that the accused is not guilty by reason of insanity. This verdict allows the court to retain some control over the accused. In *Sullivan's* case, for example, it enabled the court to make orders in respect of his receiving hospital treatment as an outpatient.

Hence, it is the absence of any more general defence that is forcing judges to categorise defendants as insane in order to be able to exercise some jurisdiction over them.

The defence of insanity can, in theory, be raised as a defence to any crime, including summary offences, requiring proof of mens rea; see *R v Horseferry Road Magistrates' Court, ex parte K* [1997] Crim LR 129 and *DPP v H* [1997] 1 WLR 1406. The question arises however, as to who would want to raise the defence? If a defendant is charged with murder and there is evidence of mental illness he will almost certainly plead diminished responsibility as defined under s2(1) of the Homicide Act 1957. A defendant charged with a less serious offence will either try to rely on automatism (see above) or will simply plead guilty, so as not to run the risk of a finding of insanity. The reality is that very few defendants today actually make use of the defence.

The main reason for this is that the defence is so narrowly drawn. As stated above a defendant can only be criminally insane in one of two situations. The first is where he is in a state of automatism – ie he does not know what he is doing. As explained he is not permitted automatism as a defence because the condition arises from a disease of the mind. This is a very extreme condition. There are many defendants who are undoubtedly mentally ill in the medical sense, but who are nevertheless aware of their actions and thus fall outside of the scope of the legal definition of insanity. Where such defendants are charged with murder they still have the defence of diminished responsibility. Where they are charged with some lesser offence they do not. The second basis for insanity is where the defendant is aware of his actions but does not realise that they are wrong: *R v Windle* [1952] 2 QB 826. The difficulty here is that 'wrong' in this context means contrary to law – again a very narrow category.

The Butler Committee Report (Cmnd 6244) (1975), recommended the introduction of a new verdict of 'not guilty by reason of mental disorder' which could be returned in two situations: (i) where the defendant was unable to form the requisite mens rea due to mental disorder; or (ii) where the defendant was aware of his actions but was at the time suffering from severe mental disorder. The difficulty lies in producing a concept of insanity which is, on the one hand, simple enough for the averagely educated man or woman on a jury to understand, but which on the other hand is sufficiently sophisticated to encompass the varying types of mental abnormality with which other modern courts are likely to have to deal.

Essentially what is needed is a general defence of mental impairment – this would cater for the many mentally ill defendants who are aware of their actions and know that they are illegal, but cannot stop themselves from engaging in such activity. The Draft Criminal Code Bill effectively supports such a conclusion.

## QUESTION TWO

'A drunken intent is sufficient to give rise to criminal liability. This is the case even when the intoxication is involuntary.'

Discuss.

University of London LLB Examination
(for External Students) Criminal Law June 1999 Q8

### General Comment

A question that would be impossible to answer without a firm grasp of the rules on intoxication and an in-depth knowledge of the ruling in *R* v *Kingston* in particular. The question requires an explanation of the operation of the rules in *DPP* v *Majewski* and the concept of drunken intent. It is not an essay on involuntary intoxication as such, but requires some focus on the narrow point concerning the House of Lords' rejecting of the putative defence of disinhibition in *R* v *Kingston*.

### Skeleton Solution

Explain the basic rules in *DPP* v *Majewski* – the specific and basic intent dichotomy – explain the various types if intoxication and the distinction between intoxication and drunkenness – provide authorities on drunken intent – show how the rules work in practice – explain the decision in *R* v *Kingston* and go through the various steps in Lord Mustill's speech whereby he explains why a defence of disinhibition is not available.

### Suggested Solution

A defendant charged with a criminal offence can raise a defence of intoxication, whether voluntary or involuntary if the offence with which he has been charged is classified as being of the specific intent variety and there is evidence that, because of the intoxication he did not form that specific intent: see *DPP* v *Majewski* [1976] 2 All ER 142. For these purposes a specific intent crime is one where the mens rea goes beyond the actus reus, for example criminal damage with intent to endanger life contrary to s1(2) of the Criminal Damage Act 1971. Where the offence is one of basic intent intoxication will not normally provide a defence. In *DPP* v *Morgan* [1976] AC 182 Lord Simon of Glaisdale explained that crimes of basic intent were those where the mens rea which did not go beyond the actus reus.

Whether the statement under consideration is regarded as correct or not depends to some extent on the interpretation given to the phrase 'drunken intent' The defendant seeking to rely on intoxication as a defence will have to provide some evidence that he did not form the necessary intent because of the effect of the intoxicant: see *R v O'Connor* [1991] Crim LR 135 and *R v Brown and Stratton* [1998] Crim LR 485. The fact that a defendant does something whilst drunk that he would not have done when sober, will not, of itself, give rise to the defence of intoxication. A drunken intent is nevertheless an intent: see *R v Bowden* [1993] Crim LR 380 and *R v Groak* [1999] Crim LR 669.

The position can therefore be summarised thus. First, if the intoxication is voluntary or involuntary and the defendant as a result does not form the specific intent required for an offence he can rely on the defence of intoxication. Whether he is convicted of a lesser offence or acquitted will depend on the wording of the offence. In the case of aggravated criminal damage with intent to endanger life the defendant would be convicted of the lesser-included offence of 'simple' criminal damage. If he were charged with theft, however, he would have to be acquitted, as there is no lesser-included offence. Second, if the intoxication is voluntary and the defendant does not form the required intent, he will not have a defence of intoxication if charged with a basic intent crime, such as assault. The recklessness required as the fault element for the assault offence is found in the reckless course of conduct in becoming intoxicated: see *DPP v Majewski*. Where the defendant's intoxication is involuntary and he is charged with a basic intent crime he should argue that he falls outside the *Majewski* principle because he was not reckless in becoming intoxicated – it was not his fault – hence there is no prior fault on which to base liability. As Lord Mustill explained in *R v Kingston* [1994] 3 WLR 519, if the intoxication was not the result of an act done with an informed will there is no intent which can be transferred to the prohibited act, so as to fill the gap in the offence. Once the involuntary nature of the intoxication is added the two theories of *Majewski* fall away, and the position reverts to what it would have been if *Majewski* had not been decided, namely that the offence is not made out if the defendant was so intoxicated that he could not form an intent – even a basic one.

As indicated above, a defendant who has voluntarily taken intoxicants but is still capable of forming mens rea and does so falls outside of the scope of the defence altogether.

What of the defendant who is duped into consuming an intoxicant with the effect that, although he forms the necessary mens rea for an offence, he only does so because of the disinhibiting effect of the drug?

The matter was considered in depth by the House of Lords in *R v Kingston*. The respondent, a homosexual paedophile who had committed an indecent assault on a 15-year-old boy, claimed that prior to these acts he had been drugged by his co-defendant, and could not recall the incident. There was a difference of medical opinion as to the extent to which the drugs, believed to have been consumed by the respondent, would have affected his ability to recall the incident. However, there was no evidence to suggest that the drugs would have made the respondent do anything he would not have done under normal circumstances. The trial judge ruled that whilst it was not open to the jury to acquit the respondent if they found that his intent to commit the indecent assault had been induced by the surreptitious administration of drugs by his co-defendant, it was open to them to find that secretly administered drugs could negative the respondent's mens rea. The respondent appealed successfully to the Court of Appeal and the prosecution appealed to the House of Lords. Allowing the appeal Lord Mustill explained that the absence of moral fault on the part of the appellant was not sufficient in itself to negative the necessary mental element of the offence. He went on to indicate further grounds for rejecting any notion of a defence based on disinhibition arising from involuntary intoxication. The first was the danger that the defence would overlap with diminished responsibility. He observed that it would be necessary to reconcile a defence of irresistible impulse derived from a combination of innate drives and external disinhibition with the rule that irresistible impulse of a solely internal origin does not in itself excuse the defendant. Second, he foresaw serious practical problems arising because the courts would have to enquire into the defendant's personality to assess the effect of the drug. Third, there would be the need for expert evidence – pharmacologists would be required to describe the potentially disinhibiting effect of a range of drugs not commonly encountered. Fourth, he noted the opportunities that would spring up for spurious defences to be advanced – particularly of the 'spiked' drink variety commonly encountered in road traffic cases. In all he thought fairness could be achieved through exercising a sentencing discretion rather than opening the Pandora's box of such a wide ranging defence.

The quotation is, therefore, correct on both counts.

## QUESTION THREE

'The distinction between sane and insane automatism is no longer of practical importance. For that matter, neither is the distinction between insanity and automatism.'

Discuss.

University of London LLB Examination
(for External Students) Criminal Law June 1997 Q2

### General Comment

An essay question which should only be attempted by the candidate who has not only a sound grasp of the law of insanity but also has an appreciation of the distinction between insanity and automatism.

### Skeleton Solution

Meaning of automatism and insanity – distinction between the defences – role of public policy – internal/external causes – conclusion.

## Suggested Solution

Criminal law punishes an offender because he is culpable and deserving of punishment. Consequently, it is a basic principle of English criminal law that an accused can only be convicted of an offence if the conduct alleged is committed out of choice. Conduct which is not committed as a voluntary act of the accused cannot give rise to criminal liability. If the accused lacks such conscious control of his conduct he is said to be acting in a state of automatism and entitled to an acquittal.

Few would doubt the principle that it would be unfair to punish the individual who was not in control or even conscious of what he was doing. Such a person may be entitled either to the defence of automatism or insanity as defined in *McNaghten's Case* (1843) 10 Cl & F 200: an accused is entitled to the defence of insanity if 'the party accused was labouring under such a defect of reason, from disease of the mind as not to know the nature and quality of the act which he was doing, or, if he did know it, that he did not know that what he was doing was wrong.'

The main practical difference between these defences is the court's power of disposal of the person acquitted. An acquittal on the grounds of non-insane automatism is a complete acquittal, the courts having no power to detain or order the treatment of the accused, who must be released from custody immediately. However, under the Criminal Procedure (Insanity) Act 1964 (until amended by the 1991 Act (see below)) an acquittal on the grounds of insanity (the 'special verdict') carried a mandatory order that that the accused should be detained for an indefinite time in a mental institution. The medical profession would then determine when the accused was fit and safe to be released back into society.

Under the 1964 Act the difference between an acquittal on the grounds of insanity and an acquittal on the grounds of non insane automatism was clear; immediate release and freedom on the one hand, and detention for an indefinite period (and possibly therefore for life) on the other.

The Criminal Procedure (Insanity and Unfitness to Plead) Act 1991 amended the 1964 Act to widen the court's powers of disposal of with respect to those acquitted on the grounds of insanity. Detention for an indefinite period is now only mandatory in cases of murder. In all other cases the court has the power make various orders such as treatment orders, supervision orders and conditional and absolute discharges.

In removing the mandatory detention order the 1991 Act may have reduced the extreme differences between the defences of insanity and automatism. However, there is still a considerable practical and legal difference between the defences; the courts still lack the power to make orders in respect of those acquitted on the grounds of non-insane automatism, who are therefore released back into the community (unless dealt under the mental health legislation) even if they pose a future threat to society. This contrasts with the wide powers of disposal available for those acquitted on the grounds of insanity (including detention at a mental institution): the mandatory detention order is still compulsory for those acquitted of murder on the grounds of insanity but no orders are available for those acquitted of murder on the grounds of non insane automatism. It should also be remembered that a person acquitted on the grounds of insanity will have to carry the not inconsiderable burden of being labelled criminally insane (especially onerous since, as will be seen below, such common conditions as epilepsy and diabetes may be considered within the ambit of the the defence of insanity). Since such important practical differences do exist, it remains important to distinguish between the defences of insanity and automatism.

It should be noted that an accused who is aware of the nature of what he is doing but does not know that it is wrong cannot be said to be acting in an unconscious state. Consequently, if his condition arises from a disease of the mind as defined in *McNaghten's Case* he will be found to be insane. However, where the accused falls under the second limb of the *M'Naghten* test (he does not know the nature of his act), he may be entitled to the defence of insanity or non-insane automatism.

The distinction between these defences has little to do with medical concepts of psychiatric conditions but is rather a product of the dictates and requirements of public policy; to acquit an accused of a serious offence on the grounds of automatism would result in the freeing of that offender to possibly commit other offences. Consequently, where the court considers the accused to pose a threat to society, a verdict of insanity will generally be preferred.

This point is well made in Lord Denning's commentary in *Bratty* (*Bratty* v *Attorney-General for Northern Ireland* [1963] AC 386) on the case of *R* v *Charlson* [1955] 1 All ER 859 in which a devoted father attacked his son with a hammer. The father was acquitted of causing his son grievous bodily harm on the grounds of automatism when evidence was presented that he was not in control of his actions due the effects of a brain tumour. Lord Denning in Bratty said:

> 'But in *Charlson* Barry J seems to have assumed that other diseases such as epilepsy or cerebral tumour are not diseases of the mind, even when they are such as to manifest themselves in violence. I do not agree with this. It seems to me that any mental disorder which has manifested itself in violence and is prone to recur is a disease of the mind [and therefore amounts to insanity]. At any rate it is the sort of disease for which a person should be detained in hospital rather than be given an unqualified acquittal.'

Following this approach the courts seemed to have adopted an 'internal/ external' dichotomy. A lack of consciousness due to an internal cause (such as disease or a psychiatric condition) will be assumed to be likely to recur and therefore constitute the defence of insanity. A lack of consciousness due to an external cause such a blow to the head or drugs will constitute automatism.

In *R* v *Kemp* [1957] 1 QB 399, *R* v *Smith* [1982] Crim LR 531, *R* v *Quick and Paddison* [1973] QB 910, *Bratty* (above) and *R* v *Burgess* (1991) 93 Cr App R 41 arteriosclerosis, extreme pre-menstrual tension, diabetic coma caused by the failure to take sufficient insulin, epilepsy and sleepwalking were all deemed to be conditions due to internal causes, likely to recur and therefore constitute the defence of insanity rather than automatism.

However, the narrow difference between insanity and non-insane automatism is illustrated by *R v Quick and Paddison* (above) and *R v Hennessy* [1989] 1 WLR 287. In the former case the accused, a psychiatric nurse, was acquitted of causing actual bodily harm to a patient in his care on the grounds of insanity. The defence of insanity applied because his hypoglycaemic diabetic fit was due to his not eating the proper amount of food to counteract the insulin he had taken as medication. His fit was therefore due to the medication which constituted an external cause. In *Hennessy* (above) the accused was acquitted of taking a vehicle without the owner's consent on the grounds of automatism. The accused had taken too much insulin and went into a hyperglycaemic fit. This was due to an external cause – the medication. It is lamentable that an accused's freedom (or the ability of society to protect itself from the accused) should depend on whether he took 10 per cent too much of his medication or forgot to eat a cheese sandwich afterwards.

In *R v Rabey* (1977) 37 CCC (2d) 461 the Canadian Supreme Court held that a lack of consciousness caused by exposure to the 'ordinary stresses and dis-appointments of life' (in this case rejection by the opposite sex) would have its roots in the accused's own psychological weakness and constitute an internal cause amounting to insanity. In *R v T* [1990] Crim LR 256 however, the Court of Appeal recognised that the exposure to extraordinarily traumatic events (in this case being the victim of rape), causing the accused to commit involuntary acts, may constitute an external cause giving rise to the defence of automatism.

In conclusion, there remain important differences between the defences of insanity and non-insane automatism. These differences may be less important today than in the past due to the relatively small number of people who raise the defence of insanity. This may be partly due to the abolition of the death penalty in 1962, before which a finding of insanity often proved an attractive alternative, and also the availability of the defence of diminished responsibility. In 1992 only three offenders charged with murder and five offenders charged with other offences were acquitted on the grounds of insanity: see *Criminal Statistics 1993*, Cmnd 2680, Table 4.8.

### QUESTION FOUR

'Involuntary intoxication prevents the defendant forming the necessary mens rea but the better way of analysing such intoxication is to regard the defendant as an automaton.'

Discuss.

University of London LLB Examination
(for External Students) Criminal Law June 1995 Q8

### General Comment

A very difficult question, not because of the subject-matter of intoxication, on which there is more than sufficient material in the leading texts and journals, but because it is confined to the relatively narrow aspect of involuntary intoxication, with a link to automatism. The question is made all the more difficult because the first part of the quotation is not necessarily always true (that a person who is involunatarily intoxicated lacks the mens rea for the offence), as the question seems to imply? this is a matter of degree and fact. This question should only have been attempted by students who had thoroughly revised both intoxication and automatism and were aware of the case of *R* v *Kingston*.

### Skeleton Solution

Definition of involuntary intoxication – outline of basic law on involuntary intoxication – discussion of *R* v *Kingston* and associated policy issues – discussion of automatism.

### Suggested Solution

The precise circumstances in which a person may be said to be involuntarily intoxicated have not been defined. It would appear that a person is involuntarily intoxicated if his or her drink has been 'spiked' with alcohol, or another drug, without their knowledge. However, the definition would seem to exclude where such a person becomes intoxicated because they underestimate the level of alcohol in their drink: *R* v *Allen* [1988] Crim LR 698. Presumably, a person who is forced to drink alcohol or consume drugs against their wishes would also be involuntarily intoxicated.

There are few authorities on the area but a number of propositions can be extracted from the cases.

The rule in *DPP* v *Majewski* [1976] 2 All ER 142 that intoxication may be a defence to a charge of specific intent where it deprives the accused of the mens rea required for the offence, but is no defence to a charge of basic intent (for example involving recklessness), would appear not to apply (*R* v *Davies* [1983] Crim LR 741) to involuntary intoxication.

According to *Davies*, involuntary intoxication will be a defence to a charge of specific intent where it deprives the accused of the required intent, and will also be a defence to a charge of basic intent since it will usually be the case, by definition, that a person who is involuntarily intoxicated is not reckless in entering this state.

If the accused had been given such large quantities of alcohol or other drugs that he could not control, and was not aware of, his actions, he may also be entitled to the defence of automatism.

The main problem in this area is that the law has provided little allowance for the accused who is involuntarily intoxicated, to the point where his or her inhibitions are lowered to cause that person to commit a crime which they would not otherwise have committed, but not so intoxicated that they are deprived of the requisite mens rea for the offence. Under the existing law such a person will be convicted: see *Davies* above.

The most recent case on the issue is *R* v *Kingston* [1994] 3 All ER 353. In this case, the accused, who was a homosexual paedophile, was lured to a house by the co-defendant. The co-defendant then surreptitiously drugged the accused and invited him to commit an unlawful sexual act with a 15-year-old boy whom the co-defendant had also drugged. The accused committed such an act.

The accused admitted that at the time of the offence he knew what he was doing and that he had the mens rea for the offence, but argued that he would not have committed the offence were he sober? the drugs had removed his inhibitions and 'caused' him to commit the crime that he would not otherwise have committed.

The Court of Appeal accepted his argument and held that a person who was involuntarily intoxicated, who would not have committed the crime were they sober, should be acquitted of the offence even though they had the requisite mens rea for the offence.

The Court of Appeal's decision can be defended by the argument that the imposition of a penal sanction can only be justified on the basis of the accused's culpability? if the accused was induced to commit an offence through no fault of his own, there is no justification for punishment.

However, the House of Lords swiftly overruled the Court of Appeal and held that the loosening of inhibitions was no defence to a criminal charge. The sole issue is whether the accused has the mens rea required for the offence? 'a drunken intent is still an intent'.

The House of Lords supported its decision by arguing that to allow such a defence as that suggested by the Court of Appeal would require the creation of a new defence, and that this was a matter better left to Parliament. It was also argued that to allow such a defence would open the floodgates to bogus claims of involuntary intoxication as a defence.

It is submitted that these problems would not be solved by classifying a person who is deprived of the mens rea of an offence because of involuntary intoxication as an automaton. If such a person loses control of his actions and lacks the mens rea, he or she would be acquitted whether the defence were classified as automatism (see *R v Bailey* (1983) 77 Cr App R 76) or involuntary intoxication: see *Davies* and *Kingston* above.

The issues which really need clarification are the scope of the definition of involuntary intoxication and the avoidance of the possible injustice which may be caused where a person commits an offence because he has been drugged against his will, or without his knowledge, and yet has the mens rea for the offence.

# Chapter 12

## General Defences – Compulsion

12.1 Introduction

12.2 Key points

12.3 Key cases and statute

12.4 Questions and suggested solutions

## 12.1 Introduction

Unlike the majority of general and particular defences, where the defendant is seeking to deny the actus reus or mens rea for the offence, the defences of necessity, duress and self-defence are perhaps more accurately seen as 'true defences' in that the defendant is seeking to justify his actions or at least seeking to be excused for having committed the actus reus with mens rea. As with other defence topics, compulsion will feature as part of a problem question but may justify an entire essay question in its own right.

## 12.2 Key points

### Necessity

At common law the courts have traditionally refused to recognise a defence of necessity: see *R v Dudley and Stephens* (1884) 14 QBD 273; *Southwark London Borough Council v Williams* [1971] 2 All ER 175; and *Buckoke v Greater London Council* [1971] Ch 655. Under various statutes a limited scope was given to lawful excuse defences which amounted to limited versions of necessity: see s5(2) Criminal Damage Act 1971 (defence to a charge of criminal damage to show that this was necessary to prevent greater damage to property).

In the exceptional circumstances offered by the dilemma facing surgeons operating to separate conjoined twins (knowing that not to operate would result in the death of both, but equally knowing that to operate would cause certain death for one of the twins), the courts have been willing to recognise a limited scope for necessity: see *Re A (Children) (Conjoined Twins: Surgical Separation)* [2000] 4 All ER 961. Brooke LJ observed that the defence of necessity could be raised, even in relation to murder, where the defendant had acted to save another's life (provided he was not taking another's life to save his own). The conditions to be met were that the defendant's act was needed to avoid inevitable and irreparable evil; was no more what was reasonably necessary for the purpose to be achieved; and was not, in the harm that it caused, disproportionate to the evil sought to be avoided.

## Duress of circumstances

During the 1980s the courts started to recognise a form of necessity, usually referred to as duress of circumstances – the defence arises where circumstances force D to commit an offence: see *R v Willer* (1986) 83 Cr App R 225; *R v Conway* [1988] 3 All ER 1025; and *R v Martin* (1988) 88 Cr App R 343. In *R v Pommell* [1995] 2 Cr App R 607 the Court of Appeal held that the defence of duress of circumstance was available in relation to all offences with the exception of murder, attempted murder and treason. The continued availability of the defence did depend, however, on the defendant desisting from the commission of the offence as soon as he reasonably could. The test for duress of circumstances can be summarised as follows::

a) Was the accused, or may he have been, impelled to act as he did because as a result of what he believed to be the situation he had good cause to fear that otherwise death or serious physical injury would result? If so:

b) Might a sober person of reasonable firmness, sharing the characteristics of the accused, have responded to that situation by acting as the accused acted? If yes, the jury should acquit.

## Duress per minas

Duress per minas arises where D is forced to commit an offence because of threats made to him by another person. The basic definition of the defence is provided in *R v Graham* (1982) 74 Cr App R 235, as amended by *R v Martin* [2000] Crim LR 615 – 'where the accused acted as he did as a result of what he honestly believed E had said or done and had good cause to fear that if he did not so act E would kill him or cause him serious personal injury'.

The nature of the threat – the threat must be to cause death or serious personal injury: *Graham* (above). A threat to damage property or expose immoral behaviour will be insufficient: *R v Valderrama-Vega* [1985] Crim LR 220.

The common law suggests that the threat must be to the accused's spouse, common law wife or 'immediate family' (*R v Hurley and Murray* [1967] VR 526), but it is submitted that a threat to any person could suffice.

The accused must have 'good cause' for fear: *DPP v Pittaway* [1994] Crim LR 600.

Note the extent to which the threat must be immediate, with the accused not having any reasonable opportunity to contact the police: *R v Hudson and Taylor* [1971] 2 QB 202; *R v Cole* [1994] Crim LR 582; and *R v Abdul-Hussain and Others* [1999] Crim LR 570 – the threat must be operating on the mind of the defendant at the time when he commits the criminal act, but the execution of the threat need not be immediately in prospect.

Duress is not available to a person charged with murder (*Abbott* v *R* [1977] AC 755), attempted murder (*R* v *Gotts* [1992] 1 All ER 832) or as an accessory to murder: *R* v *Howe* [1987] 1 All ER 771.

Where the accused voluntarily participates in a criminal offence with another person whom he knows to be violent and likely to demand that he commit other criminal offences, the accused cannot rely on the defence of duress: *R* v *Ali* [1995] Crim LR 303.

### Self-defence

Self-defence allows reasonable force to be used to defend oneself, another person or property from attack or damage.

Note the overlap between self-defence at common law and s3 of the Criminal Law Act 1967 which allows reasonable force to be used in the prevention of crime.

The force used must be commensurate with the level of the perceived attack: *R* v *Oatridge* [1992] Crim LR 205.

The reasonableness of the force must be considered in the light of the fear and pressure the accused was under at the time of the attack: *Palmer* v *R* [1971] AC 814.

The victim of an attack does not necessarily have to wait for the first blow to be struck: *R* v *Beckford* [1988] 1 AC 130.

Where the accused is charged with murder and raises the defence of self-defence or the use of reasonable force to prevent a crime or effect an arrest under s3 Criminal Law Act 1967, the accused is entitled to a full acquittal if the force used was reasonable. If the force used was unreasonable then, even though the use of some force may have been justified, the accused must be convicted of murder. In other words, under the law as it now stands, the use of excessive force where some force is justified is not a partial defence which can mitigate what would have been a conviction for murder to one of manslaughter: *R* v *Clegg* [1995] 2 WLR 80.

Note that an accused who mistakenly believes that he is under attack may still be able to raise the defence of self-defence: *R* v *Williams (Gladstone)* [1987] All ER 411.

## 12.3  Key cases and statute

*Duress per minas*

- *DPP for Northern Ireland* v *Lynch* [1975] 1 All ER 913
  Must threaten death or grievous bodily harm

- *R* v *Abdul-Hussain and Others* [1999] Crim LR 570
  Imminence of harm threatened

- *R* v *Bowen* [1996] 2 Cr App R 157
  Relevant characteristics

- *R v Cole* [1994] Crim LR 582
  Nominating the crime

- *R v Fitzpatrick* [1977] NI 20
  Duress not available to gang members

- *R v Gotts* [1992] 1 All ER 832
  Duress no defence to attempted murder

- *R v Graham* [1982] 1 All ER 801
  Standard direction on duress

- *R v Hegarty* [1994] Crim LR 353
  Being 'emotionally unstable' not a characteristic

- *R v Howe* [1987] 1 All ER 771
  Duress no defence to murder

- *R v Hudson and Taylor* [1971] 2 QB 202
  Imminence of harm threatened

- *R v Martin* [2000] Crim LR 615
  D judged on facts as he believes them to be

- *R v Shepard* (1987) 86 Cr App Rep 47
  Did D realise what sort of gang he was joining

## Duress of circumstance

- *R v Conway* [1988] 3 All ER 1025
  Elements of the defence

- *R v Martin* (1988) 88 Cr App R 343
  What D must show to plead duress of circumstances

- *R v Pommell* [1995] 2 Cr App R 607
  Need to desist from illegal conduct when possible

- *R v Willer* (1986) 83 Cr App R 225
  Duress of circumstances recognised as a defence

## Necessity

- *Re A (Children) (Conjoined Twins: Surgical Separation)* [2000] 4 All ER 961
  Where D kills A to save B

- *R v Dudley and Stephens* (1884) 14 QBD 273
  Necessity no defence to murder

## Self-defence

- *Beckford* v *R* [1987] 3 All ER 425
  Mistaken self-defence

- *Palmer* v *R* [1971] AC 814
  Need to allow a margin of error to D

- *R* v *Clegg* [1995] 2 WLR 80
  No partial defence

- *R* v *Hussey* (1924) 18 Cr App R 160
  Defence of property

- *R* v *Julien* [1969] 1 WLR 839
  Objective test

- *R* v *McInnes* [1971] 3 All ER 295
  Failure to retreat

- *R* v *Rose* (1884) 15 Cox CC 540
  Defence of others

- *R* v *Williams* [1987] 3 All ER 411
  Mistaken self-defence

- Criminal Law Act 1967, s3(1) – statutory defence of using such force as is reasonable in the circumstances in the prevention of crime

## 12.4 Questions and suggested solutions

QUESTION ONE

X, Y and Z were alone in a life boat. Their ship had sunk in a storm five days before. They had little water and food and they were 800 miles from the nearest land. They proposed to draw lots and the one who lost should go without further food and water in order to increase the chances of survival of the other two. Z drew the short straw and for two days he received no food or water. Eventually, he became desperate and tried to take some of the precious water supply but X and Y prevented this. Z became more and more desperate and that night when Y was asleep Z pushed Y over the side of the boat where he drowned. X and z shared the remaining water and were rescued by a passing ship just in time.

Advise the parties of their criminal liability. What difference, if any, would it make to your advice if Z had been hallucinating when he threw Y overboard?

University of London LLB Examination
(for External Students) Criminal Law June 1999 Q5

## General Comment

A highly unusual question – based loosely around the facts of *R v Dudley and Stephens*. Although the main issue is the homicide, some thought has to be given to possible theft offences in relation to the drinking water although this is a very academic point. The question requires a through consideration of the ratio of *R v Dudley & Stephens*. The alternative part relating to the hallucinations obviously throws up a wider range of defences, including automatism and diminished responsibility.

## Skeleton Solution

Z tries to take the water – consider theft – attempt – other use force to exclude him. Z pushes Y over the side – consider the form of homicide – necessity - unlawful act manslaughter. X and Z – possible liability for theft of the water. Z hallucinating – defences of automatism – diminished responsibility – insanity.

## Suggested Solution

By trying to take some of the water Z may have committed attempted theft, contrary to s1(1) of the Criminal Attempts Act 1981 and s1(1) of the Theft Act 1968. The water is property (s4) and belongs to Y and Z following the drawing of the lots: s5. Appropriation is defined in s3 as any assumption by a person of the rights of an owner. In *R v Morris* [1983] 3 All ER 288, Lord Roskill explained that this encompassed any assumption of any right of the owner. X and Y would not consent to Z's actions, but even if it were argued that they did, this would not prevent Z's actions amounting to an appropriation: see *R v Gomez* [1993] 1 All ER 1. Clearly Z takes steps more than merely preparatory to stealing the water – thus the actus reus of attempt is made out. Z's intended appropriation of the water must be dishonest. Resort will be had first to s2(1) of the Theft Act 1968. It provides that Z's appropriation of property belonging to another is not to be regarded as dishonest if he appropriates the property in the belief that he has in law the right to deprive X and Y of it, or he appropriates the water in the belief that he would have the other's consent if they knew of the appropriation and the circumstances of it. There is no evidence to suggest that he could escape liability under either sub-section. Failing this the trial judge could direct the jury in terms laid down in *R v Ghosh* [1982] QB 1053. The jury should first consider whether or not the prosecution has proved that Z was acting dishonestly according to the ordinary standards of reasonable and honest people. If so, did Z realise that what he was doing was by those standards dishonest? Given the extreme circumstances a jury might well have some sympathy, even though the crewmembers drew lots.

As to defences, Z might seek to raise the defence of necessity to a charge of attempted theft – as to which see below. X and Y would be have been able to argue that they were entitled to use reasonable force to exclude Z from the water as it was their property following the drawing of lots. As Lord Hewart CJ observed in *R v Hussey* (1924) 18 Cr App R 160, it is still the law that in defence of a man's property the owner or his family may kill a trespasser who would forcibly dispossess him of it, subject, of course, to the issue of whether the force used was reasonable in the circumstances. Alternatively X and Y could rely on the defence provided by s3(1) Criminal Law Act 1967, which states that a person may use such force as is reasonable in the circumstances in the prevention of crime.

When Z pushes Y over the side of the boat he causes his death in fact and in law. If he intended to kill Y or cause him to suffer grievous bodily harm he can be charged with murder. The jury would be directed that intent can be inferred by the jury from evidence that Z foresaw either consequence as the virtually certain consequence of his actions. Given that they are 800 miles from shore this would seem likely, provided Z is aware of far adrift they are. It hardly seems likely that he pushed Y overboard expecting him to live. If there were any doubt as to the mens rea for murder a manslaughter conviction could be sustained on the basis that Z committed a dangerous unlawful act —the assault and battery in throwing Y overboard – and this act caused Y's death. On the basis of *R v Church* [1965] 2 All ER 72 and *R v Dawson* (1985) 81 Cr App R 150, the prosecution would have to prove that a sober and reasonable person at the scene of the crime would inevitably have recognised a risk of some physical harm resulting to Y. The mens rea would be satisfied by proof that Z intended to do what he did. It is not necessary to prove that he knew that his act was unlawful or dangerous. It is unnecessary to prove that he knew that his act was likely to injure Y. All that need be proved is that he intentionally did what he did: see *Attorney-General's Reference (No 3 of 1994)* [1997] 3 All ER 936.

In relation to the death of Y, Z will presumably try to raise the defence of necessity. The common law does recognise such a defence. It was defined in *R v Martin* [1989] 1 All ER 652 as arising when, from an objective standpoint, the accused can be said to be acting reasonably and proportionately in order to avoid a threat of death or serious injury. There are two questions for the jury to consider. First, was Z impelled to act as he did because as a result of what he believed to be the situation he had good cause to fear that otherwise death or serious physical injury would result? If so, the second question would be whether a sober person of reasonable firmness, sharing the characteristics of Z, would have responded to that situation by acting as Z did? On the facts there is every likelihood that the defence would be made out were it not for the ruling in *R v Dudley and Stephens* (1884) 14 QBD 273 that provides that the defence is not available to a defendant charged with murder, where he kills another to save his own life. Lord Coleridge CJ expressed the view that a man has no right to declare temptation to be an excuse nor allow compassion for the criminal to change or weaken in any manner the legal definition of the crime. The court rejected the contention that a defendant should be allowed to take the life of another in order to save his own. No one life is worth more than another.

When X and Z share the remaining water they might also be committing theft in that they are drinking what was Y's share. The elements of the offence are outlined above. Again, on the facts, dishonesty is likely to be a difficulty for the prosecution, and the defendants would be able to raise a defence of necessity, as outlined above, to a theft charge.

If Z had been hallucinating at the time of the killing he may have been able to raise a number of defences. If charged with murder he might have raised the defence of diminished responsibility under s2(1) of the Homicide Act 1957. This provides that, where a person kills or is party to a killing of another, he shall not be convicted of murder if he was suffering from such abnormality of mind (whether arising from a condition of arrested or retarded development of mind or any inherent causes or induced by disease or injury) as substantially impaired his mental responsibility for his acts and omissions in causing the death.

An abnormality of the mind is, on the basis of *R v Byrne* [1960] 2 QB 396, a state of mind that the normal person would regard as abnormal. This could encompass temporary conditions such as hallucinations. If successful it would reduce Z's liability to manslaughter.

A more general defence that could be raised is that of automatism. No act is punishable if it is done involuntarily. On the basis of *Attorney-General's Reference (No 2 of 1992)* [1993] 3 WLR 982, the defence of automatism requires that there was a total destruction of voluntary control on the defendant's part. Impaired, reduced or partial control is not enough. Whether the defence succeeded would depend on the expert medical evidence as to the effect of Z's hallucinations. If the defence was made out Z would be acquitted. If the court took the view that what Z putting forward was actually evidence of insanity, it could refuse to accept a plea of automatism and only permit one of insanity. This will happen if the court is of the view that the evidence suggests that Z was suffering from a disease of the mind that manifested itself in violence and was likely to recur: see *Bratty v Attorney-General for Northern Ireland* [1963] AC 386.

QUESTION TWO

'The defence of necessity has been the mother of judicial invention. Judges have had to look to other devices to cover situations of necessity.'

Discuss.

University of London LLB Examination
(for External Students) Criminal Law June 1997 Q8

*General Comment*

A narrow question on the defence of necessity which should only be attempted by the candidate who has an in-depth knowledge of the defence.

*Skeleton Solution*

Historical development of the defence – initial reluctance of the courts to recognise the defence – gradual evolution of the defence – conclusion.

*Suggested Solution*

An accused may seek to plead the defence of necessity where he has acted in an unlawful and criminal way to avoid a greater danger than that created by his unlawful conduct. For an example of such a situation see *R v Dudley and Stevens* (1884) 14 QBD 273, where the defendants killed another person in order to cannibalise his body so that two people could survive a shipwreck. The defence might also arise where a defendant pushes a person into the sea where that person is blocking an escape ladder jeopardising the lives of many other passengers trying to board lifeboats (as in the sinking of the Herald of Free Enterprise): see further *R v Kitson* (1955) 39 Cr App R 66.

At common law English judges have, traditionally, been reluctant to recognise the defence of necessity on public policy grounds: the fear that the defence would open the floodgates to spurious claims and the difficulty in deciding whose life or property should be sacrificed (as in the *Dudley and Stephens* situation, where two survivors of a shipwreck killed and ate the cabin boy in order to survive). The defendants were convicted of murder and denied the defence of necessity.

The point is further illustrated by *Southwark London Borough Council v Williams* [1971] 2 All ER 175 in which Lord Denning said:

> 'If hunger where once allowed to be a defence for stealing, it would open a way through which all kinds of disorder and lawlessness would pass. So here, if homelessness were once admitted as a defence to trespass no one's house would be safe. Necessity would open a door which no man could shut. So the courts must, for the sake of law and order, take a firm stand. They refuse to admit the pleas of necessity to the hungry and the homeless; and trust that their discretion will be relieved by the charitable and the good.'

The defence of necessity has, however, appeared in various statutory guises, for example s5 Criminal Damage Act 1971, which permits one to damage property in order to prevent further damage to one's own or another's property. See also reg 34 Traffic Signs Regulations and General Directions 1975 (SI 1975/1536), which allows drivers of emergency vehicles to drive through red traffic lights in certain circumstances.

In the 1980s the courts began the gradual recognition and evolution of a form of the necessity defence under the title of duress of circumstances, through decisions such as *R v Willer* (1986) 83 Cr App 225 and *R v Conway* [1988] 3 All ER 1025. These cases recognised that an accused who drove recklessly in order to escape being attacked by a mob might have a defence based on the circumstances in which he found himself. The defence differs from duress per minas in that the defendant is not being directly forced to commit an offence in the sense that a person making threats is telling him which crime he must commit. The defence was also allowed in *R v Martin* (1988) 88 Cr App R 343 where the accused drove a motor vehicle while disqualified in order to prevent his wife from committing suicide.

The scope of the defence began to expand in the 1990s with the recognition (obiter) in 1994 in *R v Cole* [1994] Crim LR 582 that duress of circumstances was not confined as a defence to road traffic offences and could be raised as a defence to a charge of armed robbery. Full recognition of duress of circumstances as a general defence came in *R v Pommell* [1995] 2 Cr App R 607 in which the Court of Appeal held that a person who was charged with the unlawful possession of a firearm because he took a loaded gun from a friend in order to prevent the friend from using it to kill someone, could raise the defence of 'duress of circumstances'. The court held that duress of circumstances could be a defence to any offence (other than murder, attempted murder or treason) provided the accused acted to prevent the death or serious injury of himself or another person and he has (objectively) acted reasonably and proportionately to that threat.

In *R v Baker and Wilkins* [1997] Crim LR 497 the courts removed one of the remaining ambiguities of the defence by confirming Pommell to the effect that duress of necessity is only available where the accused has acted in order to prevent death or injury to himself or others, and is not available where the accused acts to prevent other losses such as damage to property.

In *Re A (Children) (Conjoined Twins: Surgical Separation)* [2000] 4 All ER 961 Brooke LJ observed that the defence of necessity could be raised, even in relation to murder, where the defendant had acted to save another's life (provided he was not taking another's life to save his own). The conditions to be met were that the defendant's act was needed to avoid inevitable and irreparable evil; was no more what was reasonably necessary for the purpose to be achieved; and was not, in the harm that it caused, disproportionate to the evil sought to be avoided. The case was significant for this obiter acceptance of necessity as a defence even in murder cases, but the court stressed that it was to be seen as limited to its own facts.

Thus, it can be seen that English judges have been reluctant to recognise any generally available defence of necessity but, through a process of judicial invention, have effectively done so. Although one may conclude that the courts have resorted to the device of creating a 'new' defence of duress of circumstances, the extent to which this defence differs from what is in effect the defence of necessity is questionable.

## QUESTION THREE

Q was a building society manager and was of a nervous disposition. R was aware of this and telephoned her stating that, unless Q handed over the keys to the building society and its safe, he would harm Q's daughter. In fact, R did not have custody of Q's daughter but Q did not know this. Q handed the keys to R when he came to Q's house. R tied up Q and drove to the building society and opened the safe intending to remove the contents. In fact, there was no money in the safe which was empty but for a note from Q. This stated that she had removed £200. Her employers had expressly prohibited this practice of borrowing their money from the safe. R was so annoyed that he smashed up the room before removing several 'chips' from the computers. He was arrested leaving the building society premises.

Advise the parties.

University of London LLB Examination
(for External Students) Criminal Law June 1996 Q7

## General Comment

A fairly standard problem question involving a discussion of a range of offences and the defence of duress. The question requires a broad brush approach rather than an examination of difficult academic points in detail. It is an opportunity for the candidate with a comprehensive knowledge to earn high marks.

## Skeleton Solution

R: blackmail – Q: accessory to burglary and theft; duress – R: false imprisonment; battery; burglary; attempted theft – Q: borrowing; theft – R: criminal damage.

## Suggested Solution

When R demanded that Q give him the keys to the building society he may have committed the offence of blackmail contrary to s21 Theft Act (TA) 1968. He has clearly made an unwarranted demand with a threat of menaces (*R v Clear* [1968] 1 QB 670) defined menaces as a threat which any ordinary person of reasonable firmness might give in to.

By giving R the keys to the building society Q may be charged as an accessory (contrary to s8 Accessories and Abettors Act 1861) to the offences of burglary and attempted theft subsequently committed by R. However, Q may raise the defence of duress if she could show that R had threatened to kill or cause serious harm to her or a close relative and that a sober person of reasonable firmness would have responded as she had done: *R v Graham* (1982) 74 Cr App R 235. It is submitted that a reasonable person might accede to a threat to his or her daughter. Q may have a problem in that it appears that she had an opportunity of calling the police between the time R made the threat and the time R arrived at Q's house to collect the keys. However, it is now established that the failure to negate the threat by calling the police may not necessarily be fatal to the defence of duress: *R v Hudson and Taylor* [1971] 2 QB 202. In considering the defence of duress Q is to be judged on the facts as he honestly believes them to be – ie if he believes the basis for the threat is true, he is to be judged as if it were: see *R v Martin* [2000] Crim LR 615.

By tying Q up, R will have committed the offence of false imprisonment which was defined as the unlawful intentional or reckless restraint on any person's freedom of movement: *R v Rahman* (1985) 81 Cr App R 349. R may also be guilty of battering Q by using unlawful force on her: *R v Venna* [1976] QB 421.

By entering the building society intending to steal, R will have committed burglary contrary to s9(1)(a) TA 1968 in that he has entered a building as a trespasser with the intent to steal therein. By opening the safe R has committed attempted theft contrary to s1 Criminal Attempts Act (CAA) 1981. The fact that the safe was empty and it was impossible for him therefore to commit the theft is irrelevant since impossibility is no longer a defence to a charge of attempt: see s1(2) CAA 1981 and *R v Shivpuri* [1987] AC 1.

R's attempted theft once inside the building society will render him guilty of burglary under s9(1)(b) TA 1968 as he is a person who has entered a building as a trespasser and therein has either committed theft or attempted to do so.

By borrowing £200 from her employer Q may be guilty of theft contrary to s1 TA 1968. Taking the money is clearly an act that is inconsistent with the rights of the owner and therefore amounts to an appropriation under s3 TA 1968. Even if Q intends to repay her employer £200 she will still have an intention to permanently deprive the building society of the money since she does not intend to return the actual notes taken: *R v Velumyl* [1989] Crim LR 299. Q's liability therefore is likely to depend on the court's view of whether she has acted dishonestly. Since she has acted against her employer's express instructions not to borrow money she cannot raise the defence under s2(1)(a) TA 1968 that she believed her employer would have consented. However, it is still open for a magistrate or jury to hold that borrowing money (albeit without permission) with an intention to return it, as evidenced by the note left by Q, is not dishonest under the *Ghosh* (*R v Ghosh* [1982] QB 1053) test (would reasonable people regard the act as dishonest and was the accused aware that reasonable people would regard his act as dishonest).

By smashing up the room R has committed criminal damage contrary to s1 Criminal Damage Act (CDA) 1971. In removing chips from computers R will also have committed the s1 offence. Although the computers can be repaired by inserting new chips they will still be damaged because until then R has caused the computers a permanent or temporary impairment of value or usefulness: *Morphitis* v *Salmon* [1990] Crim LR 48. If the removal of the chips caused any loss of information stored on the computer hard disc, although R could not be convicted of criminal damage to this information since this type of intangible property is excluded from the definition of property under s10(1) CDA 1971, he could be charged with criminal damage to the hard disk by rearranging the magnetic particles on the disk: *R v Whitely* (1991) 93 Cr App R 25.

## QUESTION FOUR

Jane, a young mother, noticed that her child was extremely white and covered in perspiration. Realising that the child was very ill, she picked up the baby and ran outside. She saw an unlocked car parked with its ignition key in it, placed her baby in the car and drove off to hospital. She drove through a red traffic signal. When she arrived at the hospital she discovered that her child was dead.

Discuss Jane's criminal liability.

University of London LLB Examination
(for External Students) Criminal Law June 1981 Q2

*General Comment*

The question centres on the mens rea required for the offences of taking a conveyance and dangerous and careless driving, and the important issue of the defence of necessity.

## Skeleton Solution

Section 12 Theft Act 1968 – belief: s12(6) – ss2 and 3 Road Traffic Act 1988 as amended by the 1991 Act.

## Suggested Solution

Jane may have committed an offence of taking a conveyance without the owner's consent or other lawful authority contrary to s12 of the Theft Act 1968.

There is no requirement for her to have an intention 'permanently to deprive' as there is in the offence of theft. All that is required is a 'taking' of the vehicle – this is completed when she moves it (see *R v Bogacki* [1973] QB 832 – and evidence that she has used it as a conveyance: see *R v Bow* (1976) 64 Cr App R 54). She does not appear to have the consent of the owner, neither can she point any lawful authority for the taking of the car.

However, Jane may be able to avail herself of the provisions of s12(6) of the Act if she can show that she believed that the owner would have consented had he known of the taking and of the circumstances. Given the nature of her urgent need of the conveyance Jane would very likely be able to show that she had such subjective belief.

Jane may have committed a further offence contrary to s3 of the Road Traffic Act 1988 (as amended by the Road Traffic Act 1991) by driving without due care and attention. This is an example of a crime where the mens rea required is that of negligence, ie an objective standard. The court has to consider whether the accused was exercising that degree of care and attention that a reasonable and prudent driver would exercise in the circumstances: *Simpson v Peat* [1952] 2 QB 24. Alternatively, she may have committed an offence contrary to s2 of the Road Traffic Act 1991 of dangerous driving, which involves her in being judged against that of a careful and competent motorist.

The key issue for Jane will be the defence of duress of circumstances. Despite assertions in earlier cases such as *Buckoke v Greater London Council* [1971] Ch 655, to the effect that the defence of necessity is not one recognised in English law (Lord Denning stated an opinion that the driver of a fire engine who crossed a red light to rescue someone in a blazing house would commit an offence), more recent authorities clearly indicate the existence of such a defence provided a number of conditions are met. In *R v Willer* (1986) 83 Cr App R 225 D had driven recklessly to escape from a crowd of youths who appeared intent upon causing physical harm to the passengers in his car; in *R v Conway* [1988] 3 All ER 1025 D had driven recklessly to protect his passenger from what he had honestly believed was an assassination attempt. In both cases the Court of Appeal ruled that the appellants should have been permitted to put the defence of duress of circumstances before the jury, given the apparent threat of death or bodily harm created by the circumstances. In *R v Martin* [1989] 1 All ER 652 the defence was extended to driving whilst disqualified. To permit the defence the jury must determine two questions:

a) Was the accused, or may he have been, impelled to act as he did because as a result of what he honestly believed to be the situation he had good cause to fear that otherwise death or serious physical injury would result? If so:

b) Might a sober person of reasonable firmness, sharing the characteristics of the accused, have responded to that situation by acting as the accused acted? If yes, the jury should acquit.

On this basis Jane would have good prospects of succeeding with the defence.

### QUESTION FIVE

R was climbing with his friends S and T. They were roped together and were climbing a particularly dangerous Welsh mountain. T, who was on the bottom of the rope, fell away from the face and dragged S off. R was supporting S and T but they were heavy. R was not able to hold their weight for long so he shouted to S to cut the rope below him. S said, 'But this would be murder.' R said, 'Unless you do so I will cut you both free and you will both be killed.' Reluctantly, S cut the rope and T, who was unconscious, plunged to his death several thousand metres below.

Advise the parties of their criminal liability.

University of London LLB Examination
(for External Students) Criminal Law June 1987 Q6

### General Comment

This question was relatively straightforward, although the aspect of causation was not easy. The link between necessity and duress required careful consideration.

### Skeleton Solution

S: murder; causation, necessity, duress; availability to murder – R: aid/abet murder; necessity.

### Suggested Solution

The question requires consideration of a number of difficult aspects of the law of homicide. The type of extreme situation described has never come before the courts in practice and much of the law to be considered in this situation may at first glance appear incongruous in its application as the case law involved is more obviously 'criminal' than the facts in question.

The core of the question concerns whether or not R and S can be liable under the criminal law for the death of T. There is nothing in the question to indicate that R and S have acted recklessly in relation to the mountaineering itself. Nor is there anything to indicate that they did anything that would amount to a crime in itself separate from possible liability for the death. Therefore killing by reckless conduct and constructive manslaughter do not appear to be in any way appropriate on the facts.

The most obvious charge that could apply is that of murder. Murder is established when a person unlawfully causes the death of another person with intention to kill or intention to do grievous bodily harm.

S could only be liable if he was regarded as the legal cause of T's death. Causation is a mixed question of fact and law. But for S's act T would not have died – hence he is the cause in fact of T's death. There does not appear to be any novus actus that could be said to operate as a break in the chain of causation in law – hence S can be said to have caused T's death both in fact and in law. Hastening death by even a short period of time, as may have been the case here, will suffice.

S must be shown to have intended to kill T or to have intended to cause him grievous bodily harm. The term intent here is not to be equated with desire or purpose. S may not have wanted T to die, and S's purpose may well have been to save his own life and that of R. On the facts in question the prosecution would allege that S had oblique intention to kill, ie he knew that it was certain to occur as a result of what he did even though he did not desire it. The term intention includes direct intent (desiring a particular result) and oblique intent (knowledge that a particular result is certain or virtually certain to occur). On the facts in question the prosecution would allege that S had oblique intention to kill, ie he knew that it was certain to occur as a result of what he did even though he did not desire it. The intent can be based on proof that S foresaw either consequence as a virtually certain result of his actions: *R v Woollin* [1998] 4 All ER 103. If such evidence of foresight is put before the jury it will be entitled to infer intent therefrom.

The most obvious defence to consider on these facts is that of necessity. In essence this is a plea that S's intentional conduct, which otherwise would be criminal, was not criminal because what he did was necessary to avoid some other greater evil. Traditionally English law has refused to recognise a general defence of necessity. Thus in *R v Dudley and Stevens* (1884) 14 QBD 273 the necessity for self-preservation was no defence to a charge of murder, arising out of the killing and eating of a cabin-boy by shipwrecked sailors adrift on an open boat and without food. There are however three possible argument open to S.

The first is to derive support from *Re A (Children) (Conjoined Twins: Surgical Separation)* [2000] 4 All ER 961, where Brooke LJ observed that the defence of necessity could be raised, even in relation to murder, where the defendant had acted to save another's life (provided he was not taking another's life to save his own). The conditions to be met are that S's act was needed to avoid inevitable and irreparable evil; was no more than what was reasonably necessary for the purpose to be achieved; and was not, in the harm that it caused, disproportionate to the evil sought to be avoided. S could argue that he was acting save his own life and that of R. He might add that T was already 'doomed' rather like the conjoined twin who would have died whether the doctors in *Re A* operated or not.

The second argument might be to rely on the emerging defence of duress of circumstances which is effectively a defence of necessity. The Court of Appeal accepted such a defence to a range of motoring offences in a series of cases culminating in *R v Martin* (1988) 88 Cr App R 343. In *R v Pommell* [1995] 2 Cr App R 607, however, it was held that the defence of duress of circumstance was not available in relation to murder – hence, on the facts, if S is charged with murder, this defence would be difficult to establish.

The third argument, based on the judgment of Ward LJ in *Re A*, is to the effect that S should have a complete defence of self-defence in relation to his killing T. This argument is based on the notion that T is effectively attacking S and R by dragging them to their deaths. It follows that S can use reasonable force to save his own life if it is threatened by T. The argument is bolstered by the assertion that S is also acting to save R. Ward LJ drew the analogy with a six-year-old boy indiscriminately shooting other children in the school playground – the actions of a defendant who shot the six-year-old aggressor dead would be in self-defence.

R's liability depends entirely on what happens to S. If S succeeds with the self-defence argument R should also be absolved of liability, as S's actions can be seen as having been justified. If S has no defence, however, R will be an accomplice to the murder in that he instructed S to cut the rope. The mode of participation would be as an aider and abettor, ie one who is present at the scene of the offence assisting or encouraging: *R v Coney* (1882) 8 QBD 534; *R v Clarkson* [1971] 1 WLR 1402. R clearly has knowledge of the offence committed by S, hence there will be no issue as to his mens rea.

# Old Bailey Press

The Old Bailey Press integrated student law library is tailor-made to help you at every stage of your studies from the preliminaries of each subject through to the final examination. The series of Textbooks, Revision WorkBooks, 150 Leading Cases and Cracknell's Statutes are interrelated to provide you with a comprehensive set of study materials.

You can buy Old Bailey Press books from your University Bookshop, your local Bookshop, direct using this form, or you can order a free catalogue of our titles from the address shown overleaf.

The following subjects each have a Textbook, 150 Leading Cases/Casebook, Revision WorkBook and Cracknell's Statutes unless otherwise stated.

Administrative Law
Commercial Law
Company Law
Conflict of Laws
Constitutional Law
Conveyancing (Textbook and 150 Leading Cases)
Criminal Law
Criminology (Textbook and Sourcebook)
Employment Law (Textbook and Cracknell's Statutes)
English and European Legal Systems
Equity and Trusts
Evidence
Family Law
Jurisprudence: The Philosophy of Law (Textbook, Sourcebook and Revision WorkBook)
Land: The Law of Real Property
Law of International Trade
Law of the European Union
Legal Skills and System (Textbook)
Obligations: Contract Law
Obligations: The Law of Tort
Public International Law
Revenue Law (Textbook, Revision WorkBook and Cracknell's Statutes)
Succession

| Mail order prices: | |
| --- | --- |
| Textbook | £14.95 |
| 150 Leading Cases | £11.95 |
| Revision WorkBook | £9.95 |
| Cracknell's Statutes | £11.95 |
| Suggested Solutions 1998–1999 | £6.95 |
| Suggested Solutions 1999–2000 | £6.95 |
| Suggested Solutions 2000–2001 | £6.95 |
| Law Update 2002 | £9.95 |
| Law Update 2003 | £10.95 |

Please note details and prices are subject to alteration.

**To complete your order, please fill in the form below:**

| Module | Books required | Quantity | Price | Cost |
|---|---|---|---|---|
| | | | | |
| | | | | |
| | | | | |
| | | | | |
| | | | | |
| | | Postage | | |
| | | TOTAL | | |

For Europe, add 15% postage and packing (£20 maximum).
For the rest of the world, add 40% for airmail.

## ORDERING

**By telephone to Mail Order at 020 7381 7407**, with your credit card to hand.

**By fax to 020 7386 0952** (giving your credit card details).

**Website: www.oldbaileypress.co.uk**

**By post to: Mail Order, Old Bailey Press at Holborn College, Woolwich Road, Charlton, London, SE7 8LN.**

When ordering by post, please enclose full payment by cheque or banker's draft, or complete the credit card details below. You may also order a free catalogue of our complete range of titles from this address.

We aim to despatch your books within 3 working days of receiving your order.

Name

Address


Postcode                              Telephone

Total value of order, including postage: £

**I enclose a cheque/banker's draft for the above sum, or**

charge my        ☐ Access/Mastercard        ☐ Visa        ☐ American Express
Card number

☐☐☐☐ ☐☐☐☐ ☐☐☐☐ ☐☐☐☐

Expiry date  ☐☐☐☐

Signature: ...................................................Date: ........................................